STRAINED RELATIONS

The Challenge of Homosexuality

Bill Muehlenberg

Foreword by Michael L. Brown

CultureWatch Books, Melbourne

Fourth printing, published in 2014 by

CultureWatch Books, Melbourne, Australia.

First published in 2011 by Freedom Publishing, Melbourne, Australia.

Cover design: Panage Design,
PO Box 1208, Glen Waverley, Vic. 3150.

Interior design and layout: Deborah McIlroy,
PO Box 452, Werribee, Vic. 3030.

Strained Relations: The Challenge of Homosexuality / Bill Muehlenberg – 1st ed.

Includes bibliographic references.

ISBN: 9781495969430

Contents

Foreword

by Michael L. Brown

If you want to be attacked, vilified, demonised, slandered, libelled, misrepresented and verbally abused, then write a book that takes issue with homosexual practice or that opposes the goals of gay activism. Put another way, don't even think about writing such a book unless you're prepared to be attacked in the crudest and ugliest ways imaginable, not to mention face potential boycotts or even threats to your job or career.

I can attest to this from personal experience, and it was while writing my own book about homosexuality (with a particular focus on America), that I learned of the important work Bill Muehlenberg was doing. This new book of his could be a watershed event in the culture wars in Australia, and he has displayed a commendable courage and conviction in writing it. I trust that he is prepared for the storm of criticism that will come his way as the book gains a much-deserved public hearing.

It is important, however, that I am not misunderstood here: We are not at war with people, all of whom, from a spiritual perspective, have been created in the image of God and yet are fallen and flawed. This, rather, is a battle of ideas and morals and values and standards. Is homosexual practice on the identical moral plane to heterosexual practice? Are two dads or two moms the real equivalent of a mom and a dad? Is it acceptable to hold religious views that censure homosexual practice? Are male and female distinctives something positive to be embraced, or is this part of a traditional, destructive, gender binary? Is it possible to teach children that bullying is bad without proclaiming that gay is good? Is there really a gay agenda that wants to silence all contrary opinion, be it social or educational or psychiatric or religious or popular? Have those who championed "tolerance" become the most intolerant?

I strongly encourage every reader to weigh carefully the arguments laid out in this well-documented book, processing the information both with heart and head, and always asking "Is this true?", rather than asking "Do I agree?" or "Do I like what I just read?" With such emotionally charged issues, it is all too easy to have a gut-level reaction either way, and all of us would do well to take a deep breath, get our minds clear, and then analyse the arguments presented.

We would also do well to remember the admonition of the American philosopher and theologian Jonathan Edwards, spoken in a different context in the mid-1700s but still relevant today, namely, that we should not judge the whole by the part. In other words, just because you differ with a particular statement or take issue with a particular study or find fault with a particular argument or dispute the credentials of a particular scholar cited doesn't mean that the overall thesis is wrong. To the contrary, with more than 700 endnotes and hundreds of supporting quotes, it is unlikely that you would read the entire book without taking issue with something. And I would not be the least bit surprised to see a gay activist attempt to discredit the whole book by taking issue with one reference in one endnote or with one paragraph on one page, as if that somehow discredited the whole. To the contrary, that would be a massive cop-out, perhaps even covering up a lack of willingness to engage the real issues at hand.

To be sure, in the context of homosexuality, Bill has touched on just about every single politically incorrect issue, even raising some otherwise forbidden subjects. But once again the question is not whether the topic is popular or acceptable. The question is: What are the facts? What is the truth? In light of the dramatic, gay-related changes that have taken place in America and Canada and Australia and England and beyond, it behoves all of us – parents, educators, business people, religious leaders, politicians, members of the media – to sift through these pages with a view to embracing what is true and right, regardless of the consequences.

For those interested in the theological debate, Bill has provided a useful summary of the major gay-slanted, biblical arguments and reinterpretations, providing solid rebuttals from top scholars in the field. And for those interested in the personal dimensions of homosexual attractions and the possibility of change, there are two appendices with moving stories of a formerly gay man and woman. Change indeed is possible.

So read on. Things might not be as they appear to be, and the truth might be unsettling. Dare we deny it?

Michael L. Brown, PhD, is director of the Coalition of Conscience, Charlotte, North Carolina, and author of *A Queer Thing Happened to America: And What a Long Strange Trip It's Been* (Concord, North Carolina: Equal-Time Books, 2011).

Preface

As one involved in the culture wars for more than two decades now, I have found that one of the areas of most concern to those who champion the pro-family and pro-faith causes is that of homosexuality. In so many ways both family and faith are under direct assault by militant homosexual lobbyists.

No one taking seriously their responsibility to uphold and defend faith and family can afford to ignore the wide range of challenges, threats and attacks emanating from the homosexual lobby. To overlook these major fields of activity will simply lead to further erosion of faith and family in Australia and the West.

This book has been long in the making. More than 15 years ago I first started writing seriously about this issue, and this volume is the result of many years of adding to the initial draft. Parts of it have been published in various forms, but never has the entire manuscript been published until now.

I must extend my thanks to a forbearing family, who have lost me to the keyboard for countless hours, and to many others who have contributed to this book in one fashion or another, whether by helpful suggestions, proof-reading, or by various corrections and additions. Of course, I alone take responsibility for any mistakes and shortcomings in this book.

Finally, I wish to acknowledge the invaluable role of John Ballantyne who has provided expert oversight and general editorship of the final stages of this book. Without his expertise this book simply would not exist – at least as you now find it. I can honestly say that I can think of no other Australian that I would like to have filled this role than John.

Introduction

Perhaps one of the most divisive topics of debate today is the issue of homosexuality. There is plenty of passion and emotion to be found on all sides of the debate and, sadly, heat, rather than light, seems to be generated in the main.

Yet a careful and rational look at this crucial issue needs to be undertaken. While a number of good books already exist on this topic, this volume is unique in that it highlights the Australian data and information, while examining a topic of universal interest.

This book is divided into two main sections. Section One approaches this topic solely from secular social science data. Secular concerns are addressed, and no religious arguments are brought to bear on the debate in this section.

Thus those who simply want the non-religious case for why we must be concerned about the homosexual agenda will find it here, with no excess theological baggage. While, of course, some religious thinkers and writers will be featured here (I happen to be one myself), the case is made without appeal to any religious scriptures or teaching.

Section Two, however, does address the religious arguments: specifically the case as made in the Judeo-Christian worldview. Those who want a biblical and theological foundation for what is being said in this book can find it here.

However, each section can stand alone. Those who have no religious leanings, or find them to be irrelevant to the debate, can find all they are looking for in Section One. Those who simply want a refresher course on the scriptural discussion of this topic will find it in Section Two.

My advice to those with a religious orientation, however, is to master both sections of the book. The theological and biblical case needs to be learned and argued for. But on many occasions, the debate will take place in the secular public square, and we need to learn how to utilise the secular arguments as we discuss these matters with our non-religious friends. Moreover, much of the social science data that I lay out in Section One is assumed as I make my case in Section Two.

PART 1

Social Science and Public Policy Concerns

Introduction to Part One

There is little doubt that the topic of homosexuality is one of the most contentious and hotly debated social issues around today. It is a defining feature of what are known as the culture wars, and it has galvanised opinion, created deep division and plenty of emotional reaction.

Perhaps no other issue has so polarised the Western world and led to radical upheavals of traditional social, cultural and moral norms. In a relatively short period of time the homosexual activists have managed to radically remake society in their own image.

Of course, they and their allies would see this as a sure sign of progress and advancement. However, many others would see it as a clear sign of regress and deterioration. For good or ill, the advances of the homosexual lobby have resulted in profound and long-lasting changes to the very fabric of our culture.

Before proceeding, it is worth pointing out that the issue of homosexuality is a complex and difficult one. A number of distinctions and qualifications need to be made to properly represent the position being argued for here.

The homosexual community, like the heterosexual community, is a diverse and multifaceted phenomenon. In talking about the homosexual community, one must not over-generalise but, rather, be sensitive to distinctions and differences. Several distinctions can be made at the outset.

First, the militant, vocal homosexual lobby does not represent all homosexuals. Many homosexuals simply want to be left alone, to live their lives quietly and peacefully. The homosexual lobby, on the other hand, is militant, vocal and very public. It wants to promote the homosexual way of life as an equal alternative to heterosexual lifestyles. It is very aggressive, demanding that homosexual behaviour be embraced and accepted by the so-called straight community. It publicly flaunts and promotes homosexuality, as in the Sydney Gay and Lesbian Mardi Gras. It is about this militant lobby group that we are primarily concerned when speaking of homosexuality. Most people do not mind the private, discreet activities of homosexuals or anybody else, for that matter. But most Australians do worry about the militant homosexual lobby and its never-ending catalogue of demands (see Chapter 8), demands which will have a very real effect on family and society.

Second, male homosexual behaviour and female lesbian behaviour should be contrasted. In general, male homosexuals are much more promiscuous than lesbians. They are the really great risk group in the spread of HIV. Lesbians can be promiscuous, but tend to prefer monogamous relationships – although "serial monogamy" may best describe lesbian practice. The threat of catching HIV is much, much less in the lesbian community.

Third, to use religious jargon, one must love the sinner while hating the sin. That is, all homosexuals deserve to be treated with respect, love and compassion, even though society has a legitimate right to dislike and censure homosexual behaviour and activity. Society, for example, can rightly disapprove of alcoholism, while seeking to help individual alcoholics. So too, society has a right to deem homosexual behaviour as unhealthy, a threat to the family, and not in the best interests of society, while ensuring that individual homosexuals are not vilified or roughly treated.

Fourth, one can distinguish between homosexual orientation and homosexual behaviour. This matter will be discussed more fully in Chapter 5.

Having made these distinctions, one must ask what the push for homosexual rights is all about, and how it will affect society, faith, and the family.

CHAPTER 1

Strategies of the Homosexual Lobby

The rapid advance of the homosexual movement and its acceptance by mainstream society have not happened by accident. As with all groups engaged in social reform, an active strategy has been put in place, and definite goals have been laid out. Homosexual activists know what they want, and have come a long way in achieving their aims. And the bottom line of the homosexual agenda has always been complete acceptance and social recognition of homosexuality.

One major strategy used by the homosexual lobby to achieve this goal is to present a picture that will hide the real behaviour, aims and agenda of lobby activists. Through the use of a series of half-truths or distortions of fact, they hope to convince the public on a number of points. They want to convince us that homosexuals are a persecuted minority whose civil rights are being violated. They argue that they simply want to be tolerated, to be left alone to practise their behaviour in private. They argue that homosexuals make up at least 10 per cent of the population. They argue that they are born homosexual, and that therefore no moral censure should apply to them. They argue that everything would be fine if homophobic attitudes could be stamped out. They argue that homosexual relationships are just the same as any other relationships.

> So successful has the homosexual lobby been in this campaign of deception that one has only to look at how the public perception of homosexuality has changed over the past few decades.

So successful has the homosexual lobby been in this campaign of deception that one has only to look at how the public perception of homosexuality has changed over the past few decades. Consider the following statement:

> Even in purely non-religious terms, homosexuality represents a misuse of the sexual faculty and, in the words of one ... educator, of 'human construction.' It is a pathetic little second-rate substitute for reality, a pitiable flight from life. As such it deserves fairness, compassion, understanding, and, when possible, treatment. But it deserves no encouragement, no glamorization, no rationalization, no fake status as a minority martyrdom...

And the author of this statement? Fred Nile? Jerry Falwell? No. It was uttered by *Time* magazine, on January 21, 1966. Would *Time* magazine ever dare to utter such comments today? Of course not.

The moral and intellectual climate has changed dramatically in a very short period of time. As Daniel Patrick Moynihan has put it, we are "defining deviancy downwards".[1] Deviancy has reached such huge proportions that in order to deal with the problem we have changed the way we think about normality and abnormality. What used to be regarded as deviant behaviour is now re-classified as normal, and what we used to call normal behaviour we now call abnormal. Thus, the only abnormality now is to be "homophobic". Indeed, pressure by the homosexual lobby to redefine deviancy resulted in the 1973 decision of the American Psychiatric Association to remove homosexuality from the listing in the Diagnostic and Statistical Manual, Mental Disorders (DSM-1).[2]

The mainstream media have, of course, been quite happy to champion the homosexual cause. By constant exposure of the homosexual lifestyle on television, in film, in the press, and so on, the process of normalisation and public acceptance has rapidly been taking place. The idea is to convince the rest of society that homosexuality is a fully normal, acceptable and equivalent lifestyle to any other.

Well worth reading in this regard is an important article entitled, "Selling Homosexuality to America". Written by sales and marketing consultant Paul Rondeau, it demonstrates how the homosexual lobby has cleverly utilised a deliberate and orchestrated marketing campaign to shift the thinking and feelings of Americans into accepting and embracing the homosexual agenda.[3]

> **The homosexual lobby has been very successful in reframing the issues.**

And the constant barrage of pro-homosexual imagery in the media and elsewhere is paying off quite handsomely for the homosexual lobby. Consider just one study: a research paper was presented at a conference on sexuality in Sydney recently. In the paper a professor said that images of lesbians kissing on television had made young people more tolerant of same-sex liaisons. Nearly half of adolescent girls surveyed on a Brazilian website thought that it was normal for a girl to kiss another girl on the mouth. One quarter of those describing it as normal said they had held this view since a Brazilian TV prime-time soap depicted a lesbian relationship.[4]

Indeed, the homosexual lobby has been very successful in reframing the issues. For example, an interesting article appeared in the homosexual press some years ago entitled "The Overhauling of Straight America". The article outlined a strategy by which homosexuals could best implement their goals. It included the following elements: desensitisation; portraying homosexuals as victims, rather than aggressive challengers; giving the protectors a just cause; and making the victimisers look bad.

Here are some quotes from the article:[5]

> In any campaign to win over the public, gays must be cast as victims in need of protection so that straights will be inclined by reflex to assume the role of protector. ... Our campaign should not demand direct support for homosexual practices, but should instead take anti-discrimination as its theme. ... In the early stages of the campaign, the public should not be shocked and repelled by premature exposure to homosexual behavior itself. Instead, the imagery of sex per se should be down-played, and the issue of gay rights reduced, as far as possible, to an abstract social question.

The authors of the above article expanded their strategy into a full-length book, and amplified this theme:[6]

> Our ultimate objective is to expand straight tolerance so much that even gays who look unconventional can feel safe and accepted. ... Thus our campaign should not demand explicit support for homo*sexual* practices, but should instead take *antidiscrimination* as its theme. Fundamental freedoms, constitutional rights, due process and equal protection of laws, basic features of fairness and decency toward all of humanity – these should be the concerns brought to mind by our campaign.

The authors make it clear that this is a deliberate strategy to deceive the public about the real nature of homosexuality. Indeed, in Chapter 6 of their book *After the Ball* they list "Ten Misbehaviours" of the homosexual lifestyle. They open the chapter with these words: "*After the Ball* has now detailed a comprehensive public-relations campaign that should go a long way toward sanitizing our very unsanitary image."[7]

This strategy of the homosexual community to shift attention away from homosexual behaviour and instead to focus on vague notions of civil rights, discrimination, and the like has been an ingenious and successful ploy. As Australian homosexual and reader in politics at Melbourne's La Trobe University, Dennis Altman put it:[8]

> The greatest single victory of the gay movement over the past decade has been to shift the debate from behavior to identity, thus forcing opponents into a position where they can be seen

as attacking the civil rights of homosexual citizens rather than attacking specific and (as they see it) antisocial behavior.

Thus civil rights, not behaviour, has taken the limelight. By taking attention off homosexual behaviour, a clever strategy has been successfully implemented by the homosexual community: namely, to convince the general public that homosexual relationships are just the same as heterosexual relationships, only a bit different. Indeed, the homosexual lobby argues that, except for the fact that they are in a same-sex partnership, their relationship is similar to that of any married or de facto relationship. But are homosexual relationships just the same as heterosexual ones? In a number of crucial areas, homosexual relationships are qualitatively different from heterosexual relationships.

CHAPTER 2

Homosexual Practices and Behaviour

As both homosexual and non-homosexuals have admitted, and as has been thoroughly documented by scientific studies, the homosexual lifestyle is in many respects a very risky, even dangerous, lifestyle. It is associated with numerous illnesses and diseases and at higher levels than among non-homosexuals. Much of this is associated with the promiscuous and high-risk nature of homosexuality.

In general, homosexual relationships do not offer the same stability and permanence as do heterosexual relationships. A number of studies have been conducted over the past few decades to show that the average homosexual relationship is far from stable and monogamous. Indeed, it can instead be characterised as highly unstable and promiscuous. "Sexual promiscuity is one of the most striking, distinguishing features of gay life in America," wrote homosexual authors

Many homosexuals have openly admitted to this highly sexualised lifestyle

Silverstein and White.[1] They say that homosexuals represent hedonism in its most extreme form, with one-night stands and brief flings offering constant excitement and variety.

Many homosexuals have openly admitted to this highly sexualised lifestyle, and plenty of other examples could be cited here. Let me offer just two more. Homosexual writer and sex columnist Dan Savage put it this way: "Gay people know more about sex than straight people do, have more sex than straight people do, and are better at it than straight people are."[2]

And Marshall Kirk and Hunter Madsen, authors of *After the Ball,* mentioned earlier, state quite plainly: "Alas, it turns out that, on this point, public myth is supported by fact. There *is* more promiscuity among gays (or at least among gay men) than among straights."[3]

Because of this much greater promiscuity, sexually-transmitted disease "occurs among gay men at a rate five to ten times higher than average".[4] But I will speak further about the unhealthy homosexual lifestyle shortly. Let me return to the issue of multiple partners and the like.

An exhaustive 1978 Kinsey Institute study of homosexuality showed that 28 per cent of homosexual males had sexual encounters with 1,000 or more males over a lifetime. And 79 per cent said more than half of their sex partners were strangers. Only one per cent of sexually active men had fewer than five lifetime partners.[5]

The study concludes: "Little credence can be given to the supposition that homosexual men's 'promiscuity' has been overestimated. ... Almost half of the white homosexual males said that they had at least 500 different sexual partners during the course of their homosexual careers."[6]

A 1982 study of AIDS victims by the U.S. Centers for Disease Control found that 1,100 sexual partners were about average, with some reporting as many as 20,000 partners.[7] One homosexual reported:[8]

> I believe my estimate of 4,000 sex partners to be very accurate. I have been actively gay since I was 13 (31 years ago). An average of two or three new partners per week is not excessive, especially

when one considers that I will have ten to twelve partners during one night at the baths.

Bell and Weinberg found that 28 per cent of white homosexual males claimed 1,000 or more partners, while 84 per cent claimed 50 or more partners over the course of a lifetime. They found that the average homosexual had 550 different sexual partners.[9]

Thomas Schmidt has meticulously gone through all of the available evidence on this subject. At the time of writing (1995) he had some of the best and most recent data available about the health risks of homosexuality. The information he used was taken only from primary, not secondary, sources. And it all came from secular, scholarly sources, virtually all of which are "either neutral or affirming of homosexuality".[10] This is how he summarises the issue: "Promiscuity among homosexual men is not a mere stereotype, and it is not merely the majority experience – it is virtually the *only* experience. ... Tragically, lifelong faithfulness is almost nonexistent in the homosexual experience."[11]

But it can be rightly asked, has not the AIDS epidemic slowed down homosexual promiscuity rates? Yes, it has, but only marginally. An article in the March 1987 issue of the *Journal of the American Medical Association* reports that both heterosexuals and homosexuals reduced their sexual contact due to fear of AIDS, but that homosexuals continued to have significantly more partners on average than the heterosexuals did.[12]

Indeed, a recent study of the sexual profiles of 2,583 older homosexuals published in *Journal of Sex Research* found that only 2.7 per cent claimed to have had sex with one partner only. It also found that homosexual men had a mean lifetime number of 251 partners.[13]

More revealing, however, is this quote from a Los Angeles-based psychologist who counsels homosexual men, as recorded in an April 1994 issue of a homosexual magazine:[14]

Gay men are discovering new ways of being intimate with another man without excluding the possibility of outside erotic experiences. ... They're relaxing a bit about what seems like a normal and healthy

11

interest in sex outside relationships, after having been shamed in the early days of AIDS. With all the talk about legalising marriage for gays, there's an assumption in the minds of most people I talk to that only rarely does that legalization include monogamy.

In the same issue of the magazine, a homosexual couple spoke about how having outside affairs was the key to their relationship. Said one of the partners: "Pretty early on we had the monogamy discussion. I felt I wanted to be with him, but the idea of having sex with only one person was a little daunting. I mean, I was a real slut, and I didn't want to give that up."[15]

It is quite common in the homosexual press in Australia to find similar remarks. For example, one writer says that to assume monogamy is "a part of every healthy relation-

> **Long-term homosexual relationships are rare, and for those male couples who do actually stay together for longer periods of time, the prevalence of monogamy is quite low.**

ship is just plain wrong". He continues: "Let's face it. Monogamy is a bizarre human invention. Sure, some animals practice it but usually when survival is tough, and teamwork is required to eat. In fact, it's a human invention designed (on a cynical level) for the possession of women."[16]

Or as Australian homosexual activist Dennis Altman puts it: "Large-scale luxurious pleasure palaces where everyone is potentially an immediate sexual partner are a common sexual fantasy; only for gay men they are a commonplace reality."[17] Elsewhere Altman writes:[18]

> … monogamy is not a realistic choice for many of us … we don't find one partner sufficiently fulfilling. People who argue that there would be no problem if all gay men would just be monogamous are ignoring both medical and emotional realities; with an unknown number of people already exposed to 'the virus' and an unknown incubation period, such advice is just too restrictive.

Altman goes even further, saying that "it does seem clear that among gay men a long-lasting *monogamous* relationship is almost unknown. Indeed both gay women and gay men tend to be involved in what might be called multiple relationships, though of somewhat different kinds."[19]

He continues by making the startling admission that "in practice most gay males accept that fidelity to a relationship is not to be measured in sexual terms. A large-scale study of gay male couples in San Diego concluded that every couple together more than five years had outside sexual contacts as a recognized part of the relationship."[20]

As Schmidt has put it:[21]

> Even if we set aside infidelity and allow a generous definition of 'long-term relationships' as those that last at least four years, under 8 per cent of either male or female homosexual relationships fit the definition. In short, there is practically no comparison possible to heterosexual marriage in terms of either fidelity or longevity.

Thus long-term homosexual relationships are rare, and for those male couples who do actually stay together for longer periods of time, the prevalence of monogamy is quite low. Studies continue to document this fact. In a study of 156 males in homosexual relationships, only seven couples claimed to have a totally exclusive sexual relationship. But these seven were in relationships lasting less than five years. The authors comment: "Stated another way, all couples with a relationship lasting more than five years have incorporated some provision for outside sexual activity in their relationships."[22] Thus the norm is having outside sexual activity.

Also, a recent study of homosexual men in Amsterdam found that the "duration of steady partnerships" was 1.5 years.[23] If that is a steady partnership, one wonders what a non-steady one is like. Moreover, the study noted that homosexual men with a "steady partner" have eight casual sexual partners a year.[24]

It should be pointed out that lesbians are much less promiscuous, but they still have a large number of partners. One study found that about 55 per cent of lesbians had between one and ten partners ever, while 35 per cent had between 10 and 100 partners.[25]

Australian findings are quite similar to the overseas research. One of the best sources of Australian information is the SMASH report (*Sydney Men and Sexual Health*), published in five volumes in 1995.[26] This is a very revealing look at the demographics, behaviours, practices, promiscuity rates and health of homosexual and bisexual men in the Sydney area. It is the result of a joint research project of the National Centre in HIV Social Research (Macquarie University), the National Centre in HIV Epidemiology and Clinical Research (University of New South Wales), and the AIDS Council of New South Wales (ACON).

The report found, for example, that 26 per cent of homosexual men had 21 to 100 partners in a lifetime; nearly 41 per cent had 101 to 1,000 partners; and 17 per cent had more than 1,000 partners.[27]

The 1996 *Sydney Gay Community Periodic Survey* reported similar findings. It found that 43 per cent of male homosexuals had engaged in sex with two to 10 partners in the previous six months; 21 per cent had engaged in sex with 11 to 50 partners in the last six months; and five per cent had engaged in sex with more than 50 partners in the past six months.[28] A study of Melbourne homosexuals reveals slightly higher figures, with 24 per cent of respondents saying they had sex with 11 to 50 partners in the last six months, and 6.5 per cent having sex with more than 50 partners.[29]

The National Centre in HIV Social Research released a study in 1998. It found that in 1996, 17.5 per cent of homosexual men had 101 to 500 partners in a lifetime; 7.7 per cent had 501 to 1,000 partners in a lifetime; and 7.8 per cent had more than 1,000 partners in a lifetime.[30]

Or consider an even more recent study. *The Melbourne Gay Community Periodic Survey February 2000* found that in the previous six months 26.2 per cent of male homosexuals had 11-50 sexual partners, while 7.8 per cent had more than 50 partners.[31]

Despite education campaigns, "safe sex" initiatives, and hundreds of thousands of taxpayers' dollars going into HIV/AIDS clinics, the practices continue. One of the most recent SMASH reports, issued in January 2000, reports that things have not changed very much.[32] In a study of sexual relationships with men over four years it found that 77.2 per cent were never celibate.[33] Only 5.3 per cent of male homosexuals over four years never had casual partners.[34]

Queensland studies reveal similar findings. A 1999 study found that in the previous six months, 46 per cent of male homosexuals had 2 to 10 partners, 20 per cent had 11 to 50, and 5.6 per cent had 50 or more sexual partners.[35]

One of the most recent, and largest, national studies (involving 20,000 Australians) found that 35.3 per cent of homosexuals had 10 to 49 same-sex partners in a lifetime, while 38.2 per cent had 50 or more sexual partners in a lifetime.[36]

Indeed, high rates of multiple partnering continue. As one recent report notes: "The majority of the 2006 respondents had engaged in sex with between one and 10 partners in the six months prior to the survey [over 63 per cent], while almost 20% of the men reported having had sex with more than 10 partners."[37]

The problem of cruising and sexual encounters in public places also needs to be pointed out.

The academic studies are backed up by the popular homosexual press. A casual perusal of the homosexual press reveals a predilection for this kind of behaviour. Consider but one recent example. A Melbourne writer, reflecting on a New Year's Eve celebration, speaks of "the essential tragedy of the heterosexual condition". He explains:[38]

> Heterosexuals, it seems, simply do not know how to pick up total strangers in the street and have uncomplicated animal sex with them. The world would undoubtedly be a happier place if they did. Certainly the den of depravity where I found myself at 3am was a considerably happier place. I had already had uncomplicated animal sex with two attractive men – at least, they looked pretty attractive in the dark – and was hot on the trail of number three. I did not expect to marry them, fall in love with them or even find out their names. All around me groans and grunts indicated that a thoroughly happy new year was being had by all.

Even pro-homosexual marriage author Jonathan Rauch admits that "male-male couples put a somewhat lower value on sexual fidelity within a relationship than do male-female couples," although he goes on to say that the "somewhat" may not be that much of a big deal.[39]

The problem of cruising and sexual encounters in public places also needs to be pointed out. A recent newspaper report noted that a Myer department store had to close customer toilets due to rampant homosexual activity taking place there.[40] A homosexual website claims to list more than 15,000 locations around Australia "where gay and bisexual guys meet for sex". These include well-known Sydney buildings, parks and beaches, even the Sydney Opera House toilets.

According to a Sydney security guard who works in the Myer store, the problem was due to men using the toilet as a hook-up point. He said: "The whole city has got that problem." Indeed, other public places have been locking their toilets as well to prevent this from happening.[41]

As the above makes clear, for homosexual couples to have long-term monogamous relationships seems pretty rare. But one might be asking, so what? If it is a matter of consenting adults, it's up to them. That may be true, but given that same-sex marriage and adoption rights are on the homosexual agenda, then a third party enters the equation: children. (A recent survey found that 90.5 per cent of Australian homosexuals and lesbians wanted legal changes to allow them to adopt children.)[42]

Most people recognise that children have a right to be raised in loving, stable, committed relationships. Homosexual relationships do not seem to provide that stability and permanence.

True, not all heterosexual marriages are loving or stable, but that is the exception, not the rule. And that is why the marriage contract is so important: it provides some assurance that society recognises the importance of permanence in male/female relationships when children are involved.

And social science evidence bears this out. Numerous studies have found that heterosexual spouses are much more faithful and monogamous than homosexual couples. Consider but three studies. The authors of the definitive *Sex in America* report that 90 per cent of wives and 75 per cent of husbands claim never to have had extramarital sex.[43] It also found that 83 per cent of heterosexual couples were monogamous, while fewer than two per cent of homosexual couples were.[44]

A nationally representative survey published in the *Journal of Sex Research* found that 77 per cent of married men and 88 per cent of married women had remained faithful to their marriage vows.[45] And another national survey found that 75 per cent of husbands and 85 per cent of wives never had sexual relations outside of marriage.[46]

Consider again the issue of children in all this. Children need parental stability in their lives, and the general lack of it in homosexual relationships is another reason why we should not encourage, endorse or promote such relationships. Not only are they less stable, less monogamous and less committed, but they are less likely to last, as well.

Research on this issue is also quite clear. Let me draw upon just one representative study. A major Swedish research study into same-sex unions and divorce rates found these alarming figures: homosexual couples were 50 per cent more likely to divorce than married heterosexual couples, and lesbian couples were 167 per cent more likely to divorce than married heterosexual couples.[47]

Before moving on, it will be noted that much of the above information mostly pertains to male homosexuals. Lesbians experience fewer health risks, but still face higher than average risks when compared to heterosexual women. Consider just three examples. A recent University of California study found that lesbians are at greater risk of heart disease than heterosexual women. Australian data have come up with similar findings.[48] A study of nearly 2,300 adults found that lesbians are more than twice as likely to be overweight and obese as heterosexual women.[49]

And researchers using a British survey of 6,399 women found that:[50]

> … compared with women who reported sex exclusively with men, women who reported sex with women and men reported

significantly greater male partner numbers, unsafe sex, smoking, alcohol consumption, and intravenous drug use and had an increased likelihood of induced abortion and sexually transmitted infection diagnoses. For women, a history of sex with women may be a marker for increased risk of adverse sexual, reproductive, and general health outcomes compared with women who reported sex exclusively with men.

Unhealthy practices and lifestyle concerns

A second area that distinguishes homosexual relationships from heterosexual ones is in the kinds of activities in which each engage. Undoubtedly, some heterosexual relationships involve unhealthy or dangerous practices. But they don't seem to be the norm, whereas in homosexual relationships, a number of unhealthy and dangerous practices seem to be widespread and fairly common.

A lot of medical evidence, as recorded in such journals as *The Lancet, The Journal of the American Medical Association* and *The British Medical Journal,* has shown how unhealthy homosexual practices can be. According to Dr Bernard J. Klamecki, a rectal specialist of 30 years' experience, the sexual practices of the average homosexual typically affect "the oral cavities, lungs, penis, prostate, bladder, anus, perianal areas outside of the rectum, rectum, colon, vagina, uterus, pelvic area, brain, skin, blood, immune system, and the other body systems".[51]

A number of practices – some which are too offensive to be described in detail here – entail serious health risks.[52] Such behaviours are not unknown among heterosexuals, but are far less frequently practised. For example, a 1992 study found that "fisting" or "handballing" is practised by some 42 per cent of the male homosexual community, but only by two per cent of the male heterosexual community. Twenty-nine per cent of male homosexuals report being involved in "golden showers" while only four per cent of male heterosexuals have practised it. Also, 37 per cent of male homosexuals indulge in sado-masochism, contrasted to five per cent of heterosexual males.[53]

The Australian SMASH report found that 70 per cent of homosexual men with regular male partners engaged in "rimming", 20 per cent engaged in sado-masochism, and 20 per cent engaged in group sex.[54] It found that in sexual behaviour with casual male partners, 47 per cent engaged in group sex.[55]

A more recent SMASH report found these trends continuing, and getting worse. Over a four-year period more than 21 per cent of male homosexuals had more than 50 sexual partners.[56] Also over a four-year period, 40 per cent of male homosexuals engaged in sado-masochism, and 25 per cent engaged in "watersports" with regular partners.[57] And with casual male partners, 45 per cent engaged in S&M and 20 per cent engaged in "watersports".[58] Finally, more than 82 per cent had engaged in group sex with casual partners over the last four years.[59]

> **Various studies show that homosexuals account for the majority of new cases of sexually-transmitted diseases.**

The Gay Report, a book much praised in homosexual communities, contains testimonials without adverse comment of homosexual encounters with labrador retrievers, cows and horses.[60] The 1992 report mentioned above found that 15 per cent of male homosexuals and 19 per cent of male bisexuals had sex with animals, compared with three per cent of male heterosexuals.[61] As lesbian activist Sara Cohen puts it: "What's wrong with a little bestiality?"[62]

And another classic homosexual volume, *The Joy of Gay Sex* became so popular that it was updated in 1992 to become *The New Joy of Gay Sex*. Written by a New York clinical psychologist, this volume was published by mainstream publisher HarperCollins. In the book the author says:[63]

> Moralists condemn sex with animals as disgusting, immoral, and generally horrible. ... Like other inexperienced city dwellers, we may not so readily fathom the mechanics of cow-, sheep- or horse-f***ing, but see no reason to condemn it out of hand.

Moreover, various studies show that homosexuals account for the majority of new cases of sexually-transmitted diseases.[64] For example, a male homosexual is 14 times more likely to have syphilis than a male heterosexual, and eight times more likely to have hepatitis.[65]

The picture is similar in Australia. In Victoria, for example, there has been a huge rise in cases of syphilis in the homosexual community. Rates have "sky-rocketed", according to one report in a homosexual newspaper. While there were zero cases in 1999, there were 60 cases in 2003 and 50 cases in the first half of 2004. A doctor who works in a St Kilda clinic said that "it appears to be occurring predominantly, almost completely, inside the men who sleep with men community". The doctor said that there had been a jump in gonorrhoea and chlamydia diagnoses as well.[66]

And a study released at the annual conference of the Australasian Society for HIV Medicine held in Canberra in 2004 found that syphilis outbreaks had increased among homosexual men in all Australian capital cities.[67]

The epidemic of sexually-transmitted diseases is further intensified by recreational drug use. Homosexuals – both male and female – have significantly higher percentages of drug and alcohol problems. American research has found that 47 per cent of male homosexuals have a history of alcohol abuse (compared to 24 per cent of males generally), and 51 per cent have a history of drug abuse (compared to seven cent of males generally). Thirty per cent of homosexuals – both male and female – are problem drinkers, as compared to 10 per cent of the general population.[68]

The SMASH report found that 82 per cent of Australian homosexuals some-times use recreational drugs.[69] An update of the SMASH report found that 21 per cent of those surveyed used amyl at least weekly; 33 per cent used marijuana at least weekly; 16 per cent used heroin, cocaine or speed at least monthly, and 12 per cent injected other drugs.[70]

A recent study conducted by the Alternative Lifestyle Organisation (ALSO) and the Australian Drug Foundation found that homosexuals have a much higher rate of drug usage than does the general population. For example, "65 per cent of gay, lesbian, bisexual and queer men aged 20 to 29 and 36 per cent of women in the same category have used ecstasy. This is compared to

19 per cent of men and 12 per cent of women in the same age group in the national survey".[71]

And a much more recent admission from AIDS Council of NSW (now known as ACON) chief executive Nicholas Parkhill further makes this point: "… people in ACON's communities have higher rates of drug use than the mainstream Australian population and … they are at elevated risks of harms as a consequence."[72]

Also, a study of 16,000 adolescents in America, as reported in the *Archives of Paediatrics and Adolescent Medicine*, found that lesbian and bi-sexual teenagers are more likely to smoke and are more vulnerable to cigarette marketing than their straight sisters. Almost 40 per cent of lesbians and bisexuals smoked, compared to just six per cent of heterosexual teenage girls. This finding is in keeping with previous studies on the subject.[73]

In addition, according to the *International Journal of Eating Disorders*, homosexual men are at a greater risk of developing eating disorders, such as anorexia and bulimia, than heterosexual men.[74]

Also, researchers using data from the California Quality of Life Survey of 2,272 adults found that "gay men and bisexual and homosexually experienced heterosexual individuals had higher levels of psychological distress compared with exclusively heterosexual individuals".[75]

And a major recent study by the Center for Health Policy Research at the University of California, Los Angeles, found that older homosexual men and women "in California are more likely to suffer from chronic physical and mental health problems than their heterosexual counterparts".[76]

As a report in the *New York Times* put it:[77]

> Older gay and bisexual men – ages 50 to 70 – reported higher rates of high blood pressure, diabetes and physical disability than similar heterosexual men. Older gay and bisexual men also were 45 percent more likely to report psychological distress and 50 percent more likely to rate their health as fair or poor. In addition, one in five gay men in California was living with HIV infection, the researchers found.

And a recent study reported in the journal *Cancer* reported that homosexual men were twice as likely to have cancer as non-homosexual men. The study of more than 120,000 people in the state of California found that homosexual men were 1.9 times more likely to have cancer and were diagnosed with cancer 10 years earlier than other men. Said the study: "The greater cancer prevalence among gay men may be caused by a higher rate of anal cancer, as suggested by earlier studies that point to an excess risk of anal cancer."[78]

The result of all this is lessened life expectancy among homosexual men.

One writer has summarised the situation this way: "For the vast majority of homosexual men, and for a significant number of homosexual women – even apart from the deadly plague of AIDS – sexual behaviour is obsessive, psychopathological and destructive to the body."[79]

The result of all this is lessened life expectancy among homosexual men. A number of studies have demonstrated this. For example, a study in the *International Journal of Epidemiology* found that homosexual men, because of HIV/AIDS and other diseases, can expect a life up to 21 years shorter than other men. The authors state:[80]

> In a major Canadian centre, life expectancy at age 20 years for gay and bisexual men is 8 to 20 years less than for all men. If the same pattern of mortality were to continue, we estimate that nearly half of gay and bisexual men currently aged 20 years will not reach their 65th birthday. Under even the most liberal assumptions, gay and bisexual men in this urban centre are now experiencing a life expectancy similar to that experienced by all men in Canada in the year 1871.

Let me conclude with two final citations. Even though I have referred to numerous medical and scientific journals here, and plenty of research conducted by the homosexual community itself, there will still be critics who will want to discount all this, and/or attempt to shoot the messenger.

So let me present two final witnesses as I make my case, both coming from the Gay and Lesbian Medical Association (GLMA). They have issued two publications warning of the health risks associated with both homosexual and lesbian lifestyles.

Each one lists ten major areas of concern. Let me list just a few of these here. For male homosexuals, the GLMA says that they have "an increased risk of HIV infection" and have "an increased risk of sexually transmitted infection with the viruses that cause the serious condition of the liver known as hepatitis".[81]

Also, homosexuals "use substances at a higher rate than the general population" and "depression and anxiety appear to affect gay men at a higher rate than in the general population". It also says that "gay men have higher rates of alcohol dependence and abuse than straight men" and that "gay men use tobacco at much higher rates than straight men".[82]

Lesbians are also warned about their risky behaviour: "Lesbians have the richest concentration of risk factors for breast cancer than any subset of women in the world." Also, lesbians "have the highest risks for many of the gynaecological cancers". In addition, "alcohol use and abuse may be higher among lesbians."[83]

However, given that so many people – for ideological reasons – will wish to dismiss all of the evidence provided above, let me conclude by offering more medical testimony, as presented in the homosexual press, and by a homosexual doctor. People can dismiss my remarks, or those of straight people, but when homosexual doctors writing for the mainstream homosexual press make this case, then perhaps we do need to listen carefully.

I refer to homosexual MD Frank Spinelli who wrote an important article for the major American homosexual publication, *The Advocate*. He begins this way:[84]

> Imagine for a moment that you're a doctor – a gay doctor with a practice that predominantly treats gay men. Now guess how many text and phone calls you might receive during any given weekend involving questions that have to do with recreational drugs, penile discharge, or the risk of contracting HIV from unprotected sexual encounters. Now take that number and multiply it by 10 if that

weekend should occur around Gay Pride, Folsom Street Fair, Gay Days at Disney, or any one of the Atlantis cruises. Welcome to my world.

He continues:

> Over the years I have monitored and treated gay men with curiosity. I've concluded that some of the most telling insights into the gay mind come from watching my own (presumably) heterosexual nephews. At age 15 and 16, they don't always listen to their parents, they're eager to push the limits set by their teachers, and when confronted about their risk-taking behavior, they invariably roll their eyes to show their disinterest in having a rational conversation. That's because teenagers, like gay men, are a conundrum, baffling to scientists and doctors.

> I'm not alone. My colleagues in Manhattan and Los Angeles give similar reports about their patients. We scratch our heads and wonder why the rates for syphilis are at an all-time high among men who have sex with men. And with all the media attention paid to HIV prevention and risk modification, the majority of new HIV cases in the United States are among gay men.

His description of a homosexual cruise ship experience is worth recounting at length:

> Of course, the obvious culprit is that we are fueled by our desires, whether these are sexual or drug-fueled escapes, especially when these desires have been liberated after years of confusion and confinement. Who wouldn't want to go on a sex, drug, and alcohol binge while drifting through the Caribbean on a gay cruise where there are no judgmental eyes watching your every move?

> On February 6 the Royal Caribbean ship *Allure of the Seas* set sail from Port Everglades, Fla. In what was billed as the largest gay cruise ever, Atlantis hosted more than 5,400 passengers. 'Where does it go?' I asked one patient as he reviewed a list of prescriptions he would need for his upcoming trip: Cialis, Xanax, and Ambien. ... 'Who cares,' he said. 'I'm never getting off the boat.' Several days later the text messages started to arrive, 'This trip is a disaster. Guys

are overdosing left and right. The authorities boarded the ship and arrested a drug dealer. They have dogs and they're making surprise room searches.'

Agents who searched a suspected dealer's cabin reported finding more than 140 ecstasy pills, nearly three grams of methamphetamine, a small quantity of ketamine, and about $51,000 in cash. While waiting for the suspect in his cabin, two more passengers stopped by seeking drugs, according to agents.

When I read the article online and spoke to passengers upon their return, I felt angry. In a time when gay men and women want to be taken seriously so that we can serve openly in the military and have the legal right to marry, isn't it counterproductive to read about the drug busts and overdoses on a floating circuit party? Or maybe we just want it all – the rights we deserve and the option to choose which, if any, fit into our particular circumstances and plans.

He concludes with these telling words:

If 5,400 people, mostly gay men, go on an Atlantis cruise, what percentage will succumb to the impulses of the reward system by using recreational drugs, drinking alcohol, and engaging in unsafe sex? Now take that number and multiply it by 10. Despite the arrest, Atlantis announced that it will repeat the trip in 2012. I hope it's over a weekend when I'm not on call.

Similar stories by other doctors – both heterosexual and homosexual – can be repeated time and time again. What we have here is a reckless, irresponsible and unsafe lifestyle that no one should be engaging in, let alone promoting and seeking to normalise.

Violence

Mention can also be made of violence in the homosexual community. The media often report cases of homosexuals attacked by heterosexuals.

Of course, such attacks are to be condemned, and no physical or verbal abuse of homosexuals is to be countenanced. However, the research makes it clear that much of the violence against homosexuals is perpetrated by other homosexuals.

Indeed, so prominent is the problem that a number of books have been written devoted to this subject. As an example, consider the book, *Men Who Beat the Men Who Love Them: Battered Gay Men and Domestic Violence*. In this volume authors David Island and Patrick Letellier report that "the incidence of domestic violence among gay men is nearly double that in the heterosexual population".[85]

Numerous articles in the scholarly literature also bear this out. For example, a recent study reported in the *American Journal of Public Health* discovered higher rates of partner abuse among men who have sex with men (MSM). The study, conducted in four major American cities between 1996 and 1998, found that "rates of battering victimization among urban MSM are substantially higher than among heterosexual men and possibly heterosexual women".[86]

It appears that lesbian relationships also contain a high level of abuse. For example, one study found that a third of lesbians surveyed reported physical abuse from their lesbian partners.[87] And a survey of more than 1,000 lesbians found that "slightly more than half of the [lesbians] reported that they had been abused by a female lover/partner. The most frequently indicated forms of abuse were verbal/emotional/psychological abuse and combined physical-psychological abuse."[88]

And in a book discussing the problem of violence in female homosexual relationships, the author concludes with these words: "In short, friends and the community itself must recognize that battering is a problem among lesbian couples, and that its consequences are as serious as those of heterosexual battering – perhaps more serious."[89]

The homosexual press itself also highlights this problem. For example, in Australia the New South Wales Anti-Violence Project has warned homosexual people about "dangers of violence from members of their own community". It spoke of a "series of recent gay-on-gay attacks around Oxford Street" in Sydney. A spokesman for the group said that in addition to violence from without, "we should be prepared to respond to violence from within the community as well" and that these actions should be reported.[90]

Concerning those Oxford Street incidents, some tried to downplay the violence, with one homosexual venue owner saying this was just a "spat" between homosexual men. This prompted one homosexual writer to complain to a homosexual newspaper: "Does this mean that violence against gay men by straights is violence, but violence against gay men by other gay men is just 'a tiff'? Where does that leave gay domestic violence?"[91] Good questions indeed.

In sum, this is not a safe lifestyle.

Another homosexual writer admits that "up until recently, violence by gay people against their partners was effectively a taboo topic in the community."[92] A counselling manager at the Victorian AIDS Council said she found a "lot of gay men coming to her had issues with violence. ... It's been too difficult in the community to talk about it until now."[93] A homosexual men's health educator said: "The reality is it hasn't been accepted because of the view that 'gay men won't be violent'."[94]

In sum, this is not a safe lifestyle. And to list such unhealthy behaviours is not, of course, being homophobic. The more honest homosexual organisations make similar warnings. For example, just prior to the November 2002 Sydney Gay Games, there appeared an article in the homosexual press predicting a sharp rise in sexually-transmitted diseases (STDs) as a result of the games. According to the article, the Victorian AIDS Council/Gay Men's Health Centre warned that Australia's low syphilis levels could rise sharply at the gay games. And they warned that the rampant gonorrhoea epidemic could get much worse at the games. With an influx of thousands of homosexual men and HIV-positive men to Australia, the STDs are sure to increase, they warned. And Health Promotion team manager Colin Batrouney said that STDs among Australian homosexual men were bound to rise. He said syphilis was unlikely to be prevented by condom use for anal sex and can infect different parts of the body including the throat.[95]

It has been a major victory of the homosexual movement to deflect attention away from homosexual behaviour and practice, and to re-focus it on more neutral areas like "rights" and "discrimination". This is all according to plan. As one influential homosexual activist manual put it: "The public should not be shocked and repelled by premature exposure to homosexual behavior itself."[96]

Pedophilia

Finally, and most disturbingly, one must examine the issue of pedophilia. While not every homosexual engages in, nor approves of, this practice, there is a significant percentage – of both individuals and organisations – that does seem to. Aside from the obvious clues, such as banners at homosexual rallies with phrases like "We're here, we're queer, and we want your children" and "Sex before eight, or else it's too late", there is more reliable information.

A survey done by two homosexual authors revealed that three-fourths of homosexuals had at some time had sex with boys 16 to 19 or younger.[97] A coalition of homosexual groups since as early as 1972 has sought the repeal of age-of-consent laws, arguing that children as young as eight years have a right to decide whether they enter into a sexual relationship with an adult.[98]

Groups like the North American Man-Boy Love Association (NAMBLA), which have regularly marched in Gay Pride parades in the past, have gone on record as wanting pedophilia legalised:[99]

> NAMBLA takes the view that sex is good, that homosexuality is good not only for adults, but for young people as well. We support all consensual sexual relationships regardless of age. As long as the relationship is mutually pleasurable and no one's rights are violated, sex should be no one else's business.

The pedophile connection is not confined to North America. For example, a Dutch social psychologist and pro-pedophilia lecturer describes in an article, "Pedophilia and the Gay Movement" how influential pedophiles have been in the homosexual movement in the Netherlands.[100]

One Australian surveyed 30 issues of the *Gay Community News*, from 1980 to 1983. He found that 16 issues carried one or more articles or news stories on pedophilia.[101] Other Australian homosexual magazines also contain similar levels of coverage on pedophilia. At a 1982 conference in Canberra for Lesbians and Homosexual Men, a workshop leader said, "Pedophiles will be free when kids are free and not before", and urged that the effort to undermine public resistance to pedophilia be continued.[102] Dennis Altman has weighed into the argument, describing pederasty (male paedophilia) as among the "safest" of stigmatised forms of gay sexuality, one that "often amounts to no more than acts of mutual masturbation".[103]

> **And then we have had pro-homosexual authors writing in praise of lowering age-of-consent laws.**

Indeed, early conferences on homosexuality regularly held sessions on paedophilia. However, public pressure resulted in such courses being phased out. For example, a planned workshop on paedophilia was cancelled at an Annual Conference of Lesbians and Homosexual Men at the University of Queensland in September of 1984. However the then-president of the university student union condemned the cancellation, saying it was an attack on freedom of speech![104]

And then we have had pro-homosexual authors writing in praise of lowering age-of-consent laws. One university press published a book by Judith Levine arguing that it was harmful to protect children from sex. In it she said age-of-consent laws should be reduced to 12 for sexual relations between children and adults.[105]

Moreover, homosexual behaviour seems to be associated with child abuse. A recent review of the child molestation literature as it appears in medical and psychological journals concluded that between 25 and 40 per cent of all recorded child molestation was homosexual.[106] A Family Research Institute's national (US) random survey of 4,340 adults found that about a third of those who reported having been molested were homosexually molested. Other polls have come out with similar findings.[107] Also, homosexual paedophiles victimise far more children than do heterosexual paedophiles (150 to 20).[108]

One research project discussed the "high prevalence of homosexuality in pedophiles (25% in this study)".[109] The researchers went on to say that "the prevalence of homosexuality is about 10 times higher in paedophiles than in teleiophiles [those attracted to adults]".[110]

In addition to the research, anecdotal evidence can also be marshalled. Just one recent Melbourne case will suffice. The founder of an under-18 homosexual disco was charged with 11 counts of sexual assault involving a child under 16 years. He no longer holds a position on the board of the underage dance party organisation, which caters especially for homosexuals and lesbians.[111]

Australian expatriate Peter Tatchell, a leading British homosexual activist, has made his views clear on underage sex: "The age of consent should be reduced to 14 for everyone – gay and straight –

> Enough people, both within and without the homosexual community, have acknowledged that these unsafe practices are a common feature of the homosexual lifestyle, that such an exposé seems necessary.

and consensual sex involving people under 14 should not be prosecuted providing there is no more than three years' difference in the partners' ages."[112]

In fairness, however, it should be noted that a good number of homosexuals do not want to be associated with pedophiles, and some have sought to distance themselves from the pedophilia movement. For example, the International Lesbian and Gay Association (ILGA) has recently voted to expel the North American Man/Boy Love Association from its membership.[113] It is a fair question to ask, however, why the association was granted membership in ILGA in the first place. Moreover, as jilted association leaders were quick to point out, ILGA still contains dozens of member groups that support man/boy lovers or have paedophile or pederast subgroups.[114]

In sum, the purpose of mentioning all of these facts on unhealthy practices is not to judge individual homosexuals nor to imply that all homosexuals share some of the negative traits described above. But enough people, both within and without the homosexual community, have acknowledged that these unsafe practices are a common feature of the homosexual lifestyle, that such an exposé seems necessary, especially since the mainstream media often will not delve into these sorts of issues. If for no other reason than the broad issue of public health and safety, these facts need to be accessible and need to be acted upon for the general good.

Given that the Federal Government is spending tax dollars to try to convince Australians to be tolerant and understanding of various "alternative" lifestyles, one has to ask why it carries on a double standard. Why does it spend millions of dollars on campaigns to get Australians to give up unsafe practices like smoking or drink-driving, but when it comes to dangerous homosexual behaviour, not only does it not try to warn the community about such high-risk behaviour, but it actually seems to be promoting it, by granting homosexuals legal recognition and, as a result, social endorsement.

Indeed, governments are quite happy to show graphic images of what smoking does to people, or bloody images of road accidents. Yet it presents no such picture of the high-risk homosexual lifestyle. Part of the reason for this, of course, is that it is exactly what the homosexual lobby has been actively involved in: keeping their harmful practices hidden from the public.

As one leading homosexual activist manual states: "Gays must launch a large-scale campaign – we've called it the Waging Peace campaign – to reach straights through the mainstream media. We're talking about propaganda." And to do this, the media campaign should "portray only the most favorable side of gays".[115] They go on to speak of "the wide range of favorably *sanitized* images that might be shown in the media" (italics added). This strategy is obviously paying off.

Such a double standard can only lead many to believe that the homosexual lobby has far greater influence with the media and the Federal Government than first imagined. It will also lead to some deadly consequences.

31

Homosexual suicide

Finally, a word about suicide. It is often claimed by homosexual activists and their sympathisers in the media that pro-homosexual education and legislation is needed because of high levels of homosexual suicide. It is claimed that "homophobia" in society is driving many homosexuals to suicide. But are these claims true?

One general observation is in order. Yes, there are more suicides among homosexuals than in the heterosexual community, just as there are greater occurrences of depression, mental illness, substance abuse, and so on. But the common line that this is due to homophobia just does not stand up. A simple way to test this is to look at places where homosexuality is very much accepted, such as in nations like Holland or cities like San Francisco or Sydney. One would expect less suicide and fewer mental health problems among homosexuals in these places. But that is not the case. As much if not more suicide and related problems occur in these localities. So homophobia cannot be to blame.

As one commentator puts it: "Studies done in the Netherlands and New Zealand, for example, where there is generally high tolerance of sexual 'diversity,' found the same high rates of psychological difficulties as those done elsewhere."[116]

More specifically, the claim is often made that homosexual and lesbian teenagers are two to three times more likely to attempt suicide. Another version of this oft-quoted "statistic" is that 30 per cent of teenage suicides are committed by homosexual youth. Often it is claimed that this is a "government statistic". In point of fact, however, this is just not true. It is neither a correct figure nor is it a government figure. So where does this figure come from?

The myth of homosexual teen suicide mainly derives from a study by a San Francisco social worker named Paul Gibson. His study, "Gay Male and Lesbian Youth Suicide" was incorporated into a 1989 report published by the U.S. Department of Health and Human Services (HHS). This study has been criticised for methodological weaknesses. Dr David Shaffer, a psychiatrist at Columbia University, said that Gibson's study "was never subjected to the rigorous peer review that is required for publication in a scientific journal".[117] For example, he did not properly distinguish between suicide attempts and actual suicides. Also, he began by taking statistics from homosexual sources, then applied them to the general population by using the discredited Kinsey figures. Sexologist Alfred Kinsey had claimed that 10 per cent of the population was homosexual – a figure now widely rejected. These and other shortcomings prompted the then-HHS Secretary Louis Sullivan to distance himself from Gibson's study: "... the views expressed in the paper entitled 'Gay Male and Lesbian Youth Suicide' do not in any way represent my personal beliefs or the beliefs of this department".[118]

The claims of high homosexual suicide rates are therefore unfounded.

Other authorities have also condemned the study. Peter Muehrer of the National Institute of Mental Health said: "There is no scientific evidence to support this figure"[119]. A 1994 panel – convened by such groups as the Centers for Disease Control and Prevention, the American Psychological Association, and the American Association of Suicidology – made this finding: "There is no population-based evidence that sexual orientation and suicidality are linked in some direct or indirect manner."[120] One study published in *Pediatrics* in 1991, entitled "Risk factors for attempted suicide in gay and bisexual youth", examined 137 youths who deemed themselves "gay". Says the study: "In this sample, bisexuality or homosexuality per se was not associated with self-destructive acts."[121] This study found that fewer than one in 10 homosexual youths attempted suicide because of their homosexuality. Bear in mind again that attempts are always much more common than completed suicides.

The claims of high homosexual suicide rates are therefore unfounded. But these myths keep being repeated because they serve the overall cause of the militant homosexual lobby: to get mainstream acceptance of homosexuality. Indeed, by using skewed statistics, homosexual activists are seeking to win over societal acceptance. This strategy is outlined in the influential homosexual publication, *After the Ball*, by Marshall Kirk and Hunter Madsen. In this book the authors urge homosexuals to cast themselves as victims and "invite straights to be their protectors".[122] Such a strategy is obviously working.

Indeed, it has resulted in many schools inviting homosexuals into the classroom to tell students that homosexuality is normal, and that students need to overcome their "homophobia". Polished videos have been produced by the homosexual lobby to convince teachers to invite in homosexuals to help change children's perceptions of homosexuality. A number of elementary schools in America have done just that, and there is pressure on for Australian schools to do the same.

It is important therefore that the myths of homosexual teenage suicide be exposed. As one pro-family leader has commented: "Teen suicide is always a tragedy. But tragedies should never be manipulated in order to advance an agenda – especially one that lures youth into an immoral, disease-ridden lifestyle."[123]

CHAPTER 3

The Politics of AIDS

Aside from all of the above-mentioned problems, there still remains the tragic issue of HIV/AIDS. This has been a problem of plague proportions in the homosexual community and needs to be addressed.

Perhaps the ultimate indicator of unsafe and unhealthy activities practised by homosexuals can be found in their average life expectancy. A study of 5,371 obituaries of homosexuals revealed that the average age of death of a homosexual with AIDS is 39 years, and the average age of one without AIDS is 42 years.[1]

Other studies vindicate such findings. For example, a study published in the *International Journal of Epidemiology* found that the life expectancy of homosexuals is eight to 20 years less than that of heterosexual men.[2]

And some of the most recent research shows what high levels of HIV there are among homosexual men. One large-scale study found that one-fifth of all U.S. homosexuals have HIV. This is how one report covered the news:[3]

> One in five gay men in the United States has HIV, and almost half of those who carry the virus are unaware that they are infected,

according to a new Centers for Disease Control and Prevention study.

The study tested more than 8,000 men in 21 cities in 2008, making it the most comprehensive such research by the CDC. It found that young, sexually active gay men and those in minority groups are least likely to know their health status, even as infection rates are climbing among men who have sex with men, while the rates of other at-risk groups – heterosexuals and intravenous drug users – are falling.

Surely such tragic statistics show how homosexual behaviour has very unhealthy outcomes. As Australian government statistics have made quite plain, it is homosexual activity that accounts for the majority of HIV cases. More specifically, 94 per cent of people known to be HIV-positive are men, and at least 85 per cent of cases of AIDS in Australia are attributed to male homosexual or bisexual contact.[4]

More recent reports show similar, if not worse, trends. As described in the homosexual press, according to recent reports, "there has been a 17% increase in HIV transmissions in 2002, a trend that has continued in 2003. Over 90% of reported transmissions were related to homosexual sex. There also has been a 24% increase since 1998 in the number of men in Sydney having unprotected sex with casual partners."[5]

Even more recent reports show the same trends. According to a 2006 report issued by the National Centre in HIV Epidemiology and Clinical Research, there has been a 41 per cent rise in cases of persons diagnosed with HIV between 2000 and 2005.[6] Time has not altered this. The rise later still remains at 41 per cent.[7]

And according to the April 2006 *Australian HIV Surveillance Report*, exposure to AIDS was mainly through male homosexual contact, and injecting drug use. Indeed, 90.3 per cent of people diagnosed with HIV in 2005 were male.[8]

Altogether, 80.5 per cent of cases in 2005 were due to male homosexual/bisexual contact; 4.9 per cent were due to male homosexual/bisexual contact and drug use; and 3.4 per cent were due to injecting drug use. Thus homo-sexuality and drug use accounted for 88.8 per cent of all cases. Heterosexual contact amounted to a mere 8.8 per cent.[9]

Of even newer figures (from the January 2007 *Australian HIV Surveillance Report*), 93.3 per cent of new cases of HIV infection diagnosed in the third quarter of 2006 were through "homosexual contact".[10]

Nearly half of all young homosexual men have unprotected sex.

A 1996-97 survey of homo-sexual men in Sydney found that although 97 per cent were aware of AIDS, nearly half said they had not changed their behaviour in response. Said the report: "The results of the ... survey indicate a decreasing concern for HIV/AIDS and a state of global complacency. This ... severely inhibits real progress in the fight against AIDS".[11] The 2000 SMASH report found that over a four-year period only 18.9 per cent of male homosexuals never had anal intercourse without a condom with regular male partners.[12]

In fact, even simple precautions like condom use are ignored. Recent stud-ies in the U.S. have shown that nearly half of all young homosexual men have unprotected sex.[13] Studies conducted in Australia show similar results. A SMASH spokesman said years of post-epidemic proactive education are inducing a level of "safe sex fatigue".[14] In Victoria, medical authorities have warned of a new AIDS crisis, with a 67 per cent HIV increase among homosexual men.[15] And a Queensland study found that only 20.8 per cent of homosexuals always used a condom with regular partners.[16]

More recent reports indicate HIV/AIDS infection rates continue to rise in NSW and Victoria. Carelessness, belief that the virus has been cured, and the practice of "bare-backing" have lead to the increase. Bare-backing (sex without condoms), coupled with safe-sex fatigue, has become a new concern among some homosexual commentators.[17]

Indeed, many homosexual websites feature homosexual men who proudly proclaim they are into bare-backing. And a recent Health in Men study by the National Centre in HIV Social Research found that 55 per cent of homosexual men did not disclose their HIV status to casual partners at any stage during the six months prior to the survey.[18] And according to reports found in extreme homosexual literature, some healthy homosexual men have actively sought HIV-positive partners so they could become infected.[19]

It may not be politically correct to say so, but if we seriously discouraged homosexual activity, we would greatly reduce the number of deaths due to AIDS in the Western world. Says one authority:[20]

> AIDS is a preventable, behavior-related disease. And we know what works in preventing the spread of AIDS. The virus is primarily spread by having sexual contact with an infected person or by sharing hypodermic needles or syringes with an infected person. Avoiding such behavior greatly reduces – indeed it almost entirely removes – the chances of becoming infected. Given the awful consequences of contracting the AIDS virus, it should be clear enough that public officials as well as members of the public health community have a basic responsibility to speak up for the true and time-honored, for things like restraint and responsibility on matters of sexual behavior.

Instead of claiming victim status, shouting homophobia, and blaming the rest of society, homosexuals need to take responsibility for their own actions. The simple truth is, if we want to see a real reduction in the number of AIDS cases, homosexuals will need to stop their high-risk sexual practices.

This is a truth that even some homosexuals have acknowledged. Consider this forthright comment by an American homosexual:[21]

> By continuing to engage in sexual practices that spread HIV, we are contributing to our own massacre. What is wrong with us? Are we so self-hating that we welcome death, that we would trade 10 minutes of pleasure for a lifetime of illness? ... The gay men who are now contracting HIV through unsafe sex are not victims. They have consciously decided to disregard their own health and the welfare of their community.

Who is really at risk?

Initially, the homosexual community and its supporters tried to convince the rest of society that AIDS could be caught by anyone. Even they no longer run this line. As one homosexual activist recently admitted: "Between 1983 and 2001 there was [sic] over 8,000 people with AIDS in Australia, of whom over 6,000 died. The great majority of these were gay men. More than 20,000 people, again mostly homosexual men, have been diagnosed with HIV infection ..."[22]

> In the West, homosexual activity is the main way the AIDS disease is passed on, along with intravenous drug usage.

The truth is, in Australia in particular, and the West in general, AIDS is primarily a homosexual disease. Indeed, back in 1981 when it was first being recognised in America, it was called GRID: Gay-Related Immunodeficiency Disease. It was only after protests from the homosexual community that the name was changed to AIDS (Acquired Immuno-Deficiency Syndrome).[23]

In the West, homosexual activity is the main way the AIDS disease is passed on, along with intravenous drug usage. Avoid the homosexual lifestyle, and intravenous drug use, and you have a greatly reduced chance of getting AIDS. As one author put it, "as rare as male breast cancer is, more native-born American males are diagnosed with the disease *each year* than the total number who have contracted AIDS through heterosexual intercourse since the AIDS epidemic began".[24]

Thus the early campaigns designed to convince heterosexuals that they were equally at risk of getting AIDS were exercises in propaganda and political correctness. When people like Madonna exclaimed that "AIDS doesn't discriminate", she was being disingenuous at best. So too were those who put out the Grim Reaper ads in Australia in the early days of the epidemic. It was patent nonsense and misinformation then, and still is. As Michael Fumento writes: "The slogans have a nice ring to them, but quickly fall apart under scrutiny. Bullets and knives don't discriminate either, but you're far more

39

likely to catch one walking through a dark South Bronx alley than strolling down a well-lit street on Manhattan's Upper East Side."[25]

The medical community has been unnecessarily politicised here:[26]

> Self-interest groups, as exemplified by the gay community, have influenced representatives of the medical community, politicians, and a sympathetic national press in a misguided effort to obscure public focus and protect a lifestyle. This effort has necessarily emasculated existing public health policies and effectively made AIDS the first politically-protected disease in history.

And it is not just conservative writers who have made these points. Consider a recent article in the UK *Guardian* newspaper. Not exactly known as a right-wing news source, the paper ran an important article in June 2008 that deserves wide reading.

Entitled "The Exploitation of AIDS", Brendan O'Neill argued that the "AIDS scare was one of the most distorted, duplicitous and cynical public health panics of the last 30 years".[27] He began his article with these words:[28]

> Finally we have a high-level admission that there is no threat of a global AIDS pandemic among heterosexuals. After 25 years of official scaremongering about western societies being ravaged by the disease – with salacious, tombstone-illustrated government propaganda warning people to wear a condom or 'die of ignorance' – the head of the World Health Organisation's HIV/AIDS department says there is no need for heterosexuals to fret.

He continues:

> Kevin de Cock, who has headed the global battle against AIDS, said at the weekend that, outside very poor African countries, AIDS is confined to 'high-risk groups', including men who have sex with men, injecting drug users, and sex workers. And even in these communities it remains quite rare. 'It is very unlikely there will be a heterosexual epidemic in countries [outside sub-Saharan Africa]', he said. In other words? All that hysterical fear-mongering about AIDS spreading among sexed-up western youth was a pack of lies.

He goes on to discuss how "the AIDS bureaucracy" knew for decades that this disease was not going to spread into the general community, but for various reasons went along with the deceptive panic-mongering anyway. "Instead of being treated as a sexually transmitted disease that affected certain high-risk communities, and which should be vociferously tackled by the medical authorities, the 'war against AIDS' was turned into moral crusade."

And a crusade it was. Those who dared to question the conventional wisdom were denounced and censored:

> Those who challenged the idea that AIDS would devour sexually promiscuous young people and transform once-civilised western societies into diseased dystopias were denounced as 'AIDS deniers' and 'heretics'. Anyone who suggested that homosexuals were at greater risk than heterosexuals – and therefore the focus of government funding and, where necessary, medical assistance should be in gay communities – was denounced as homophobic. Nothing could be allowed to stand in the way of the glorious moral effort to make everyone submit to the sexual and moral conformism of the AIDS crusaders.

> Even in Africa – where there is a serious and deadly AIDS crisis in some countries – the international focus on AIDS has been motivated more by pernicious moralism than straightforward charity. Diseases such as malaria and tuberculosis are bigger killers than AIDS. Yet focusing on AIDS allows western governments and NGOs to lecture Africans about their morality and personal behaviour. It also adds a new gloss to the misanthropic population-control arguments of western charities, which now present their promotion of condoms in 'overly fecund' Africa as a means of preventing the spread of disease.

O'Neill concludes:[29]

> The relentless politicisation and moralisation of AIDS has not only distorted public understanding of the disease and generated unnecessary fear and angst – it has also potentially cost lives. James Chin estimates that UNAIDS wastes around $1bn a year in activities such as 'raising awareness' about AIDS and preventing

the emergence of the disease in communities that are at little risk. How many lives could that kind of money save, if it were used to develop drugs and deliver them to infected or at-risk communities? It is time people treated AIDS as a normal disease, rather than as an opportunity for spreading their own moral agendas.

AIDS and public policy

Based on somewhat older figures, the average hospitalisation of an AIDS patient runs for four months and costs $80,000.[30] A much newer Australian figure provided by the Australian Federation of AIDS Organisations says "it would cost in the order of $240,000 to treat a PLWHA [people living with HIV/AIDS] over their lifetime in Australia".[31]

Homosexual acts, therefore, are not "victimless crimes", and the consequences must be borne by the entire community. In the 1997-98 financial year, HIV and AIDS treatments cost taxpayers $59 million, more than two per cent of the total cost of the Pharmaceutical Benefits Scheme.[32]

More recent figures are somewhat harder to come by. A recent briefing paper put out by the Australian Federation of AIDS Organisations (AFAO) concerning the 2006-2007 Federal Budget said this:[33]

> Previous federal budgets specified a budget for HIV/AIDS. For example, in 2002, this figure was $38 million. However, specific figures for sectoral spending are not included in this budget – a chart shows approximately $425 million in indirect and $325 million in direct spending in health. If calculating the 13% health expenditure from the total ODA [Official Development Assistance] (minus the one-off Iraq debt cancellation), the figure is $338 million. If using this figure to calculate the 28% of the health budget (down from 32% last year) allocated to STD control including HIV/AIDS, then spending is approximately 95 million.

Some 30 per cent of the health budget "allocated to STD control including

HIV/AIDS" is a very sizable percentage indeed. Obviously, illnesses suffered by heterosexuals are also borne by the community, but as the above has made clear, it seems the homosexual minority absorbs an inordinate proportion of public finances to deal with homosexual-related diseases and problems. The medical research just canvassed makes it clear that homosexual relationships are more than just private activities between consenting adults, but a public health problem of serious proportions.

Of course, in one sense no one is begrudging health care to any person for any reason. Thus taxpayers subsidise health care to cigarette smokers who bring upon such problems as lung cancer due to their lifestyle choices. Thus I am not denying the right of governments to provide health care for all their citizens. But the point being made is that private morality does have public consequences, and we all pay for these high-risk lifestyle choices.

Even though homosexual behaviour brings on so much sickness and death, it must be remembered that the number of AIDS cases, compared to some other health problems, is relatively low in Australia. Yet governments seem to spend disproportionate amounts of taxpayer funds on AIDS. Indeed, health issues have become politicised in Australia, with some issues appearing to be more politically correct than others. This can be seen in the way govern-ments allocate funding for various health problems. For example, the Federal Government spends much more money on AIDS, which takes the lives of about 600 Australians each year, than it does on breast cancer, which takes the lives of about 2,600 Australians each year. Consider the following facts from a decade ago:

- Every year 6,500 Australian women are told they have breast cancer; [over 2,600] a year die of it.[34]
- In 1992, 643 people died of AIDS-related causes.[35]
- The National Program for the Early Detection of Breast Cancer – Commonwealth outlays of $25.6m in 1993-94. AIDS Control: $54.3m in 1994-95 budget.[36]
- Some 4,000 women die each year of gynaecological cancer (cancers of the cervix, ovaries, uterus and vulva) and breast cancer. About 2,500 Australians in total have died of AIDS since the early 80s. $32

million has been set aside for three years to combat these cancers, but $62 million a year for AIDS.[37]

A call to Australia's federal Department of Health and Ageing (its present title) reveals that these figures have changed very little in the past few years. (Actual figures have not been sent to me, as was promised). Clearly, such a discrepancy indicates a political agenda at work. Such is the clout of the homosexual lobby that they have managed to take issues of life and death and skew them in their favour, and away from others.

This problem is not confined to Australia. Many West-

> **AIDS has become the nation's first politically-protected disease.**

ern countries have similar biases in their health funding. In America, for example, in the early 1990s, federal spending on AIDS per death was about $50,000, while it was $3,500 for cancer, $2,300 for breast cancer, and $900 for heart disease.[38]

Former U.S. President Bill Clinton admitted to such imbalance as he addressed a homosexual lobby group on November 8, 1997: "Since I became president, we're spending 10 times as much per fatality on people with AIDS as people with breast cancer or prostate cancer."[39] It's not just conservatives who are concerned about such mistaken priorities. Michael Johnston, a former homosexual who was dying of AIDS, said the president's remarks put him in a difficult position:[40]

> What do I say to the person who has breast cancer or prostate cancer when they find out that the president is pandering to homosexuals and is spending 10 times more on their disease – AIDS – when primarily it is the result of our foolish and immoral choices, as opposed to those who have breast cancer or prostate cancer through no fault of their own.

And given that the normal procedures associated with infectious diseases have not been used on AIDS, for fear of homosexual protests, it is clear, as some have put it, that AIDS has become the nation's first politically-protected disease. But AIDS should be treated as a medical issue, not a political one. AIDS is a health epidemic, requiring stringent measures. This should include all the normal means of prevention of transmission: public health departments should be able to know who has the disease through case-monitoring and contact-tracing; routine testing must be undertaken; and notification of carriers should be mandatory. As one author says, "we must stop romanticizing AIDS".[41]

As a co-founder of the Children's AIDS Fund in America put it:[42]

> Never before in medical history have we made it the responsibility of the individual exposed to a contagious or infectious disease to end such an epidemic. With HIV/AIDS, the medical and public health communities during the first fifteen years of the epidemic largely removed themselves from the intervention through aggressive diagnosis and reporting consistent with their approach to similar diseases.

It is because we have refused to treat HIV/AIDS as we have any other public health risk that we now are paying a terrible price. One doctor puts the situation in striking terms:[43]

> If a foreign nation were to attack our shores and kill 10,000 Americans, it would be considered an act of war. Yet, millions of Americans have already been unnecessarily infected in this epidemic and they will almost all die. The tragedy is that this epidemic should never have occurred.

At bottom, AIDS is not primarily a health issue but a behaviour issue. Stop the behaviour (homosexual activity, and needle-based drug use) and you pretty well stop the disease. These are not just the thoughts of bigoted right-wingers. Here is how one practising lesbian puts it:[44]

> Let's be honest. There is a way to stop the spread of AIDS – it's called abstaining from sex. Unlike with Alzheimer's disease, Parkinson's disease, or diabetes, you can make a decision to not get AIDS (with a few unfortunate exceptions, like the child of an infected mother or the victim of a contaminated blood transfusion). Considering its preventability, there is no excuse for AIDS being the biggest health crises we as a people face.

Another homosexual, writing in a leading American homosexual magazine, *The Advocate*, says that young homosexual men are ignorant of "a disease that has been around over 20 years. And if they are gay and male, they doubly deserve it. We've seen firsthand what it can do but choose to ignore that in favor of our own carnal desires."[45]

Fortunately, a bit of sanity is re-entering the debate. A leading Californian homosexual group has decided to go straight – that is, decided to get back to the truth about AIDS. The Los Angeles Gay and Lesbian Center is trying to reach the many homosexual men who have become complacent about HIV and AIDS. They have launched a major ad campaign with the frank admission: "HIV is a gay disease."

It is running this message on billboards and magazines, with the tag line "Own It. End It." The campaign is a major departure from the many years in which homosexuals "vigorously fought the contention that HIV is a disease of homosexuals".[46]

And a few brave voices are being heard in Australia as well. One is homosexual John Heard. He does not mince his words when it comes to the reckless behaviour of many fellow homosexuals:[47]

> Twenty-five years after Gay Men's Health Crisis, ACT-UP and Australian-based anti-HIV activism first kicked off, someone has to take the blame for this outrageously long-lived, unbelievably reviving, preventable epidemic. It is time to state that a reasonably well-educated, Western gay man who contracts HIV in 2006 because of sex is at least a reckless fool, and if he deliberately brings it upon himself, at best a suicidal sociopath.

He continues:

> Yes, believe it or not, there is a whole gay subculture that rests upon 'bug-chasing', or the despicable sport of actively seeking out or passing on HIV infection for the satisfaction of sexual or other perverse fantasies. A great effort from within and without the gay community is needed to counter these rising infection rates and the lifestyles and political ideas that support them, not least because of the strain they put on the health system. It is time the love got tough.

CHAPTER 4

How Many Homosexuals Are There?

A staff reporter with *The Australian* once began an article on homosexuality claiming there were one million homosexuals in Australia. Where did she get this figure? As it turns out, she took the word of a member of Significant Others Marketing Consultants, who is later quoted in the article as saying there "are more than one million gays and lesbians in Australia".[1] A month later, again in *The Australian,* the same spokesman for Significant Others was quoted in an article saying that there are "1.4 million gay and lesbian adults in Australia".[2] That was a jump of 400,000 in one month. At that rate there should have been 24 million homosexuals in Australia in the year 2000!

Homosexual activists have confirmed this to be a case of deliberate deception

Now, do these numbers seem a bit high? They should. An issue of *Newsweek* admitted that the 10 per cent figure that sexologist Alfred Kinsey used was highly inflated:[3]

Activists seized on the double digits to strengthen their political message. ... Policymakers and the press adopted the estimate – despite protests from skeptical conservatives – citing it time and time again. But new evidence suggests that ideology, not sound science, has perpetuated a one-in-ten myth.

Homosexual activists have confirmed this to be a case of deliberate deception:[4]

Based on their personal experience, most straights probably would put the gay population at 1% or 2% of the general population. Yet ... when straights are asked by pollsters for a formal estimate, the figure played back most often is the '10% gay' statistic which our propagandists have been drilling into their heads for years.

What is the evidence? The 10 per cent figure is actually about eight to 10 times too high. Let's look at Kinsey's findings, for example. An article in *The American Journal of Psychiatry* claims that Kinsey's work suffered from "severe methodological limitations" and that his sample group – male prisoners and sex offenders included – was "far from representative". The authors of the article say that the actual figure should be about 1.1 per cent.[5]

Furthermore, Kinsey never actually said that 10 per cent of the population was homosexual. He claimed that four per cent of white males were exclusively homosexual throughout their lives after adolescence, and that 10 per cent were "more or less" exclusively homosexual for parts of their lives.[6]

Finally, while most people seem to know about Kinsey's original study, very few know about a more recent Kinsey Institute study conducted in 1970 and released in 1989. This study found the number of homosexual males to be only 1.4 per cent. It also found that lesbians are far fewer than male homosexuals.[7]

Some years ago the *Wall Street Journal* presented a summary of some of the recent studies on the extent of homosexuality.[8] All the findings present similar low figures. In the United States a 1989 University of Chicago study found that only 1.2 per cent of both male and female adults reported homosexual activity. And a 1993 survey found only 1.1 per cent of men who claimed to be exclusively homosexual. Furthermore:

- In France a 1992 government study of over 20,000 adults found that 1.4 per cent of men and 0.4 per cent of women had had homosexual intercourse in the five years preceding the survey.

- In Britain a 1991 nationwide survey of 19,000 adults found that 1.4 per cent of men aged 16 to 59 had homosexual contact in the past five years.

- In Canada a nationwide survey of 6,000 first-year college students found that one per cent were homosexual and one per cent were bisexual.

- In Norway a 1987 nationwide poll found that 0.9 per cent of males and 0.9 per cent of females had homosexual experiences within the previous three years.

- Finally, a 1989 study in Denmark found fewer than one per cent of males aged 18-59 were exclusively homosexual.

More recent American studies have demonstrated similar figures. A 1993 study of the sexual behaviour of men based on the National Survey of Men found that "2 percent of sexually active men aged twenty to thirty-nine ... had had any same-gender sexual activity during the last ten years. Approximately 1 percent of the men (1.3 percent among whites and 0.2 percent among blacks) reported having had exclusively homosexual activity."[9]

A year later the most scientifically rigorous study to date of American sexual practices was released. A condensed version of the study, *Sex in America*, reported that there were "few homosexuals" in its survey, and the nationwide incidence of male homosexuality was only 2.8 per cent, while lesbianism was just 1.4 per cent.[10]

And a major study released in 2000 in *Demography* found more of the same. Based on three large sets of data (the General Social Survey, the National Health and Social Life Survey, and the U.S. Census), it found that the number of exclusive male homosexuals in the general population was just 2.5 percent, and the number of exclusive lesbians just 1.4 percent.[11]

Recent Canadian research has found similar sorts of figures. The 2003

Canadian Community Health Survey, a comprehensive study of 135,000 Canadians on a wide range of health issues, was released in mid-June 2004 by Statistics Canada. It found that among Canadians between 18 and 59 years, about 1.0 per cent considered themselves homosexual; another 0.7 per cent said they were bisexual.[12]

If the homosexual lobby is willing to use faulty statistics to support its cause, just how reliable is it in other areas?

Also, the largest and most recent survey in the UK has found the numbers to be remarkably low. The Office of National Statistics received nearly a half million responses to its new Integrated Household Survey. The data showed that just one per cent claimed to be homosexual or lesbian, while another half of a per cent claimed to be bisexual.[13]

And a much more recent American study reported in 2011, conducted by UCLA's Williams Institute on Sexual Orientation and Public Policy, found that just 1.7 per cent of Americans identify themselves as being gay or lesbian. The research was based on five earlier major studies on this topic.[14]

Unless Australians are significantly different from their Western counterparts, it seems clear that the claim that one million Australians are homosexual is overstated at least five-fold. But as all good propagandists know, throw a figure around long enough, and pretty soon the general public won't even question its validity.

If the homosexual lobby is willing to use faulty statistics to support its cause, just how reliable is it in other areas? As one homosexual warned: "If you say a number that you can't prove, there's always the chance that by disproving one part of your argument, your opponents weaken you overall. I think that's dangerous."[15]

While it is understandable that a movement would want to overestimate its importance and influence, it is reprehensible that such large sections of the media parrot these figures, without doing their homework first.

But the truth is, those who have sought to do the figures in Australia have come out with quite low figures. A study by Monash University entitled

"How Gay is Australia?", based on 2001 census figures, found very low numbers indeed. It found that only 37,774 persons are in same-sex couples; persons in same-sex couples are only 0.2 per cent of the total population; and persons in same-sex couples are only 0.47 per cent of all persons in couples.[16]

A 2008 Victorian government report found similar numbers. According to *The State of Victoria's Young People*, 97.9 per cent of Victorians aged between 12 and 24 regarded themselves as heterosexual; 1.5 per cent identified as bisexual; and 0.6 per cent identified as homosexual.[17]

And a recent study of sexuality in Australia has confirmed that the 10 per cent figure is greatly overblown. In a study of nearly 20,000 Australians, La Trobe University researchers found that 97.4 per cent of Australians said their sexual identity was heterosexual. A mere 1.6 per cent identified as homosexual, and a paltry 0.9 per cent identified as bisexual. So much for the 10 per cent myth.[18]

The same study found that those who had an exclusively same-sex sexual attraction amounted to 0.6 per cent for men and 0.2 per cent for women. And those who had sexual experience exclusively with the same sex came to 0.6 per cent for men and 0.1 per cent for women.[19]

In a book-length retelling of the study, two of the authors involved in the original research go on to say: "When questions about homosexuality have been asked in rigorous scientific sexual behaviour surveys in the United Kingdom and the United States, results similar to those in Australia have been found."[20]

Incredibly, however, in the face of all this hard evidence to demonstrate the very low percentage of homosexuals in society, the two authors put this rather unscientific spin on things: "It is too simple to say '10 per cent of the population is gay', but it is true that at least 10 per cent of the population is a little bit gay-ish"![21]

We need to put the spin aside, and stick to the facts. And the fact is: homosexuals have never made up 10 per cent of the population. But it has been a convenient lie to peddle, making it easier to convince gullible heterosexuals and governments alike to grant even more special rights to homosexuals.

CHAPTER 5

Once Homosexual, Always Homosexual?

Is homosexuality a genetic condition in which people have no choice? Are people born homosexual? Can a homosexual break free of homosexuality? Can one make a distinction between homosexual orientation and homosexual behaviour? These and related questions deserve careful attention. The answers to these questions will help determine the way the homosexual rights arguments are assessed. For example, if homosexuals are born that way, then it would be harder to argue for legislation that discriminates against something they have no choice over.

First, one must make a distinction between homosexual orientation and behaviour. It is clear that not everyone with a homosexual orientation acts out this orientation. That is, some may have feelings of sexual attraction to another member of the same sex without acting on those feelings. Just as some may have an orientation to other activities, one need not act them out. As one author put it:[1]

> The question about choice and homosexuality is often asked the wrong way. It is not so much that one chooses to engage in

homosexual acts as it is that one can choose not to. We are all predisposed to some things, and frequently tempted. But we make choices every day not to engage in certain activities, for any number of reasons.

The cause of homosexual orientation is far from clearly known and would appear to be multi-factorial. It is apparent that social, psychological and cultural factors are involved as well as the aggressive promotion of homosexuality. In this it may be similar to the development of alcoholism. In the case of homosexuality, many studies have noted the influence of weak or absent father figures as an important factor in offspring becoming homosexuals. Also, studies indicate that homosexual men and lesbian women report a significantly higher rate of childhood molestation than do heterosexual men and women.[2]

> **Weak or absent fathers, and/or childhood abuse, seem to be the main common themes in the histories of many – if not most – homosexuals.**

For example, one study noted that abused adolescents, "particularly those victimized by males, were up to 7 times more likely to self-identify as gay or bi-sexual than peers who had not been abused".[3] Another study of 1,001 adult homosexual and bisexual men found that 37 per cent recorded that they were "encouraged or forced to have sexual contact before age 19 with an older or more powerful partner; 94 per cent occurred with men".[4]

Indeed, weak or absent fathers, and/or childhood abuse, seem to be the main common themes in the histories of many – if not most – homosexuals. One counsellor puts it this way: "I have spoken with hundreds of homosexual men. Perhaps there are exceptions, but I have never met a single homosexual man who said he had a close, loving, and respectful relationship with his father."[5]

Of course, this concept has been around for quite some time now. Freud noted a century ago that domineering mothers and weak or absent fathers were closely associated with their offspring's homosexual behaviour. Studies have long confirmed this.

As one main example, Irvin Bieber and his team of researchers released an important study in the early 1960s which showed how excessive mothering coupled with paternal absence influenced the development of homosexuality in males:[6]

> The 'classical' homosexual triangular pattern is one where the mother is CBI [close-binding-intimate] with the son and is dominant and minimizing toward a husband who is a detached father, particularly a hostile-detached one. From our statistical analysis, the chances appear to be high that any son exposed to this parental combination will become homosexual or develop severe homosexual problems.

Decades later, similar findings were still being reported. As one 1993 study reports:[7]

> The literature suggests that many, perhaps a majority, of homosexual men report family constellations similar to those suggested by Bieber et al. to be causally associated with the development of homosexuality (e.g., overly involved, anxiously over-controlling mothers, poor father-son relationships). This association has been observed in non-clinical as well as clinical samples.

And consider more closely the area of abuse. Far too many homosexuals seem to have unfortunately undergone this tragedy as children. As one lesbian puts it: "Almost without exception, the gay men I know (and that's too many to count) have a story of some kind of sexual trauma or abuse in their childhood – molestation by a parent or an authority figure, or seduction as an adolescent at the hands of an adult."[8]

This lesbian goes on to make this revealing point: "The gay community must face the truth and see sexual molestation of an adolescent for the abuse it is, instead of the 'coming-of-age' experience many regard it as being."[9]

Two psychologists who surveyed the latest scientific research on the question of possible causation concluded as follows:[10]

> Homosexual persons are not subhuman robots whose acts are predetermined. They are moral agents who inherit tendencies

from biology and environment, and who share in shaping their character by the responses they make to their life situations. Like all persons, they must ask, 'This is what I want to do, but is it what I should do?' The existence of inclinations or predispositions does not erase the need for moral evaluations of those inclinations.

Dr Elizabeth Moberly has worked with homosexuals for decades now, and she has found a very common theme: "The homosexual – whether man or woman – has suffered some deficit in the relationship with the parent *of the same sex*; and ... there is a corresponding drive to make good this deficit – through the medium of same-sex or 'homosexual' relationships."[11]

One counsellor who has spent decades working with adult men dissatisfied with their homosexuality said this:[12]

> At the root of almost every case of homosexuality is some distortion of the fundamental concept of gender. ... Self-deception about gender is at the heart of the homosexual condition. A child who imagines that he or she can be the opposite sex – or be both sexes – is holding on to a fantasy solution to his or her confusion. This is a revolt against reality and a rebellion against the limits built into our created human natures.

And a study designed by the Kinsey Institute for Sex Research concluded with these words: "Childhood gender nonconformity turns out to be a very strong predicator of adult sexual preference among the males in our sample."[13]

Whatever the factors associated with the development of homosexuality, in each individual case certain factors will need to be weighed so that treatment – if desired – can be tailor-made to the individual and his or her needs.

Born that way?

Nonetheless, what about the claim that homosexuals are born, not made? This is the common claim by homosexual lobbyists. It is not a question of choice, they argue, but who a person inherently is. The Victorian AIDS Council president, for example, recently repeated the claim that homosexuals "did not choose their homosexuality".[14] Such remarks can be multiplied at length.

The term for this overall perspective on homosexuality is "essentialism". It states that one's homosexuality is essential to who one is. It is not an added feature but an intrinsic part of one's person. It is grounded in biological or genetic reality, and cannot be altered. It is an unchangeable reality.

Not everyone goes along with this concept. There are those who hold to the "social constructionist" theory. For example, one very important book strongly rejects essentialist theories: Daniel Greenberg's, *The Construction of Homosexuality*.[15] It is a major contribution to this debate and is well worth reading. Perhaps the best way to quickly sum up its thrust is to make use of the opening paragraph of one review of it:[16]

> This is the most extensive and thorough world history of homosexuality ever written. Yet it is more accurate to call it a work of sociology than a work of history, for it develops a specific and arresting sociological thesis. David Greenberg argues, against popular opinion, that homosexuality is not a static condition; it is not like being black or white or left-handed. It is not, for the most part, even a deep-seated psychological 'orientation'.

The essentialist/constructionist debate cannot here be entered into. Suffice it to say that for many reasons, the essentialist view seems inadequate. In America, for example, there are about 200 centres which help homosexuals to go straight, and there are thousands of former homosexuals who now are straight, many of them happily married with children. I know personally a number of these individuals.

And it is not just "religious" organisations that are involved in helping homosexuals go straight. The decidedly non-religious Masters and Johnson Clinic in St Louis has treated hundreds of homosexuals and bisexuals. Masters reports that they have successfully "changed" more than half of their homosexual clients, and more than 75 per cent of bisexuals.[17]

One New York University psychologist, Dr Robert Kronemeyer, puts it this way:[18]

> With rare exceptions, homosexuality is neither inherited nor the result of some glandular disturbance or the scrambling of genes or chromosomes. Homosexuals are made, not born that way. From my twenty-five years' experience as a clinical psychologist, I firmly believe that homosexuality is a learned response to early painful experiences and that it can be unlearned.

It must be noted that a very small percentage of people are in their own category, and are quite different. I refer to the intersex condition, where genetic abnormalities results in sexual confusion. There can be ambiguous genitalia, chromosomal imbalances – e.g., having an extra sex chromosome – and so on. These can be found in conditions such as Congenital Adrenal Hyperplasia, Turner Syndrome, Klinefelter's Syndrome, and Androgen Insensitivity Syndrome. Intersex conditions are mostly innate, whereas the unusually low concordance rates in identical twins (who have identical genes and an essentially identical prenatal environment) show that causes of homosexuality are predominantly post-natal.

Jeffrey Satinover, a psychiatrist who has taught at Yale University and is a past president of the C.G. Jung Foundation, after examining the evidence, says this: "The desire to shift to a biologic basis for explaining homosexuality appeals primarily to those who seek to undercut the vast amount of clinical experience confirming that homosexuality is significantly changeable."[19]

A two-year study involving nearly 860 individuals and 200 therapists found that change is clearly possible. The study found that:[20]

> ... before counseling or therapy, 68% of the respondents perceived themselves as exclusively or almost entirely homosexual, with another 22% stating they were more homosexual than heterosexual. After treatment, only 13% perceived themselves as exclusively or almost entirely homosexual, while 33% described themselves as either exclusively or almost entirely heterosexual.

One male respondent said: "Change is extremely difficult and requires total commitment. But I have broken the terrible power that homosexuality had over me for so long. I haven't been this light and happy since I was a child. People can and do change and become free".[21]

> **It is an aggressive homosexual lobby, along with the pressures of political correctness, that has robbed many of a chance to go straight.**

More recently, a study found that psychotherapy has helped a large percentage of American homosexuals to change. Of 200 homosexuals and lesbians given the treatment, 78 per cent of males and 95 per cent of females reported a change in their sexuality. The author concludes: "This study provides evidence that some gay men and lesbians are able to also change the core features of sexual orientation."[22] It is worth noting that the man who led the study, Professor Robert Spitzer, was instrumental in having homosexuality removed from the American Psychiatric Association's list of mental disorders in 1973.[23] (The story of homosexual pressure and intimidation both within and without the APA to make this change is recounted in a book penned by a pro-homosexual author, *Homosexuality and American Psychiatry: The Politics of Diagnosis.*)[24]

But it is an aggressive homosexual lobby, along with the pressures of political correctness, that has robbed many of a chance to go straight. As psychologist Joseph Nicolosi, author of *Reparative Therapy of Male Homosexuality*, points out, "Psychology and psychiatry have abandoned a whole population of people who feel dissatisfied with homosexuality."[25]

Indeed, political correctness and the homosexual lobby have had such an influence that, in the mid-90s, delegates of the American Medical Association voted to scrap the association's 13-year-old policy of encouraging practitioners to alert homosexual patients to "the possibility of sex preference reversal in selected cases".[26] The new policy calls instead for attitudinal adjustment for medical personnel, saying that health care is improved by a "non-judgemental recognition of sexual orientation and behavior".[27] Physicians involved in assisting homosexuals to change their sexual behaviour criticised the new policy as a "political maneuver".[28]

In America a recent study has found that while various factors might contribute to a person's homosexual orientation, biological factors alone cannot be substantiated. After an in-depth review of the literature, the study makes this observation: "Recent studies postulate biological factors as the primary basis for sexual orientation. However, there is no evidence at present to substantiate a biological theory, just as there is no compelling evidence to support any singular psychosocial explanation."[29]

A stronger statement comes from Dr Charles Socarides, professor of psychiatry at the Albert Einstein College of Medicine in New York. He says theories seeking to relate sexual orientation to brain structure and hormones are "completely erroneous. There's no possibility of someone developing homosexuality from hereditary or organic causes. It's just impossible ... a cluster of the brain cannot determine sexual object choice. We know that for a fact."[30]

Closer to home, Australian homosexual activist and La Trobe University lecturer Dennis Altman wrote this uncomfortable fact in 1986:[31]

> To be Haitian or a hemophiliac is determined at birth, but being gay is an identity that is socially determined and involves personal choice. Even if, as many want to argue, one has no choice in experiencing homosexual desire, there is a wide choice of possible ways of acting out these feelings, from celibacy and denial ... to self-affirmation and the adoption of a gay identity.

"Being gay," says Altman, "is a choice".[32]

A leading Australian feminist and lesbian has also made it clear that choice is a major component of the lifestyle. Melbourne University academic Sheila Jeffreys became a feminist in her twenties, when she was involved in "perfectly good" relationships with men. She then decided to become a lesbian: "At the time," she says, we "made the decision to become political lesbians, as we called it."[33]

She says that "you can learn to be heterosexual and you can learn to be lesbian". When challenged by an interviewer that sexuality is more innate than that, she continues, "I don't think there's anything natural about sexuality; you do learn it. And you can unlearn it, go in a different direction, change it." She says that her own experience proves this, as does that of many other women who decided to switch to lesbianism in the '70s.[34]

Also, consider the words of lesbian writer Dr Camille Paglia:[35]

> Homosexuality is not normal. On the contrary it is a challenge to the norm. ... Nature exists whether academics like it or not. And in nature, procreation is the single relentless rule. That is the norm. Our sexual bodies were designed for reproduction. ... No one is born gay. The idea is ridiculous. ... [H]omosexuality is an adaptation, not an inborn trait.

Another American homosexual also rejects the "born gay" idea, but nonetheless acknowledges its usefulness. Homosexual activist and gender studies professor John D'Emilio put it this way: "What's most amazing to me about the 'born gay' phenomenon is that the scientific evidence for it is thin as a reed, yet it doesn't matter. It's an idea with such social utility that one doesn't need much evidence in order to make it attractive and credible."[36]

The recent confessions of another homosexual activist are also quite revealing. Peter Tatchell is an Australian-born, British-based homosexual activist, who spills the beans on the "gay gene". There is none, he asserts, and says homosexual desire is not genetically determined.

Writing for *Spiked Online*, in 2008, he makes some very interesting remarks about homosexual determinism. He says there may well be biological influence in one's sexuality, but nothing more. He argues that:[37]

> ... an influence is not the same as a cause. Genes and hormones may predispose a person to one sexuality rather than another. But that's all. Predisposition and determination are two different things. There is a major problem with gay gene theory, and with all theories that posit the biological programming of sexual orientation. If heterosexuality and homosexuality are, indeed, genetically predetermined (and therefore mutually exclusive and unchangeable), how do we explain bisexuality or people who, suddenly in mid-life, switch from heterosexuality to homosexuality (or vice versa)? We can't. The reality is that queer and straight desires are far more ambiguous, blurred and overlapping than any theory of genetic causality can allow.

Indeed, he is honest enough to admit that the jury is still out on the science of all this:

> The relative influence of biological versus social factors with regard to sexual orientation is still uncertain. What is, however, certain is that if gayness was primarily explainable in genetic terms we would expect it to appear in the same proportions, and in similar forms, in all cultures and all epochs. As the anthropologists Clellan Ford and Frank Beach demonstrated in *Patterns Of Sexual Behaviour* (1965), far from being cross-culturally uniform and stable, both the incidence and expressions of same-sex desire vary vastly between different societies.

He concludes his piece with this interesting remark: "The homophobes are thus, paradoxically, closer to the truth than many gay activists."[38] Of course, he does not go all the way and admit that people can leave their homosexual lifestyle for a heterosexual one. He says: "For most of us, it is impossible to subsequently change our sexual orientation."[39] But notice that he does not say "all of us", but "most of us". That is a very telling choice of words.

Other homosexuals have admitted that choice plays at least a partial role in the overall equation.

Other homosexuals have admitted that choice plays at least a partial role in the overall equation.[40] Indeed, there is even an entire website devoted to those who say they have chosen the homosexual lifestyle. The site says it is "a radical gathering place for people who have chosen to be queer".[41]

However, the tendency is to deny choice, to make it appear that homosexuals cannot help it, and to argue that any criticism of the homosexual lifestyle is as silly as criticism of being left-handed or red-haired.

And this has been a deliberate strategy by homosexual activists. They have done a very good job to convince a gullible public that homosexuals are born that way and cannot change. Consider this revealing quote from a homosexual activist manual:[42]

The public should be persuaded that gays are *victims of circumstance*, that they no more chose their sexual orientation than they did, say, their height, skin color, talents, or limitations. (We argue that, for all practical purposes, gays should be considered to have been *born gay* – even though sexual orientation, for most humans, seems to be the product of a complex interaction between innate predispositions and environmental factors during childhood and early adolescence.) To suggest in public that homosexuality might be *chosen* is to open the can of worms labelled 'moral choice and sin'.

As Thomas Schmidt has noted, "a large component of homosexual activists applaud biologic causation theories for their effect on public opinion, but are philosophically committed to *personal choice* as opposed to any deterministic theory, biologic or environmental".[43]

Even if there is a genetic predisposition to homosexuality, one can overcome this just as one can overcome a predisposition to, say, overeating, anger, or even alcoholism. We are not animals, and can therefore, as Altman points out, make choices about how we live out the life that nature accords us.

Or, as one science writer reminds us, "even if genetic determinism is shown to be very powerful, we are still left having to decide what we want to do with it. After all, genetics can give someone a predisposition to cancer, but we don't applaud cancer."[44] And as another commentator remarks, "the influence of non-volitional forces on *any* human activity is no help in determining the ethical status of that action. ... To the degree that these external or nonvolitional factors influence one's actions, they moderate the degree of personal culpability (or personal credit in the case of good behavior) but they do not change the assessment of the behavior itself."[45]

Even some homosexuals admit to this. John Corvino, a homosexual and philosophy professor, puts it this way:[46]

> The fact is that there are plenty of genetically influenced traits that are nevertheless undesirable. Alcoholism may have a genetic basis, but it doesn't follow that alcoholics ought to drink excessively. Some people may have a genetic predisposition to violence, but

they have no more right to attack their neighbors than anyone else. Persons with such tendencies cannot say 'God made me this way' as an excuse for acting on their dispositions.

Or as Michael L. Brown rightly argues:[47]

> ... virtually all behaviours or orientations or tendencies have at least some biological or genetic component (or, aspect of hereditability), and yet this does not justify or normalize these behaviors or orientations or tendencies, nor does it mean that people with these behaviors or orientations or tendencies or temptations should not try to change.

He notes a possible genetic link to obesity, then argues:[48]

> Based on gay activist logic, however, this discovery should lead to the *embracing* of obesity and even the public *celebration* of obesity. Perhaps we should now hold Fat Pride events in our cities? After all, most name-calling in our schools has to do with appearance, and so kids who are overweight are subject to all kinds of cruel taunts from their classmates, not to mention their inability to compete well in sports, leading to further ostracization.

> This, of course, underscores why all name-calling and bullying is wrong, while the discovery of this 'obesity gene' should produce greater sympathy for those who struggle with their weight. But does this cause us to embrace and celebrate obesity or to downplay its harmful effects? Absolutely not! Why should it? Obesity remains a dangerous condition.

Quite right. There are plenty of behaviours or dispositions which may have some biological component to them, but simply giving in to any and every one of these is hardly how civilised society operates. Some people may be born with a predilection, predisposition or tendency to anger, overeating or unfaithfulness. But simply embracing and condoning these is, however, hardly acceptable.

Social commentator William Bennett reminds us that:[49]

> ... a decent, humane, self-governing society will reject the belief

that most human beings – homosexual *or* heterosexual – are slaves to their passions, their desires, their genetic predispositions. Our identities are not defined by sex, nor is sex itself an irresistible force. To believe otherwise is to vitiate the concept of individual responsibility and free will. Although our struggles are not all the same, we all do struggle against every sort of human desire, against our biological impulses, against our emotional luggage. We do not abjure the struggle because it is difficult or because we seem to be battling against something deep within us – even if that something is as powerful as sexual desire; even if it seems fundamental to who we are.

In the genes?

A few scientific studies have been heralded by a sympathetic press recently as evidence that homosexuality is genetically based. Studies by National Cancer Institute researcher Dean Hamer and homosexual researcher Simon LeVay are two such studies. While both studies urged caution in the interpretation of the findings, the media featured headlines claiming a genetic basis for homosexuality. Both studies have been heavily criticised for methodological shortcomings and other problems.[50]

> **Studies on twins in fact make it perfectly clear that there can be no genetic basis for homosexuality.**

Indeed, later attempts to verify these studies have proven a failure. A study of 52 homosexual brothers by a team of clinical neurologists "found no evidence of linkage of sexual orientation to Xq28", the so-called "gay gene" identified by Hamer in 1993.[51] Another study of 54 pairs of homosexual brothers also failed to find the link.[52]

Homosexual activist Peter Tatchell, cited earlier, says this about Hamer: "One of the main original proponents of the gay gene theory, Dr Dean Hamer, now concedes that it is unlikely that something as complex as human sexuality can be explained solely in terms of genetic inheritance.

He seems to accept that while genetic factors may establish a predisposition towards homosexuality, a predisposition is not the same as a causation."[53]

Studies on twins in fact make it perfectly clear that there can be no genetic basis for homosexuality. As one researcher in the field explains:[54]

> Identical twins have identical genes. If homosexuality was a biological condition produced inescapably by the genes (e.g., eye color), then if one identical twin was homosexual, in 100% of the cases his brother would be too. But we know that only about 38% of the time is the identical twin brother homosexual. Genes are responsible for an indirect influence, but on average, they do not force people into homosexuality. This conclusion has been well known in the scientific community for a few decades.

Jeffrey Satinover has dealt with this question extensively. He concludes that "hard science is far from providing an explanation of homosexuality, let alone one that reduces it to genetic determinism".[55] And homosexuals themselves have criticised these "gay gene" studies. For example, Edward Stein PhD, a homosexual activist, has written a whole book on the subject.[56] In an interview with a homosexual magazine, he says this:[57]

> There are serious problems with the science itself. ... My training had taught me that a lot of what was being said was, well, highly unscientific. ... Many gay people want to use this research to promote gay rights. If gay people are 'born that way,' then discrimination against them must be wrong. ... A gay or lesbian person's public identity, sexual behaviors, romantic relationships, or decisions to raise children are all choices. No theory suggests that these choices are genetic.

But homosexual activists continue to insist that homosexuality is genetically based, and nothing can be done about it. Science, again, begs to differ. One person who should know is Oxford University's Richard Dawkins, author of *The Selfish Gene*. Dawkins argues that "the body of genetic determinism needs to be laid to rest". Says Dawkins: "Whether you hate homosexuals or whether you love them, whether you want to lock them up or 'cure' them, your reasons had better have nothing to do with genes. Rather admit to prejudiced emotion than speciously drag genes in where they do not belong."[58]

Indeed, scientists involved in genetic research are becoming increasingly convinced that "genetic determinism" is a fallacy. One distinguished Harvard University professor, Dr Ruth Hubbard, recently wrote a book denouncing genetic determinism.[59] One summary of the issue concluded by saying that scientists are coming to realise one truth at least: "DNA is not destiny."[60] And the two men most responsible for the humane genome project, Francis Collins and Craig Venter, have both argued that their discoveries imply the end of genetic determinism. Their discoveries about the human genome have made any simplistic statements about one or two genes predisposing someone to complex areas of behaviour such as gayness or schizophrenia appear untenable.[61]

> **Many homosexuals themselves reject the idea that homosexuality is genetically based.**

In an article in *Science* magazine, Charles Mann said this:[62]

> Time and time again, scientists have claimed that particular genes or chromosomal regions are associated with behavioral traits, only to withdraw their findings when they were not replicated. 'Unfortunately,' says Yale's [Dr Joel] Gelernter, 'it's hard to come up with many' findings linking specific genes to complex areas of human behavior that have been replicated. '...All were announced with great fanfare; all were greeted unskeptically in the popular press; all are now in disrepute'.

And many homosexuals themselves reject the idea that homosexuality is genetically based. Many could be cited here. Let me mention a few. Homosexual activist Edward Stein has penned an entire book on the issue. This is what he has to say:[63]

> Genes in themselves cannot directly specify any behaviour or psychological phenomenon. Instead, genes direct a particular pattern of RNA synthesis, which in turn may influence the development of psychological dispositions and the expression

of behaviors. There are necessarily many intervening pathways between a gene and a disposition or behaviour, and even more intervening variables between a gene and a pattern that involves both thinking and behaving. The terms 'gay gene' and 'homosexual gene' are, therefore without meaning. ... No one has presented evidence in support of such a simple and direct link between genes and sexual orientation.

An Australian homosexual activist has said similar things about homosexuality and genetics:[64]

> I think the idea that sexuality is genetic is crap. There is absolutely no evidence for it at the moment, and I think it is unhealthy that people want to embrace this idea. It does reflect a desire to say, 'it's not our fault', as a way of deflecting our critics. We have achieved what we have achieved by defiance, not by concessions. I think we should be recruiting people to homosexuality. It's a great lifestyle and something everybody should have the right to experience. If you believe it's genetic, how are you going to make the effort?

Or as he put it elsewhere:[65]

> On the question of recruiting to homosexuality – well, of course, I am in favor of this. I believe homosexuality to be a perfectly valid lifestyle choice. ... I am naturally keen to encourage people to participate in [the gay lifestyle].

Yet the Victorian AIDS Council president said that homosexuality is "just a fact of life. The concept of someone becoming a homosexual because of something they see or hear is something I find quite bizarre". He rejected the idea that young people could be seduced into homosexuality by homosexual propaganda and recruitment.

But if this is so, why do we keep hearing statements like this coming from the homosexual movement?[66]

> We shall sodomize your sons, emblems of feeble masculinity, of your shallow dreams and vulgar lies. We shall seduce them in your schools, in your dormitories, in your gymnasiums, in your locker rooms, in your sports arenas, in your seminaries, in your

youth groups. ... Your sons shall become our minions and do our bidding. They will be recast in our image. They will come to crave and adore us.

If young people cannot be seduced, why this statement from a homosexual activist?[67]

> I have found that even many of my most unbiased straight friends grow skittish with my homosexual candour – say, kissing my mate – when their children are around. Underneath it all, they too understand that sexually free ideas are infectious and that, once introduced to the suggestion of same-sex love, their kids might just try it and like it.

There are very real dangers of homosexuals seeking to recruit impressionable youth. The promotion of homosexuality, in the schools, for example, will result in a number of young people being enticed to experiment with anal intercourse and other practices endemic in the homosexual community. Public policy should seek to discourage this kind of promotion of the homosexual lifestyle. The health and well-being of our children is at stake. Indeed, a war is waging over the minds and hearts of our young people.

As one commentator puts it:[68]

> From history, sociology, and anthropology, what we learn is 1) that it's not just Judeo-Christian Western culture that has scorned homosexual behavior; and 2) that in those (rare) cultures where homosexual behaviour has *not* been scorned, gayness didn't stop at some hypothetical 10 per cent, but ended up being virtually an epidemic. Homosexual behavior throughout a society is not static, but fluid. It can change radically in either direction, depending upon societal attitudes toward it. Isn't that what sexual taboos have always been about? Both society and the individual have a say in the matter. Society can ban it or bless it; and whatever society decides, it is likely that its individual citizens will choose to go as far as they are permitted to go.

To conclude this chapter, perhaps the best argument that can be made against the "once gay, always gay" mentality is to hear from former homosexuals themselves. As I have noted, countless thousands of homosexuals have known the experience of liberation from the homosexual lifestyle. And hundreds of organisations around the world are helping homosexuals make that change. Many books have been written document-ing these changed lives.[69]

One such book, *Coming out of Homosexuality*, tells the

> **It is not just the lifestyle, but the orientation as well, that can be changed.**

story of how the book's co-authors went through the difficult but rewarding path of change. They also speak of many others who have taken this tough journey: "We have witnessed solid, substantial healing in so many men and women over the years that we can say without hesitation, 'There is a way out of homosexuality'."[70] They continue:[71]

> During the past fourteen years, we have become personally acquainted with hundreds of men and women who have left behind the gay and lesbian lifestyle. ... Now some of these men and women have been free from homosexual involvement for ten or twenty years. They are not just suppressing their strong homosexual or lesbian longings. There has been a true resolution of this issue in their lives.

And it is not just the lifestyle, but the orientation as well, that can be changed, albeit slowly and painfully. Another former homosexual, Jeff Konrad, puts it this way:[72]

> Despite what we hear from the media and the world at large, your homosexual orientation can be changed. I want you to know there is hope. ... And I'm not just talking about behaviour or surface stuff. I'm talking about deep-down change. I no longer have the feelings, desires, temptations, orientation, or identity of the past. I am convinced you can experience this also.

Or as one former British lesbian says, "It is possible for your sexual orienta-tion to change. It is also possible for a former lesbian to marry and to be happily married. I am."[73]

The thousands of individuals who have left the homosexual lifestyle comprise the most important counterweight to the claims of the homosexual activists and their demands for preferential treatment. As Robert Knight puts it: "The greatest threat to the gay rights movement is the ex-gay movement, with its message of compassion, hope and healing."[74] That is why militant homosexuals try so hard to shout down and deny the message of those who have left the ranks of homosexuality. Their transformed lives belie the claims of the homosexual lobby.

In conclusion, there is remaining uncertainty about the exact causes of homosexuality. But putting it all – or mostly – down to genetics or biology is clearly incorrect. The research on this will continue, and we would do best to affirm what one professor of neuropsychiatry and behavioural medicine who has published 80 academic articles and book chapters on this has said: "The precise sequence and interaction of variables involved in the etiology of homosexual orientation are not yet completely understood."[75]

He continues:[76]

> At the present time, we may tentatively conclude that the main source for gender and sexual behaviour is found in social learning and psychological development variables, although we should recognize that there remains the theoretical possibility that biological abnormalities could contribute a potential vulnerability factor is some indirect way. A great deal more exacting research is needed to clarify the causes of homosexuality.

CHAPTER 6

Homosexual Rights and Discrimination

The push for homosexual rights, as we have seen, is the main means by which the homosexual lobby seeks to further its agenda. By talking about discrimination, civil rights and minority status, the impression is created that homosexuals lack basic human rights that others enjoy, and that they are a persecuted minority.

There are several things wrong with regarding homosexuality as a civil right. For example, homosexuals enjoy the same protections under law of basic civil rights as does anyone else.

Moreover, one's behaviour should not be the basis of civil rights legislation. Homosexuality is not a benign factor like race or gender, but is primarily a behaviour-based activity. We do not extend special rights to other behaviour-based groups, like smokers or stamp collectors.

Analogies between homosexuality and race have proven to be insupportable. Special protected status has historically been granted when three criteria are met: first, where a group are denied economic, educational and cultural opportunities. While this has been true of various races in the past, it is not true of homosexuals. Homosexuals as a class have higher than average annual incomes, are more often college-educated than non-homosexuals, and especially predominate in culture and in the arts world.

As a recent example, a study of 20,000 Australians found "associations between homosexual identity and experience and higher socio-economic status as marked by profession and education". The authors of this study say that such findings are "consistent with some previous national studies".[1] For example, a 2001 American study of nearly 6,000 homosexuals and lesbians found that they were "overwhelmingly high-income, highly educated, professionally employed, urban-dwelling and property-owning".[2] The findings left an Australian homosexual to ask: "This is an oppressed minority?"[3]

> **Shouts of discrimination, so often heard from homosexuals, need to be examined more closely.**

Under the second criterion, protected classes must be identifiable by obvious, immutable traits. Again, this is true of race, but not of the homosexual community. Blacks cannot help being black but, as we have seen, homosexuals can help being homosexual. Moreover, some characteristics are immutable but not protected. Height, good looks and predispositions to obesity are also immutable, but do not warrant in themselves special protection. Homosexual behaviour is not innate or immutable, so again, it fails the test.

As General Colin Powell has noted: "Skin color is a benign non-behavioral characteristic. Sexual orientation is perhaps the most profound of human behavioral characteristics. Comparison of the two is a convenient but invalid argument."[4]

Under the third criterion, protected classes should demonstrate political powerlessness. Just the opposite is the case in Australia. The amount of influence one to two per cent of the population has over the rest of the population is staggering.

Shouts of discrimination, so often heard from homosexuals, need to be examined more closely. Often we hear lesbians talking about a right to children, or homosexuals talking about being denied the right to marriage. But discrimination means the denial of a right that one really has. It makes no more sense for a same-sex couple to talk about the right to have children than it does for me to talk about the right to be five metres tall. If two people decide to place themselves outside the conditions that make procreation possible, then it is silly to talk about discrimination and the denial of rights.

Homosexual rights laws, in summary, meet none of the traditional criteria for human rights protection.

Also, it needs to be stressed than whenever you grant special rights to homosexuals you have to take rights away from other people. If homosexuals are granted special rights to force home-owners to rent to them, those home-owners will have lost certain rights – the right, for example, to conscientiously choose whom one wishes to rent to. If a homosexual is granted the right to teach sex education in schools, the parent of the child in that school loses the right to have a say in the moral calibre of the teacher.

Admittedly, morality and law are not based on numbers, but how is it fair that one and a half per cent of the population should be granted special rights at the expense of the other 98.5 per cent? Why should Australia's four and a half million families be forced to concede rights to Australia's 300,000 or so homosexuals?

The truth of the matter is this: almost all societies and cultures throughout history have recognised the importance that the institutions of marriage and family offer to society.

Let's illustrate the situation this way. Mrs Murphy is renting a room. A student applies. Mrs Murphy asks him, "Do you like the music of J.S. Bach?" "Yes" he replies. "Then you will never rent from me," she retorts. Next come two men dressed in female clothing. Mrs Murphy eyes them over and tells them to get lost. What are the rights of each? Roger Magnuson puts it this way: "Before the passage of a gay rights law, both the student and the homosexuals have the same rights: none."[5] Mrs Murphy may be opinionated, bigoted or confused, but she can reject both applicants. Neither party has the right to claim special protection of the law for its preference for Bach or for homosexuality. However, after a homosexual rights law is passed, says Magnuson, "the homosexuals win a privilege for their unnatural sexual practices that the student does not have for his baroque musical tastes, or the average citizen for his normal preferences. The homosexuals can sue, and win."[6]

The truth of the matter is this: almost all societies and cultures throughout history have recognised the importance that the institutions of marriage and family offer to society.[7] Especially in the raising, teaching and protection of children, families, preferably cemented by marriage, offer the most secure, stable and loving context for preparing the next generation for their role in society. Societies thus have a vested interest in promoting marriage and family. Indeed, societies have therefore granted special recognition to marriage and family. In this sense they have positively discriminated in favour of marriage and family. But such discrimination is both desirable and healthy.

In the same way that society "discriminates" against eight-year-olds by not granting them licences to drive, so society "discriminates" against those who choose to remain outside of the institutions of marriage and the natural family. A homosexual relationship is just that, a relationship. It has never been, nor can it ever be, considered to be a family. Thus if a person wants the benefits and privileges of family life, then he or she needs to meet the criteria and responsibilities thereof.

But it is nonsense for a person to eschew male-female relationships in favour of same-sex ones, and then complain of discrimination. If I choose to lop off both my arms, and then demand that the Boston Celtics hire me as a basketballer, they have every reason to tell me to get lost. Even if I retain my arms, my shortness and my inability to throw a ball may disqualify me as well.

Society is like that. It is full of distinctions, of differentiations. I may complain bitterly that I am not able to breastfeed, but that is life. Nature itself discriminates. The word discriminate simply means to differentiate, to distinguish. When I chose my wife over millions of other women, I discriminated. When a professional basketball team chooses a two-and-a-half-metre athlete over me, it is discriminating. When societies pass laws saying seven-year-olds cannot get a driver's licence, they are discriminating. When a nation says a four-year-old does not have the right to vote, it is discriminating.

Thus it does no good for the homosexual lobby to forever complain about discrimination and inequality when such is the very fabric of living in a democracy. (Genuine unjust discrimination – e.g., racial discrimination – of course is another matter.)

Nor will it do for homosexual activists to argue that they are the objects of all kinds of economic and social discrimination based on their sexuality. A homosexual activist once made just this claim in a radio debate with me. He bewailed the fact that as a taxpayer he was denied access to all kinds of government benefits because he was homosexual. He challenged me to name just one area where I was being discriminated against.

Unfortunately, I was not given the right of reply. I could have produced a very long list. There are all kinds of benefits that I as a taxpayer also do not get. I do not receive the youth allowance. I do not get a single-parent benefit. I do not get a widow's pension. I do not get maternal health benefits.

The point is, there are all sorts of benefits that, as a married heterosexual male, I am not qualified for. Yet I am a taxpayer like everyone else. I am just as much a victim of discrimination in this regard as any one else. Yet I do not hear of male taxpayers saying they will withhold part of their tax because they do not directly get the benefits of breast cancer screening or gynaecological services.

The issue of rights is often one of whoever shouts the loudest gets the most attention. Homosexual activists have made many noisy demands over the years and have done quite well, often at the expense of other groups who may in fact exhibit more genuine need. Anthony Butcher offers this example: "In 1992, with some 250,000 Australians suffering from major mental illness, approximately $8.2 million was spent on psychiatric research. In the same year $10.6 million was spent on AIDS research, even though by December, 1994, the total number of AIDS cases diagnosed had reached only 5,732."[8] For a "poor persecuted minority group", homosexuals have done quite well out of the public purse.

Pro-homosexual discrimination

Moreover, if there is discrimination against homosexuals taking place, it is not just the heterosexual community that is doing the discrimination. Homosexuals seem to have a pretty good track record of discriminating against each other, in Australia, as elsewhere. For example, organisers of a lesbian festival in Victoria sought to exclude not only male homosexuals, but transsexuals as well. The organisers wanted to ban everyone except female-born lesbians. They even managed to persuade the Victorian Civil and Administrative Tribunal (VCAT) to grant the organisers exemption from state equal opportunity laws.[9]

While this blatant example of discrimination went largely unnoticed in the mainstream community, there was a huge uproar within the homosexual community.[10] Various sides took to the debate, in numerous heated and acrimonious exchanges, as recorded in the homosexual press. The infighting lasted for several weeks until VCAT withdrew its exemption, saying that such a ban was illegal after all.[11] In the end the so-called "Lesfest" was cancelled because organisers did not want to accept the VCAT decision.[12]

During this kerfuffle, one homosexual writer penned an interesting article in the homosexual press. He spoke of rampant discrimination within the homosexual community, and said that the "bickering and infighting that I have witnessed" within the gay, lesbian, transgender, transsexual and intersex community in Queensland "in the last 12 months is atrocious". He continued, "the gay and lesbian community continues to discriminate, ignore or even ostracise bisexual, transgender, transsexual or intersex people. ... I can cite many examples where the gay and lesbian community has done the above either accidentally or deliberately. It still does."[13]

As another example of pro-homosexual discrimination, the same VCAT recently ordered that Melbourne homosexuals could get special rights over the rest of the community. It allowed an exemption for a homosexual hotel to have men-only dance parties. It also ruled that similar men-only parties could be held throughout the state.[14]

VCAT allowed a further exemption to the Equal Opportunity Act by allowing homosexuals at three university campuses to have their own space. They will be able to refuse admittance to students who don't identify as homosexual.[15] And yet again, VCAT once more ruled in favour of pro-homosexual discrimination. It allowed a Melbourne pub yet another exemption from the Equal Opportunity Act, allowing the pub to refuse entry to heterosexuals.[16]

Many other cases could be cited. For example, in Australia's north Queensland city of Cairns there is a homosexual-only resort. Interestingly, however, it has been forced to allow straights to come in as well, because of low returns from the homosexual travel market.[17] And in Victoria VCAT has again ruled in favour of pro-homosexual discrimination. A party company that specialises in lesbian dances was granted the right to ban men.[18]

The discrimination continues. A more recent VCAT decision said women could be banned from a homosexual "cruise club". VCAT said only males could be employed at Club 80 in the Melbourne suburb of Collingwood. The ruling said women were banned both from employment at the sex club and from even being on the premises.[19]

And another homosexual venue in Collingwood, Sircuit Bar, was also granted special rights to exclude women who might seek to "turn gay men straight". VCAT said such discrimination was justified, on the grounds that homosexuals need a place where they are not subject to "misunderstanding and disparaging remarks".[20]

It appears, then, that our ruling elites really don't have a problem with discrimination, as long as it is pro-homosexual discrimination. As Brent Bozell put it regarding the situation in America: "In other words, the gay left now can have it both ways. They can force 'anti-discrimination' rules on everybody else, but they don't have to follow them."[21]

Discrimination against religious groups

While many groups are disadvantaged when special rights for homosexuals are legalised, this is especially true for religious groups that may find themselves forced to renounce their own beliefs and practices to accommodate pro-homosexual legislation.

> **Homosexual activists falsely claim that no religious person or group will be adversely affected by pro-homosexual legalisation.**

Homosexual activists falsely claim that no religious person or group will be adversely affected by pro-homosexual legalisation, not least of which is the legalisation of same-sex marriage. I have documented numerous such cases on my own website.[22]

They are becoming increasingly frequent and flagrant. More and more cases are being reported of religious liberties put under threat or being denied because of homosexual activism. In but one such example, an article in *National Public Radio* focused on nine different areas where this has occurred.

In an article entitled, "When gay rights and religious liberties clash", Barbara Bradley Hagerty looks at how homosexual activists have targeted housing, youth groups, wedding services, adoption services, medical services and parochial schools, among other religious bodies and services.[23]

Let me focus on just one recent overseas example. Catholic Charities in Washington DC have had to radically alter their policies because of the recent introduction of same-sex marriage there. As social commentator Charles Colson explains, "In connection with the new law, the DC Council insisted that, as a city contractor, Catholic Charities had to offer the same benefits to same-sex couples that it did to heterosexual ones. Catholic Charities had to choose between church teaching and ministering to the city's neediest residents" as a result.[24]

And here are several recent Australian examples. The Ten Network in Australia dumped a long-running U.S. Christian television program when just one person (presumably a homosexual activist) complained that one episode aired at three in the morning was offensive. On the program it was simply said that "God does not approve of homosexuality", yet that was enough for Ten to dump it altogether![25]

And a Christian camping ground in Victoria that refused to rent out its premises to homosexual activists was fined $5,000 by VCAT. County court judge Felicity Hampel, sitting at VCAT, said this: "They are not entitled to impose their beliefs on others in a manner that denies them the enjoyment of their right to equality and freedom from discrimination in respect of a fundamental aspect of their being."[26]

How in the world is this discrimination against a fundamental aspect of their being? Not only is this pushing the pro-homosexual myth that homosexuals cannot change, but it is a complete furphy. There would be hundreds of camping grounds around Melbourne to choose from. Why did this homosexual group insist on just this one?

Whenever a new right is created, corresponding obligations come into play as well. If a state decrees that same-sex marriage is legal, then every individual and organisation dealing with marriage will be forced to ensure that these new rights are met and facilitated. Jews, Christians, Muslims and numerous other religious groups will all be forced to violate their own beliefs and teachings in this regard.

An important article on all this was written recently by Roger Severino. Entitled "Or for poorer? How same-sex marriage threatens religious liberty", it examines a number of past cases and potential future cases of how religious institutions suffer from the expansion of homosexual rights.[27] He is worth quoting at length:[28]

> The legal definition of marriage does not exist in isolation; changing it alters many areas of the law. For example, the definition of marriage plays an important role in the law of adoption, education, employee benefits, health care, employment discrimination, government contracts and subsidies, taxation, tort law, and trusts and estates. In turn, these legal regimes directly govern the ongoing daily operations of religious organizations of all stripes, including parishes, schools, temples, hospitals, orphanages, retreat centers, soup kitchens, and universities. Moreover, current law provides no room for non-uniform definitions of marriage within a state, it is all or nothing. ...

> Changes in marriage law impact religious institutions disproportionately because their role is so deeply intertwined with the public concept of marriage. ... The specific consequences that will likely flow from legalizing same-sex marriage include both government compulsion of religious institutions to provide financial or other support for same-sex married couples and government withdrawal of public benefits from those institutions that oppose same-sex marriage. In other words, wherever religious institutions provide preferential treatment to husband-wife couples, state laws will likely require them to either extend identical benefits to same-sex married couples or withdraw the benefits altogether.

Yet homosexual activists keep insisting that if same-sex marriage were legalised nothing would change, and religious people will face no ill-effects. This is blatantly false, and the activists know it. As U.S. law professor David Orgon Coolidge notes, "Of course the legalization of same-sex marriage will have dramatic effects; it is supposed to. The real debate is about whether these effects will be good."[29]

He looks at a number of such changes. Consider just the legal impact:[30]

> This includes federal benefits, but the main effects will be at the state level, in the areas of marriage-related benefits, anti-discrimination laws based on marital status, adoption and child custody laws, public and private school curricula, non-profit contracts with State and local government, private groups using public facilities, and professional licensing standards for lawyers, doctors, social worker and teachers, among others.

Obviously, people with religious convictions who are concerned about same-sex marriage and the like will find themselves being discriminated against and penalised if they do not embrace and affirm this raft of legal and social changes. As already documented, this is already happening, and it will only get worse as more and more special rights are granted to homosexuals.

CHAPTER 7

Judicial Activism and Homosexuality

Activist judges and courts are increasingly siding with the homosexual lobby, bypassing normal democratic processes as they implement radical social change. Often these judges are unelected and unaccountable, allowing them to more readily spurn the concerns of the majority as they side with the minority activist groups.

As the Victorian Civil and Administrative Tribunal (VCAT) examples above make clear, various courts and tribunals have, in many instances, been aiding and abetting the homosexual agenda. Indeed, along with complicit media organisations, and pro-homosexual activities in our educational system, the judiciary is a leading body of pro-homosexual activism. Increasingly judges and courts of various kinds are using their judicial powers to promote and implement the homosexual agenda, often against the express wishes of the majority.

A number of examples could be mentioned. Let me begin with some major cases from overseas. In December of 1999 the Vermont Supreme Court ruled that same-sex couples must be granted the full rights and privileges of heterosexual unions. In June of 2003 the Ontario (Canada) Court of Appeals declared that same-sex couples had the right to legally marry. In the same month the U.S. Supreme Court decided that the laws banning sodomy in Texas were unconstitutional. Somehow the U.S. Constitution is now interpreted to mean that every American has the right to homosexual relations. And in November of 2003 the Massachusetts Supreme Court ruled that a state ban on same-sex marriage was unconstitutional.[1] (Some of these cases will be further discussed below.)

In Australia, similar judicial activism continues apace, where judges are able to interpret and apply value-laden legislation or to develop the common law with an eye to the promotion of an "equal rights" agenda.

In July 2000 a landmark court case in effect struck down state laws on IVF access by saying they violated the federal Sex Discrimination Act (1984) by banning single women and lesbians.[2] In April 2002 a High Court ruling threw out an appeal to that ruling.[3] This decision ignored or minimised the lengthy and careful consultative processes that resulted in the legislation of reproductive technology in several states. And taxpayers will have to foot the bill for allowing lesbians access to expensive IVF treatment.

In October 2001 Justice Richard Chisholm of Australia's Family Court ruled that, in effect, two women could marry. A woman who decided to become a man, and renamed herself Kevin, had taken up a relationship with another woman, Jennifer, and took steps to marry in 1999. The judge ruled that "man" could mean a variety of things, and not just be related to the constraints of biology. Psychological and social considerations, in other words, could also be considered when we define (or redefine) "male" and "female".[4] The full bench of the Family Court later upheld that decision.[5]

Some recent cases occurred in December of 2003. In that month the Family Court granted a Melbourne homosexual couple parental responsibility for a baby boy born to a surrogate mother in the U.S. Justice Sally Brown (now retired) ruled that it was in the "best interests" of the child to be looked after by the homosexual couple![6]

Also in December, the Australian High Court declared that homosexuals who might suffer persecution overseas were entitled to refugee status in this country. In a 4-3 ruling, the court declared that a homosexual Bangladeshi couple could win the right to be refugees. It was a world-first ruling, and will likely have ramifications in other similar cases.[7]

In April 2004 Chief Justice Alastair Nicholson of the Family Court declared that a 13-year-old girl could undergo a sex-change procedure because she felt that she was really a boy.[8] Also in April 2004, in Auckland, New Zealand, the Family Court ruled that a toddler could have three parents: the lesbian mother, her female partner, and the Sydney male sperm donor.[9]

> It should be clear that various judges, courts, commissions and tribunals are attempting to align themselves with the homosexual agenda.

A glaring example of government-sponsored pro-homosexual activity is the conduct of the Victorian Equal Opportunity Commission (EOC). It regularly goes out of its way to advocate on behalf of the homosexual community, encouraging homosexuals to be more active. Instead of being an impartial observer, it seems the EOC wants to stir up trouble. Dr Diane Sisely, who headed the EOC from 1994 to 2004, complained that only 77 out of nearly 3,500 discrimination cases taken to the commission in 2003 were about sexuality. She was unhappy with that, and wanted to see more such cases. She said the 77 complaints were "only the tip of the iceberg". But how does she know that? Never mind that maybe it is just not as huge a problem as the Equal Opportunity Commission hopes it is. Nonetheless, the commission has set up booths at homosexual festivals, informing people there of their rights, and encouraging them to make complaints if need be.[10]

Numerous other examples could be cited. But it should be clear that various judges, courts, commissions and tribunals are attempting to align themselves with the homosexual agenda, regardless of whether such actions are in the best interests of the community, or in fact reflect the desires of the majority of its citizens.

CHAPTER 8

The Homosexual Agenda

We have already examined homosexual strategies. However, a few more words must be devoted to what homosexual campaigners actually want. What are their demands? What changes do they propose? How will the family be affected by such changes?

Since Australian groups like GLAD (Gay [men] and Lesbians Against Discrimination) quote freely from their American counterparts, let me mention some of the agenda items listed in the U.S.A. The homosexual lobby's list of demands, as presented at the 1993 March on Washington, includes the following:[1]

- Recognition of same-sex "marriages" and "domestic partnerships".
- Adoption of children by homosexual couples.
- The implementation of homosexual, bisexual and transgendered curricula at all levels of education.
- Repeal of all sodomy laws.
- Passage and implementation of graduated age-of-consent laws for sexual relations.

Much of this is already happening in Australia. An earlier list of demands

84

stated similar goals:[2]

- Repeal of all laws prohibiting private sexual acts involving consenting persons.
- Repeal of all laws prohibiting prostitution, both male and female.
- Repeal of all laws governing the age of sexual consent.
- Repeal of all legislative provisions that restrict the sex or number of persons entering into a marriage unit; and the extension of legal benefits to all persons who cohabit, regardless of sex or numbers.
- Enactment of legislation that child custody, adoption, visitation rights, foster parenting and the like shall not be denied because of sexual orientation or marital status.
- Encouragement and support for sex education courses, prepared and taught by gay women and men, presenting homosexuality as a valid, healthy preference and a lifestyle that is a viable alternative to heterosexuality.

It should be noted that many of these proposals have been put forward in Australia, and many have already been adopted. Indeed, one way to see how the homosexual agenda is being implemented is to examine earlier proposals made by the homosexual community and to see just how many of their demands have been met.

Consider several earlier documents that list some of the demands that the homosexual lobby have been making. One source of information is from comments made by the homosexual community during a two-day Senate hearing concerning the Sexual Conduct Bill held late in 1994. Homosexual representatives at the hearing were quite frank about what they wanted achieved in the near future. For example, Mr Michael Alexander, of the Australian Federation of AIDS Organisations, mentioned three areas that needed changing. The first area, he said, was the issue of criminal law (overthrowing anti-sodomy laws, etc.); "... anti-discrimination legislation or equality is the second thing, and I think the whole recognition of relationships is a third thing."[3] He mentioned a number of laws that could be affected: "laws on intestacy, laws on family provisions, challenging wills – that sort of stuff. There is a whole range of laws".[4]

Changes to the definition of marriage and family are part of the package. The late Catholic Archbishop Eric D'Arcy of Hobart pointed out that in a letter that former Attorney-General Michael Lavarch wrote to D'Arcy, Lavarch made this admission: "The bill does not purport to endorse nor condemn any alternative to the dignity of marriage and the procreation of children, but it does appear to equate them."[5] Exactly, and this is just the point homosexual activists will seize on in their next set of claims. Indeed, as one witness said, well-placed homosexuals had informed him that "this bill was just the beginning of a wide range of things that will come before parliament".[6]

In fact, in a number of submissions by the homosexual community, such demands were already being made. For example, Mr David Buchanan of the Lesbian and Gay Legal Rights Service stated at the committee hearing that his group had argued that "the age of consent is excessively conservative ... [and] the age of consent should be reduced to 16".[7]

Some of the most revealing comments came from Tasmanian homosexual activist Rodney Croome. Concerning homosexual relationships being as valid as marriage, he said: "I think it is a form of chauvinism to elevate heterosexual relationships, be they sanctioned with marriage or not, to a position that is superior in some way to relationships between members of the same sex."[8]

Concerning hiring and education, he said:[9]

> If the Tasmanian government was to introduce legislation to protect us from discrimination in employment and housing, goods and services some time in the distant future, then we would ask that there be no exemption in that for people who have care or responsibility over children, for instance, teachers.

Most frightening was his answer to Senator Eric Abetz who asked him if he would make an exemption for religious organisations and religious schools:[10]

> In principle, Senator, we would argue that if a religious school found it acceptable to employ people of a different denomination or different religion who may not share the convictions and may actually disagree with the convictions of the people who run

the school, then we could see no difference between that and employing homosexual people if those people were good teachers, regardless of the convictions of the people who ran the school.

Another document that is quite revealing is a paper put out by the Australian Democrats in 1995 entitled "Prohibiting Discrimination on the Grounds of Sexuality: Issues Paper No. 1". The paper was "designed to collect the views of individuals and groups in the gay community"[11] concerning a private member's bill to be introduced in Federal Parliament.

The section dealing with the ambit of the bill says this:[12]

One option here would be to design a bill which aims at a modest advance only i.e. one which included sufficient exemptions from the prohibition of discrimination to make it more palatable to a greater number of people and therefore more likely to pass. The preferred alternative was to develop a piece of legislation which comprehensively, decisively and as effectively as possible prohibits discrimination in all spheres of our communal life.

Concerning same-sex couple relationships, the late Australian Democrat Senator Sid Spindler said in that document that "legal equality with heterosexual defacto relationships is in my view achievable".[13]

> **Many of these demands have now been met.**

Of most interest is the section on exemptions. It reads:[14]

Exempting controversial areas, e.g., employment as teachers in religious institutions was generally rejected despite superficial attraction as a strategy to reduce opposition to the bill. The crucial role of teachers in perpetuating (or removing) stereotypical prejudices was emphasised.

Many of these demands have now been met. Indeed, the extent to which the homosexual agenda is being implemented is nicely laid out in a recent book by Australian homosexual activist Graham Willett. In his book *Living Out Loud* he presents a history of homosexual activism in Australia. His book shows how successful the homosexual lobby has been in achieving its ends. Indeed, the author expresses amazement at how quickly and easily its ends have been attained.[15]

A few representative quotes set the tone. He begins his book by noting "how very different" attitudes are today

> **"The triumph of liberal tolerance is now more or less complete"**
> **– Graham Willett.**

compared to not so very long ago: "Anti-gay ideas still exist in society, of course, but a basic liberal tolerance is the dominant mood. ... It is a startling indication of just how far we have come that the moral crusaders' demands are widely regarded as silly and unfair."[16]

His concluding chapter offers more of the same:[17]

> Never have homosexuality, the gay and lesbian community and their issues been more visible or more seriously dealt with by the mainstream, or more entrenched in social and political life. ... One of the great changes of the past 40 years has been the growing visibility of lesbians and gay men in Australian society. ... This visibility is reinforced by the role of the mainstream media.

"The triumph of liberal tolerance is now more or less complete."[18] Indeed, so successful has the homosexual offensive been that Willett argues the real problem for the homosexual community may be internal fragmentation due to its own diversity and acceptance.

After Willett made those comments, new and more ominous developments have occurred. In June of 2003 the Ontario Supreme Court declared that exclusive heterosexual marriage laws violated the human rights of Canadian homosexuals and lesbians. In the same month the U.S. Supreme Court decided that Texan laws against sodomy were unconstitutional. And also in June of that year, English Anglicans and Australian Uniting Church members debated the ordination of homosexual clergy.[19]

All of this encouraged one homosexual commentator writing at that time to express amazement at how rapidly and easily the homosexual agenda was being implemented. He said he had previously doubted whether same-sex marriage was a "worthwhile or attainable objective for gay and lesbian activism. How wrong I was. This is clearly now the last great frontier of the 40-year struggle for gay and lesbian equal rights." He went on to say, "Progress in this area has been much faster, and has met much less resistance, than I or anyone else anticipated."[20]

After mentioning a number of legal victories granting special rights to homosexuals, he says this: "I hope all those clever post-modern academics and nostalgic Marxists who have been arguing all these years that we will never achieve equality or liberation under patriarchal capitalist bourgeois democracy have been paying attention."[21]

Elsewhere the same commentator makes these remarks:[22]

> It is astonishing how in recent years the dynamics of gay rights law reform have changed. In the old days (before about 1990), it took years of patient lobbying, petition writing, fundraising and occasional violent demo-going to bring about change. ... But in recent years, no sooner does the gay and lesbian community think of some new reform, some new right, than gay-friendly politicians positively ... rush to put it into law for us. We scarcely even have to ask.

Australian homosexual activist Dennis Altman concurs:[23]

> When I became a gay activist – a phrase I always disliked – in the 1970s, it was because the law and society declared me to be both criminal and inferior. Much of the major issues of discrimination we opposed have now been addressed, though there is a strong residue of dislike and fear of homosexuals, as the frequency of fag-bashing and anti-queer jokes in the media attest.

Or as he said seven years later: "For those of us old enough to remember the 60s or earlier, the changes in being homosexual are enormous".[24] And an Australian lesbian activist writing in early 2004 also remarks on the major advances being made: "In the last five years, progress in lesbian and gay law reform in Australia has seemed unstoppable".[25]

And writing in 2011, Australian lesbian Helen Razer said this about the homosexual advance:[26]

Same-sex couples are, largely, no longer discriminated against in law. In 2009, the federal Labor government passed a suite of legislative changes recommended by the Human Rights and Equal Opportunities Commission. The 58 alterations, to real estate, superannuation and sundry other acts, were a great win. I thank the Gay and Lesbian Rights Lobby for the real and practical differences they've made to the lives of myself and others.

Thus while many homosexual warriors are still claiming that they are the victims of discrimination and inequality, more forthright homosexual leaders are saying that they have come a long way indeed. It sounds as though they see things panning out quite well, and are very triumphant about all this.

CHAPTER 9

Homosexual Marriage

Perhaps the most disconcerting item on the homosexual agenda is the desire to equate same-sex relationships with normal marriage and family life. In this the homosexual lobby has been quite successful. For example, during the International 1994 Year of the Family, the Australian Government refused to even try to define what it meant by the term "family" for fear of offending the homosexual lobby. Indeed, a Labor Federal Cabinet decided to include homosexual couples in its definition of families for the purpose of future census-taking by the Australian Bureau of Statistics. Also, in New South Wales it has been decided that homosexual couples are to be recognised as "family".[1]

And this has been a deliberate strategy of the homosexual activists: to radically alter the traditional understanding of marriage and family. One

> If the institution of family is under sustained attack, the real object of this assault is the institution of marriage.

representative quote will suffice here. One Melbourne activist, discussing homosexual law reform, says that it "was not just about formal discrimination, although that was the language of the campaign. It was a battle to change the meaning of family".[2]

91

If the institution of family is under sustained attack, the real object of this assault is the institution of marriage. Homosexual activists know that this is, in many ways, the jewel in the crown. Redefine marriage and you can easily redefine and destroy family. Thus the campaign to radically redefine the institution of marriage.

Of course the Orwellian attempt to equate same-sex relationships with traditional marriage is doomed from the outset. Homosexual marriage is simply an oxymoron. However, with de facto relationships now on a near par with marriage relationships, the homosexual lobby feels it can make a strong case for equating same-sex relationships with heterosexual marriage. Indeed, we have managed to strip away the inherent uniqueness of marriage by redefining it and broadening it.

As social commentator Maggie Gallagher puts it:[3]

> Over the past thirty years, quietly, and largely unremarked outside a narrow group of specialists, American family law has been rewritten to dilute both the rights and the obligations of marriage, while at the same time placing other relationships, from adulterous liaisons to homosexual partnerships, on a legal par with marriage in some respects. To put it another way, by expanding the definition of *marriage* to the point of meaninglessness, courts are gradually redefining marriage out of existence.

Who actually wants same-sex marriage?

The identification of homosexual relationships with heterosexual marriage is a chief example of this. However, it needs to be pointed out that there has been a long debate among homosexuals over the question of homosexual marriage. Some are in favour, some are opposed, and there are many options in between. As one example, David McCarthy of the Victorian Gay and Lesbian Rights Lobby (VGLRL) puts it this way: "Obviously, while there is a lack of unanimity about gay marriage, our human rights must be the same as everyone else's. If someone wants to get married or doesn't want to get married, it's their choice."[4]

Indeed, one Australian homosexual lobby group has actually split over this issue. Two committee members have resigned from the New South Wales Gay and Lesbian Rights Lobby, claiming it has not pushed hard enough for marriage rights. But the lobby group said that marriage reform was "not a priority".[5]

Consider a number of quotes on this issue (just a few of many possible). An Australian lesbian said this about the former Prime Minister John Howard's attempts to keep marriage as the union of a man and a woman for life:[6]

> When it comes to same-sex marriages, John Howard has got us pretty well summed up. We're not cut out for it. ... [Heterosexuals are] welcome to it. 'For life'! It'd be like sitting through one of those interminable bloody Indian films but when you get to the end it starts all over again and you can't leave. Let's leave marriage and other drudgery to heterosexuals. They've had millenniums of practice. They're good at child-rearing and taking out the rubbish. I never wanted to be like them, even when I *was* one of them. ... Surely we can come up with something better: semi-marriage or quarter-marriage, which would narrow the field down to eight. Or a casual, part-time or temporary marriage. Or even a flexitime marriage.

And the same lesbian, when asked whether open relationships work, was quite candid in her response:[7]

> I don't know, but I know closed ones don't. How many good, loving lesbian relationships have floundered on the rock of sexual tedium? That's what worries me about our demands for holy matrimony because we want to be 'just like them'. If we go on demanding exclusive access to those we love, our relationships will end in anger and sadness – just like theirs.

An Australian homosexual activist puts it in even stronger terms:[8]

> I think gay marriage is an absolute non-starter as an issue. We have spent the last 40 years trying to get the state out of our bedrooms. Why are we now demanding recognition from John Howard? The notion of these extraordinary, creative, avant-garde

gay people rushing to cover themselves in grey cardigans and join their straight cousins in the suburbs with some bureaucratic document just sh*ts me.

Another Australian homosexual said much the same: "Whether we like it or not, marriage is, as John Howard memorably said, a bedrock cultural institution for heterosexuals; and most gay men seek different rules for their relationships."[9] And activist Dennis Altman even said that homosexual marriage was "a great deal of self-indulgent crap", although he later tried to tone down his remarks.[10]

Also, a letter-writer to a homosexual newspaper, commenting on Altman's remark, concurs: "Stop being selfish, and centre your efforts on bettering this world for those that still need to get recognition, acceptance and the right to survive peacefully, before you try getting the ability to get legally married so you can get legally divorced a year later."[11]

In a much more recent piece, Altman continued to decry homosexual marriage. In the article entitled "Same-sex marriage just a sop to convention", he says that it is just too stifling. He stated that he is "uncomfortable with an approach that seemed to buy into the most conventional morality".[12]

He continues: "I mourn the loss of radical critique that was central to the early gay and lesbian movement". He says that his resistance to marriage comes from a "desire to stress the particularity of homosexuality". Because of the move to same-sex marriage, he fears that we "may be approaching the end of the homosexual".[13]

Another Australian homosexual is quite clear about rejecting what he considers the straitjacket of heterosexual marriage: "[F]ull recognition for same-sex marriages will encourage all those shallow promiscuous gay men to settle down in Box Hill with Mr Right and breed shitzus. Speaking as a shallow promiscuous gay man, I remain sceptical about this."[14]

He continues:[15]

> Straight men, it seems, are quite shameless in their perverted desires, and in their enthusiasm for illicit sex of all kinds. And this

after 2,000 years of the civilising influence of Christian marriage! On the evidence so far, I think it will take more than the Ontario Supreme Court [and its support of same-sex marriage] to get the majority of gay men to get married and settle down.

And another Australian homosexual offers similar thoughts: "So we don't have 'gay marriage'. So what?"[16] He goes on to talk about all the progress homosexuals have already been making in terms of legal and social reforms. He then says, "I'm worried that people who continue to scream for the least attainable reform ... use our community's political capital up on a fruitless journey. So I call on the people in our community to stop talking about gay marriage."[17]

And a lesbian activist in Australia makes it clear that she is opposed to same-sex marriage. She does so on the grounds that marriage is a religious issue, and church and state must remain separate. She says, "I am completely against demands for the Australian government to introduce an Act for Gay Marriage."[18]

She continues: "We're approaching the battle for relationship equality from the wrong direction. ... We should be fighting for Civil Union Partnerships. It should not be a solely gay issue. This is a battle for the true separation of religion and politics."[19]

And here is what a Melbourne law professor and activist says about this issue:[20]

Ultimately, it is my view – though I acknowledge that it is not a view universally shared – that lesbian and gay rights activists in Australia should not be fighting for same-sex marriage. I hold this view not because of the legal and political obstacles to same-sex marriage (although they are significant and do raise the question of best allocation of political energy), but because I consider marriage a problematic institution and one which would have negative effects on the lesbian and gay communities in Australia; negative effects that would outweigh the positive effects of same-sex marriage.

Finally, listen to what Australian lesbian Helen Razer has to say about same-sex marriage:[21]

Affirming gay marriage has become a progressive reflex and there is no scope for debate. Supporting same-sex marriage is compulsory, rather like an objection to genetically modified food or a preference for buying organic. One cannot say that marriage, particularly the 'gay' kind, is silly without being pelted by (conventionally grown) refuse. At the risk of upsetting the workers of the world and the biodynamic markets at which they shop, I just can't get excited about the 'right' to an institution predicated on some pretty whacko old nonsense.

She continues:

Getting hitched, expensively and blithely, is not [a pressing civil equality issue]. This is not to suggest the creation of long-term intimacy is anything short of wonderful. My own partnership of 12 years is my life's central feat. It has been sanctioned by the years, by difficulty and by love. It will never be sanctioned by compliance to the terms of a rickety institution.

But 'gay' itself has become a rickety institution. Wedded to the idea of weddings, military participation and cheering on 'out' footballers, the visible gay culture retains all the radicalism of a radish. Marriage equality is not a truly progressive struggle but an effort to privilege one kind of relationship, long-term and monogamous, above all others. I wonder how is this going to play out, particularly for the many gay couples who have spent years finessing a feasible polygamy. Gay and progressive communities are selling up and buying into a market long since ruined. We are trading in a history rich in difference at the altar of absolute conformity.

Similar debates are found elsewhere. In North America for example, many homosexuals have expressed their lack of interest in marriage. In fact, there are many homosexual organisations that are fiercely opposed to the concept of same-sex marriage.

As one example, consider the U.S.-based group, Against Equality. They are quite explicit in their aims: "Against Equality is an online archive, publishing, and arts collective focused on critiquing mainstream gay and lesbian politics. As queer thinkers, writers and artists, we are committed to dislodging the centrality of equality rhetoric and challenging the demand for inclusion in the institution of marriage."[22]

Also, when Ontario legalised same-sex marriage in 2003, there was not exactly a huge rush of Canadian homosexual couples to the altar. Indeed, the *New York Times* was so intrigued with this fact that it did a major story on it. Here is one excerpt from that article:[23]

> When David Andrew, a forty-one-year-old federal government employee, heard that the highest Ontario court had extended marriage rights to same-sex couples ... he broke into a sweat. 'I was dreading the conversation,' he said, fearing that his partner would feel jilted when he told him that he did not believe in the institution. 'Personally, I saw marriage as a dumbing down of gay relationships. My dread is that soon you will have a complacent bloc of gay and lesbian soccer moms'.

The article also cites Rinaldo Walcott, a sociologist at the University of Toronto, who shared his worries about getting on board the heterosexual marriage bandwagon: "I can already hear folks saying things like: 'Why are bathhouses needed? Straights don't have them'. Will queers now have to live with the heterosexual forms of guilt associated with something called cheating?"[24]

Another telling comment comes from a Toronto homosexual magazine editor who said, "Ambiguity is a good word for the feeling among gays about marriage. I'd be for marriage if I thought gay people would challenge and change the institution and not buy into the traditional meaning of 'till death do us part' and monogamy forever. We should be Oscar Wildes and not like everyone else watching the play."[25]

In an editorial in an American homosexual magazine, Jim Rinnert says of same-sex marriage: "I'm against it". He writes, in part:[26]

> Gay marriage strikes me as, first and foremost, just another way to show the straights that we're the same as them, that we're as

'normal' as the heterosexuals with whom we share the planet and thereby are worthy of acceptance into their clubs. Well, without getting into a discourse on the social function of homosexuality in cultures ancient and modern, let me just assert that, guess what – we're not the same. We're different. Rather than try to paint heterosexual stripes on our pelts, let's examine, explore and celebrate our different coloration.

Noted Irish political commentator and homosexual Richard Waghorne has also weighed into the debate, arguing that homosexuals should leave marriage alone. He says:[27]

Actually, gay people should defend the traditional understanding of marriage as strongly as everyone else. Given that it is being undermined in the name of gay people, with consequences for future generations, it is all the more important that gay people who are opposed to gay marriage speak up.

He especially makes his case on the well-being of children, and how they deserve a mother and a father, something that same-sex marriage can obviously never provide them. His entire article is well worth reading in this regard. Thus he says homosexual marriage "is not only unnecessary, but verges on selfishness".[28]

And the percentage of homosexuals who actually want marriage rights is very small indeed. In Australia, studies have found that only about one-fifth of homosexuals and lesbians have showed an interest in same-sex marriage.[29] A major article on the subject in the homosexual press found that there are deep divisions over the issue, and same-sex marriage was far from a high priority for most.[30]

> **The percentage of homosexuals who actually want marriage rights is very small indeed.**

Perhaps the best way to see just how desirable same-sex marriage is, is to find out how many homosexuals have actually availed themselves of it when it has been made available. Consider the Netherlands where same-sex marriage has been legal since 2001. Studies have shown that only about four per cent of Dutch homosexuals have got married during the first five years of legalisation.[31]

And a new study marking the tenth anniversary of this Dutch law change found that homosexuals are still not exactly racing down the aisle. Here is how one researcher summarised the data:[32]

> After ten years of same-sex marriage, approximately nine out of 10 gay and lesbian people in the Netherlands have still not chosen to enter a legal marriage. Marriage as a social institution continues to decline, with lower rates of marriage, higher rates of divorce and out-of-wedlock childbearing among opposite sex couples.
>
> As noted above, correlation does not prove causation. At a minimum the data from the Netherlands does suggest that the hopes of those making a conservative case for gay marriage – that it will strengthen marriage generally and dramatically increase the stability and fidelity among same-sex couples – are likely to be disappointed.

Or consider the American state of Massachusetts which legalised same-sex marriage in 2004. In the first several years, perhaps as many as 16 per cent of the state's homosexuals took advantage of the law change.[33] That is a slightly higher figure, but still a very small minority indeed. And in many of these cases, percentages dropped after the initial "rush" following legalisation.

It seems that there are far more homosexual activists who are talking about marriage than actually getting married. For example, former Australian High Court judge Justice Michael Kirby is a prominent supporter of same-sex marriage, yet, ironically, has rejected pursuing this option with his own partner, saying that "marriage was not an important priority" in their lives.[34]

What sort of marriage will it be?

The truth is, for all the talk about same-sex marriage, few homosexuals actually have in mind the same thing that heterosexuals have in mind. Most seek to radically expand and alter the common understanding of marriage. Long-term monogamous fidelity is seldom part of this new understanding.

Simply reading through the homosexual press makes this clear. Many seem to want to have their cake and eat it too. Article titles such as "How to Stay

Married and Still Be a Slut" are not all that uncommon.[35] Many homosexuals happily admit that traditional heterosexual marriage constraints are not exactly their cup of tea.

I have already documented in Chapter 2 how very different homosexual relationships are from heterosexual relationships. The evidence presented there should be enough to warn us all about legalising same-sex marriage.

But more evidence can be provided as to why those in favour of same-sex marriage do not necessarily think in terms of marriage as is commonly accepted. For example, one homosexual writer, Andrew Sullivan, writes that if homosexual marriage contracts come into force, they would have to be "different": that is, they would have to allow for "extra-marital outlets" and other major changes.[36] Of course, that undermines the very essence of marriage, which is the covenant of life-long sexual faithfulness.

It is worth quoting Sullivan further here. He speaks about the "foibles of a simple heterosexual model" for homosexual relationships.[37] And then he makes this telling admission:[38]

> I believe strongly that marriage should be made available to everyone, in a politics of strict public neutrality. But within this model, there is plenty of scope for cultural difference. There is something baleful about the attempt of some gay conservatives to educate homosexuals and lesbians into an uncritical acceptance of a stifling model of heterosexual normality. The truth is, homosexuals are not entirely normal; and to flatten their varied and complicated lives into a single, moralistic model is to miss what is essential and exhilarating about their otherness.

Elizabeth Kristol offers some trenchant commentary on this:[39]

> *Rote? Stifling? Moralistic?* These are strange epithets to come upon in the final pages of a book whose goal is to convince readers that homosexuals want to marry and deserve to marry; that homosexual love is as dignified as heterosexual love; that it is inhumane not to allow the dignity of this love to find fruition in marriage; that marriage is so venerable an institution that it is single-handedly

capable of leading men out of lives of empty promiscuity into unions of commitment and fidelity. Suddenly we learn, almost as an afterthought, that the institution of marriage may have to change to accommodate the special needs of homosexuals.

Quite so. I have already noted in the chapter on homosexual practices that monogamy is quite rare in homosexual relationships. Many homosexual commentators have made it clear that if and when they do achieve the right to "marry" they will demand to radically redefine what that term means. Several more examples can be mentioned here.

Australian-born, British-based activist Peter Tatchell puts it this way in his article, "Beyond equality":[40]

> The gay community's demand for equality is often also tinged with a whiff of self-obsession and selfishness. Solely concerned with winning rights for homosexuals, it offers nothing to heterosexual people (perhaps if queers supported the interests of straights, more of them might be inclined to support gay interests too?).
>
> In contrast to this shallow reformism, queer emancipation groups like OutRage! have a post-equality agenda. We seek the extension of sexual freedom and human rights in ways that benefit everyone, regardless of sexuality. Many in the lesbian and gay community are jumping on the same-sex marriage bandwagon, endorsing either Dutch-style gay marriages or Danish-style registered partnerships (which are basically civil marriage by another name). OutRage!, in contrast, argues for a more democratic, egalitarian option. We offer a modern, flexible alternative to traditional heterosexual wedlock.

Even though he now campaigns for homosexual marriage, he still wants nothing to do with it himself:[41]

> Let's face it, marriage is the gold standard. Civil partnerships are marriage lite for queers. They are second best. No thanks. Even though I am no fan of wedlock and would not want to get married myself, I defend the right of other same-sex couples to make that choice, if they wish. We should all be equal under the law.

Like many homosexuals, he simply finds the heterosexual marriage model to be far too restrictive, sexually speaking. Thus he does not want to be like straights, nor embrace their marriage:[42]

> We get equality, but at a price. The cost to our community is the surrender of our unique, distinctive queer identity. The unwritten social contract at the heart of law reform is that lesbians and gays will behave respectably and comply with the heterosexual moral agenda. No more cruising, orgies or sadomasochism!

One Australian activist and law professor decries same-sex marriage because of its restrictive nature for homosexuals:[43]

> Why, then, would I be opposed to extending marriage to same-sex couples? The reason is that I think that the normative impact of marriage will be such that it will ultimately diminish, not enhance, the choices available to lesbians and gay men concerning their relationships. I have written about this elsewhere, as have others, so I shall not repeat the argument in depth. But it is important, in my view, to keep in mind the negative impact of marriage when considering whether legal recognition is appropriate and worth fighting for. ...
>
> Briefly stated, in my view opening marriage to same-sex couples would have a number of problematic effects related to its normative impact. For some, it would operate as 'the norm to which we must move' – that is, there would be pressure on same-sex couples to marry, just as there is pressure on different-sex couples to marry. Not only would there be overt pressure, eventually (perhaps immediately), marriage would become the 'natural' way to express commitment. Same-sex couples would want to marry (regardless of pressure), simply because marriage would be the way to celebrate a relationship. The freedom lesbians and gay men currently have in defining their own relationships would be diminished.

That last line says it all. While being rather circumspect in her language, it is quite clear what she is driving at: the monogamous long-term ideal of heterosexual marriage will simply be too limiting for most homosexuals who do not want such tight boundaries imposed upon their sexuality.

Another Australian homosexual activist also makes it clear how different same-sex marriage will be:[44]

> Feminists have long criticised marriage as the institutional basis for male supremacy and restrictive notions of monogamy, and sexual radicals have long denounced marriage as a declining and oppressive institution. The notion of marriage implies a long-term sexual and emotional commitment. Yet the two are not necessarily synonymous, and most gay men, at least, accept a whole range of sexual adventuring as co-existing with long-term partnerships. There seems something hypocritical in the rush to embrace marriage vows, which were designed to restrain any idea that commitment was to be measured entirely by sexual fidelity.
>
> Moreover the constant stress on marriage as the ultimate test of gay equality risks making invisible those homosexuals who either do not want, or cannot find, a long term relationship. There is an extensive feminist literature on the ways in which women are restricted by the emphasis on seeking a husband to the exclusion of all else. It would be ironic if the lesbian and gay movement forgot these warnings, and reified marriage as the only acceptable way of living one's life.

If need be, please read that last quote again. It is most revealing, and it is written by one of the key homosexual players in Australia. He has made it crystal-clear that marriage is a stifling, restrictive institution, and that if homosexuals enter into it, they will have nothing to do with life-long fidelity and commitment, but will include "a whole range of sexual adventuring" in such a marriage.

This same homosexual activist repeated this disdain for faithfulness and fidelity in marriage during a forum on same-sex marriage in July of 2011. Said Dennis Altman on the ABC television debate: "I am enormously proud of the fact that I am in a relationship that has been all the things you all want from relationships, with the exception of sexual fidelity which I think is crap for most people and doesn't exist by and large."[45]

Plenty of overseas homosexuals can also be quoted in this regard. American same-sex marriage proponent Richard Mohr openly affirms the importance of "flexibility" in same-sex unions. He is unashamed in saying this: "Monogamy is not an essential component of love and marriage."[46] Lesbian activist Paula Ettelbrick put it this way:[47]

> Being queer is more than setting up house, sleeping with a person of the same gender, and seeking state approval for doing so. ... Being queer means pushing the parameters of sex, sexuality, and family, and in the process, transforming the very fabric of society. ... As a lesbian, I am fundamentally different from non-lesbian women. ... In arguing for the right to legal marriage, lesbians and gay men would be forced to claim that we are just like heterosexual couples, have the same goals and purposes, and vow to structure our lives similarly. ... We must keep our eyes on the goals of providing true alternatives to marriage and of radically reordering society's views of reality.

Homosexual activists Kirk and Madsen speak about how "open relationships" are so appealing to homosexual lovers. They speak about the "wayward impulse" as being "inevitable in man-to-man affairs, as in man-to-woman, only, for gays, it starts itching faster".[48]

They go on to say that "the cheating ratio of 'married' gay males, given enough time, approaches 100%. Men are, after all, as said earlier, more easily aroused than women, who tend to act as a relatively stabilizing influence; a restless gay man is more apt to be led astray by a cute face in the subway or the supermarket. Two gay men are double trouble, arithmetically squaring the probability of the fatal affairette."[49]

William Aaron, a former homosexual, explains why concepts such as "monogamy" must be redefined by homosexuals:[50]

> In the gay life, fidelity is almost impossible. Since part of the compulsion of homosexuality seems to be a need on the part of the homophile to 'absorb' masculinity from his sexual partners, he must be constantly on the lookout for [new partners]. Consequently the most successful homophile 'marriages' are those

where there is an arrangement between the two to have affairs on the side while maintaining the semblance of permanence in their living arrangement.

American homosexual activist Michelangelo Signorile makes similar remarks, urging activists to:[51]

> ... fight for same-sex marriage and its benefits and then, once granted, redefine the institution of marriage completely, to demand the right to marry not as a way of adhering to society's moral codes but rather to debunk a myth and radically alter an archaic institution that, as it now stands, keeps us down. The most subversive action lesbians and gay men can undertake – and one that would perhaps benefit society – is to transform the notion of 'family' entirely.

Legalising same-sex marriage is not a minor or peripheral social shift. It is social change on a massive scale.

Or as he said several years later:[52]

> It is also a chance to wholly transform the definition of family in American culture. It is the final tool with which to dismantle all sodomy statutes, get education about homosexuality and AIDS into public schools, and, in short, usher in a sea change in how society views and treats us.

Indeed, legalising same-sex marriage is not a minor or peripheral social shift. It is social change on a massive scale. Advocates of homosexual marriage admit as much. In addition to the quotes just given, consider one final remark. Leading homosexual marriage advocate Evan Wolfson admits to just what will happen: "This won't just be a change in the law either; it will be a change in society. For if we do it right, the struggle to win the freedom to marry will bring much more along the way."[53]

What is at stake?

With a number of nations and some U.S. states now going the way of homosexual marriage, the issue has taken on new significance. Indeed, with the Ontario Supreme Court declaring that it is a violation of homosexuals' rights to restrict marriage to heterosexuals, a new emphasis has been made by some in the homosexual community to push for homosexual marriage in Australia.

For example, Victorian Gay and Lesbian Rights Lobby co-convener David McCarthy says that same-sex marriage should be tested here, now that the Ontario ruling has been made. He argues that if an Australian homosexual couple went to Ontario and got married, or a Canadian married couple moved here, the Australian legal system would be forced to decide on whether that marriage was valid here. (Ontario has no residence requirement for marriages celebrated in the province, unlike Holland and Belgium).[54]

And this has now happened. A Melbourne couple went to Toronto, were "married", and have now demanded recognition by Australian lawmakers. While the outcome is pending, it is now only a matter of time before the issue is brought to a head.[55]

Bear in mind that the Australian Greens and Democrats have already moved to allow amendments to the Marriage Act 1961 going in their direction. Moreover, in June of 2002 a news item reported that the Marriage Act could easily be reinterpreted by the courts. A top jurist gave confidential legal advice to the then-Attorney-General Daryl Williams saying that the Act was so wide open that courts could easily interpret homosexual and lesbian unions as legally valid marriages.[56]

Thus it is quite possible that the Australian Parliament could be by-passed altogether through a court decision instead clearing the way for homosexual marriage. Indeed, the courts are already softening things up in this regard. On October 11, 2001, the Family Court of Australia decided that a transsexual could marry.[57] That is, a woman who underwent a sex-change operation was declared to be legally able to marry another woman, according to Justice Chisholm. And in February 2003 the full court of the Family Court again decided that the 1999 marriage was valid.[58] In doing so, the justices effectively undermined the words of the Marriage Act which state that marriage is the "voluntary union of one man and one woman, to the exclusion of all others".[59]

Fortunately, in August of 2004, Federal Parliament voted to amend the Marriage Act 1961 to ensure that marriage can be only between one man and one woman. However, the battle continues, and homosexual activists have clearly not given up the fight.

If homosexual marriage were to be legalised here, it would be one of the final nails in the coffin of heterosexual marriage and family as traditionally understood. The truth is all cultures have recognised marriage, but only of the heterosexual variety. And marriage has always been associated with procreation.[60] To strip marriage of its traditional moorings is effectively to destroy it.

> **If homosexual marriage were to be legalised here, it would be one of the final nails in the coffin of heterosexual marriage and family as traditionally understood.**

Indeed, one must bear in mind the normative and educative function of the law. Whenever something is legalised, it sends out a social signal, saying that this is an acceptable and even preferable activity. In legalising same-sex marriage, we will be making a major social statement, and taking a major step forward in social engineering. Even Judge Richard Posner, who in general favours the direction of the sexual revolution, is concerned about homosexual marriage. He writes: "To permit persons of the same sex to marry is to declare, or more precisely, to be understood by many people to be declaring, that homosexual marriage is a desirable, even a noble, condition in which to live."[61]

Moreover, as same-sex marriage becomes a right, the corresponding duties will be insisted upon. That is, those opposed to homosexual marriage will be forced by the state to countenance and actively become involved in it. Opposition will, in the end, become criminalised.

Consider just one example. A recent headline said this: "Canadian Court: Marriage officials must marry homosexuals". The article begins this way: "The Saskatchewan Court of Appeal declared this morning that proposed legislative amendments that would have allowed Saskatchewan's marriage commissioners to refuse to perform same-sex 'marriages' on religious grounds are unconstitutional."[62]

107

And anthropologists who have studied the historical record have observed previous experiments in redefining sexual norms. They do not always like what they see. For example, a Boston University anthropologist remarks that anthropology "guards a treasure house of examples of what happens when a society institutionalizes *other* arrangements". He argues that if a society normalises male homosexuality through same-sex marriage, the general results "are predictable on the basis of the ethnography: heterosexual marriage will be weakened; the birth rate will decline; the status of women as mothers will further erode; and young boys will be a much greater target of erotic attention by older males".[63]

As one Canadian University professor put it, legal attempts to redefine marriage will eradicate a tried and tested good in favour of a risky social experiment. But the new hybrid will not be marriage at all:[64]

> Marriage is not merely a union of two persons. It is a gendered union with specific social goods attached. The state – which did not invent marriage and has no authority to re-invent it – rightly takes an interest in marriage on account of these goods: stability of community and property, of human reproduction and the care of children, of cross-gender and cross-generational bonding, etc.

To include same-sex couples in the institution of marriage is simply to substitute "for a gendered phrase ('one man and one woman') its genderless one".[65]

As William Bennett has written:[66]

> Marriage is not an arbitrary construct; it is an 'honorable estate' based on the different, complementary nature of men and women – and how they refine, support, encourage and complete one another. To insist that we maintain this traditional understanding of marriage is not an attempt to put others down. It is simply an acknowledgement and celebration of our most precious and important social act. Nor is this view arbitrary or idiosyncratic. It mirrors the accumulated wisdom of millennia and the teaching of every major religion.

Slippery slope

Moreover, the same arguments used for legalising same-sex marriage could be used to argue for legalising incest, polygamy and any number of other sexual combinations. If a man wanted to have a long-term sexual relationship with his daughter, or if three women wanted to do the same, how could any society, if it has already overturned the traditional understanding of marriage, argue against it?

> **If marriage is no longer one man, one woman for life, then any number of alternatives seems to be possible.**

This has been exactly the case with a Columbia University professor charged with incest with his adult daughter. His attorney put it this way:[67]

> It's OK for homosexuals to do whatever they want in their own home. How is this so different? We have to figure out why some behavior is tolerated and some is not. What goes on between consenting adults in private should not be legislated. That is not the proper domain of our law. If we assume for a moment that both parties are consenting, then why are we prosecuting this?

If marriage is no longer one man, one woman for life, then any number of alternatives seems to be possible. If homosexuals can argue that a loving committed relationship should qualify anyone for the institution of marriage, then other equally binding and loving unions should be recognised.

As Sam Schulman put it:[68]

> If we grant rights to one group because they have demanded it – which is, practically, how legalized gay marriage will come to pass – we will find it exceedingly awkward to deny similar rights to others ready with their own dossiers of 'victimization.' In time, restricting marriage rights to couples, whether straight or gay, can be made to seem no less arbitrary than the practice of restricting marriage rights to one man and one woman. Ultimately, the same must go for incestuous relationships between consenting adults.

109

Logically, one could argue for all sorts of combinations and permutations if we swallow the idea that same-sex couples have a right to marry. What about a bisexual who really does love both a man and a woman? Cannot this threesome qualify?

Indeed, there have been plenty of homosexual activists who have long argued for the removal of most, if not all, legal restrictions on sexuality. Way back in 1972 the National Coalition of Gay Organizations in the U.S. demanded the "repeal of all legislative provisions that restrict the sex or number of persons entering into a marriage unit; and the extension of legal benefits to all persons who cohabit regardless of sex or numbers".[69]

Also in this 1972 *Gay Rights Platform* was the call for the abolition of all age-of-sexual-consent laws. These proposals were endorsed far and wide in the homosexual community. Indeed, lesbian activist Judith Levine argued for all this and more (even pedophilia) in her 2003 book, *Harmful to Minors: The Perils of Protecting Children from Sex*,[70] and her famous *Village Voice* article, "Stop the Wedding! Why Gay Marriage Isn't Radical Enough".[71]

Consider another recent example of the slippery slope in action. The pro-same-sex marriage Greens in Switzerland are now happy to see the legalisation of incest. One press report says this: "The upper house of the Swiss parliament has drafted a law decriminalising sex between consenting family members which must now be considered by the government. ... Daniel Vischer, a Green party MP, said he saw nothing wrong with two consenting adults having sex, even if they were related."[72]

The truth is, when we redefine marriage all boundaries are smashed. There are even groups arguing for the right to marry one's pet! Called petrosexuality, this new sexuality group insists that a person's love for his or her pet, including sexual relations, should be made official. Thus one Dutch website encourages people to marry their pets.[73]

Such proposals are not just being made by the lunatic fringe. Consider a recent article in the *Futurist*, produced by the World Futurist Society based in America. A cultural historian wrote an article entitled "The Transformation of Marriage". Stephen Bertman, professor emeritus of languages, literatures and cultures at Canada's University of Windsor, declared that marriage may be "a semantic artefact of a lost world".[74] He argued that it is not just the transience of marriage that is at issue now: "It is the very definition of the term that futurists must now address. A radical redefinition of marriage is now underway that promises to transform its meaning for all future time."[75]

He gave as his first example same-sex marriage. He did not stop there however. He then went on to speak of other types of marriage. Seemingly with a straight face, he first raised the prospect of "interspecies marriage". This is the "potential for the sexual union of human beings and aliens".[76] From there he mentioned the option of marriages to pets. Why couldn't an "individual choose to affirm the emotional attachment he or she feels for a pet with the formality of a documented ceremony in which the human partner promises to love and honor the animal companion?"[77]

And finally, presumably still with the utmost seriousness, he speaks of the "theoretical possibility" of "the marriage of human beings to inanimate objects". He speaks of how many men love their cars, or how many people have formed an intimate relationship with their computer. "Why should not this bond of tactile intimacy be validated by more than an owner's manual?" he asks, seemingly in complete sincerity.[78]

As Bennett writes elsewhere: "Once marriage has been detached from the natural, complementary teleology of the sexes, it becomes nothing more than what each of us makes of it".[79]

Or as another commentator says:[80]

> What we are doing by creating this institution to be called 'gay marriage' is smashing marriage and replacing it with a whole new set of arrangements that apply to everybody, not just homosexuals, everybody, in which marriage is a unique contract between any two or more adults who want to enter into it and set by any rules. It makes marriage impermanent, and it turns children into commodities.

That the legalisation of same-sex marriage would radically alter and redefine the institution of marriage is, of course, widely acknowledged by homosexual activists. I have already cited some of them. Here let me offer just one more representative quote. Tom Stoddard is a leading homosexual activist in the U.S. He has been quite willing to admit that "enlarging the concept [of heterosexual marriage] to embrace same-sex couples would *necessarily transform it into something new*" (emphasis added).[81]

Slippery slope: polyamory

In fact, polyamory (group marriage) has become a new cause, championed by both grassroots groups and academic supporters. A quick search of the Web will reveal just how popular the idea of polyamory is becoming. Family law reformers, for example, are increasingly promoting this new sexual cause.[82]

And it is remarkable how the polyamory and polygamy advocates are simply latching on to and extending the very arguments made by advocates of same-sex marriage. They are rightly saying that if same-sex marriage is legalised, then certainly group marriage must be legalised as well.

They appeal to the very same arguments, logic and past court decisions used by the homosexual activists. A brief look at their websites makes this quite clear. As just one example of many, a website called Pro-Polygamy has these words flashed across its home page: "Freely-consenting, adult, non-abusive, marriage-committed POLYGAMY is the next civil rights battle".[83]

In fact, as one commentator has noted, the "case for polygamy is in some ways stronger than the case for same-sex marriage". She explains: "In contrast to same-sex marriage, there is historical and cultural precedent for it. Unlike same-sex marriage, polygamy provides a father and a mother (and then some) for children."[84]

> **The case for polyamory is being argued for all over the place.**

Consider for example the "Unitarian Universalists for Polyamory Awareness". The president of this group, Jasmine Walston, made this connection quite clear in 2004: "We're where the gay rights movement was 30 years ago."[85] She sees the struggle for polyamory rights to be the logical extension of the homosexual rights struggle.

And the case for polyamory is being argued for all over the place, with plenty of academics, organisations and universities rushing to champion the cause. Indeed, you know it is becoming something of substance when a mainstream magazine like *Newsweek* devotes a major story to it.[86]

Consider how one Australian university academic makes the case for polyamory in an article entitled, "Poly is the new gay". She makes it clear that, just as society has welcomed homosexuality and same-sex marriage, it is now time to welcome polyamory. This is how she puts it: "The more aware and accepting of diversity in relationships the more healthy our society is. ... I look forward to a society where any loving family, irrespective of how many people it includes or what sex they are, feels safe to be open about who they are."[87]

Slippery slope: case study

If all the quotes mentioned above have not yet convinced the reader about the radical nature of the homosexual demands, let me cite just one more activist. This writer makes it abundantly clear that a slippery slope of massive proportions will result from the legalisation of same-sex marriage.

It is such a revealing – and bizarre – admission of how radical the marriage overhaul and dismantling is intended to be, that it is worth spending a bit of time on this one. It involves Australian writer Katrina Fox. In 2008 she co-edited a book called *Trans People in Love*, but I want to focus on an incredible piece she wrote for the Australian Broadcasting Corporation in 2011.

Entitled, "Marriage needs redefining",[88] she made it perfectly clear how all the boundaries surrounding marriage must be smashed. You can tell things will be going downhill fast when she begins her article this way: "A more inclusive option is to allow individuals to get married whatever their sex or gender, including those who identify as having no sex or gender or whose sex may be indeterminate."

She informs us that monogamy is clearly just not on, and she even cites a 2010 book informing us that "monogamy may not be natural to humans". She claims it is "unrealistic" for people to expect to remain in lifelong sexually faithful relationships.

She then goes on to speak approvingly of "non-monogamy" and "open relationships". Says Fox: "Surely it makes more sense to expand the definition of marriage to include a range of relationship models including polyamory, instead of holding up monogamy as the gold – indeed only – standard."

But wait, there's more: "Marriage would also benefit from being expanded to include non-sexual, non-romantic relationships, like the existing Tasmanian relationship register which allows anyone who is in a 'personal relationship involving emotional interdependence, domestic support or personal care' to register that relationship."

And it gets even more interesting. If it were not for the lack of consent, there really might be no limits at all: "I'm not suggesting we goes [*sic*] as far to sanction people marrying inanimate objects like the German woman who married the Berlin Wall and was utterly devastated when her 'husband' was destroyed in 1989. Nor am I advocating marrying animals since they cannot consent, but simply extending marriage to reflect the broad range of loving relationships between consenting adults."

She is also quite indignant at homosexual activists who claim they won't force churches to perform same-sex marriages: "These tactics have horrified many gay, lesbian and queer people, including me. It's hard to imagine any person of colour advocating for religions to have the right not to marry non-white people, so why some gay campaigners think so little of themselves and the broader queer community to sanction what *is* bigotry beggars belief."

And just in case we have not got her drift, she also says: "In 2011 it's time to redefine marriage to include a diverse range of relationships between one or more people of any sex or gender (including not specified or indeterminate). Those desperate to cling on to outmoded traditions would do well to heed the moniker used by motivational speakers: 'Adapt or die'."

114

Her concluding line is perhaps the most bizarre of all: "Opening up marriage to be more inclusive, progressive and representative of the realities of our relationships today is not a threat to the institution, but rather an opportunity to preserve it."

This is of course an incredible self-contradiction. She has just spent the entire article demonstrating how she plans to massacre marriage, transforming it out of existence, and now she wants to tell us that this is somehow going to "preserve" marriage.

Let me simply follow in her footsteps, and give an analogy as to what she is proposing. Let's do to the Australian Football League (AFL) what she wants to do to marriage. We all know that Australian Rules football is a hidebound, archaic institution that really needs to get with the times.

It has been hampered by outdated tradition and needless rules and regulations. It certainly does not reflect current realities of where we want to go with sport. So let us make a few obvious changes. First of all, it is silly – and quite discriminatory – to allow just two teams at a time to play the game.

Thus from now on I suggest any number of teams be allowed to enter into the action at the same time. Monoteams are just so passé, and polyteams are really the way to go. And how sexist and species-ist is it to exclude women and animals from the game. No more men-only AFL.

And having just one ball is so repressive and intolerant. From now on any number of balls can be used during the game. And it is the worst form of oppression to have just two sets of goal posts, so from henceforth anyone can set up goalposts anywhere they like.

Moreover, restricting the game to an oval is just so unfair and oppressive. The game should be allowed to be played wherever one chooses: in an office, the toilet, at church, or in the centre of Parliament House, Canberra.

And given that rules, umpires, and the like are evidence of rigid conformity, outmoded authoritarianism and bourgeois morality, all games from now on will be played completely free of any rules, and all umpires will be forever banned from the game.

115

Isn't this just so very liberating, progressive and modern? Why be slaves to old-fashioned laws and morals? Let's go with the times and end all unjust discrimination and restrictions on rights. After all, the name of the game is equality, freedom and justice for all.

Oh, and by the way: "Opening up football to be more inclusive, progressive and representative of the realities of our sporting relationships today is not a threat to the institution, but rather an opportunity to preserve it."

Adapt or die, AFL. I guess that all makes perfect sense. So foolish of me to think that a bit of tinkering around the edges of marriage would be a big deal. I can thank Katrina Fox and her buddies for clearing this up for me.

Discrimination

Let me here mention a few words about the complaint often made by homosexuals that they are discriminated against under current marriage laws. As an example, Australian comedian and television personality Julie McCrossin gave an address to the Sydney Institute in July of 1999. Entitled, "Always a bridesmaid, never a bride: recognising same-sex relationships", she spoke of how she and her lesbian partner were denied marriage rights in Australia.

> **These arguments are as fallacious as they are common.**

She complained that she was being discriminated against, and made this impassioned statement: "Until we're able to get married, gay and lesbian couples don't have equality before the law."[89] Such an argument is common, of course, among homosexual rights activists.

However, these arguments are as fallacious as they are common. The truth is, no one has the kind of "equality before law" that the homosexual activists are clamouring for. In this case, for example, homosexuals are no more (and no less) being discriminated against than are all kinds of other people.

Yes, it is true, a homosexual cannot now legally marry a person of the same sex. But neither can a whole lot of other folk. A five-year-old boy cannot marry. Three people cannot get married to each other. And even if an attractive young woman were to fall in love with me and want to marry me (a highly unlikely scenario, I might add), she cannot, because I am already married.

Moreover, a girl cannot marry her pet goldfish, no matter how much she might love it. A father cannot marry his daughter, regardless of his affection for her. A football team cannot enact group marriage, no matter how close, committed and bonded they are. The list is endless.

However, under the law, almost all of us can marry, given certain conditions. If I should decide to reciprocate the affections of this young woman, I could divorce my current wife and marry her (also an unlikely scenario, I must emphasise). The five-year-old could wait for around a dozen years, and then he will be free to marry. The threesome can decide to give one the boot, and then get married (provided they are an opposite sex pair).

And a homosexual too can marry. There is no law saying a homosexual cannot marry, if he decides to find a woman and settle down (or if a lesbian finds a man and seeks marriage). But it is nonsense for a person to eschew male-female relationships in favour of same-sex ones, and then complain of discrimination.

In the same way, it is disingenuous to complain about rights being taken away, when they never existed in the first place. Homosexual activist Rodney Croome, for example, displayed a case of sour grapes after the passage on August 19, 2004 of the Australian Marriage Amendment Act, which reaffirms in law what has always been the case: that marriage is to be only between a man and a woman, and no other combination. He wrote an op-ed piece a few days later, which opened with these words: "For the first time since federation, an Australian Parliament

> **Not all homosexuals see the case against same-sex marriage as being discriminatory.**

has voted to deprive gay and lesbian people of their rights."[90] Sorry, but there never was such a right in the first place, so the government did no such thing.

You cannot take something away if it was not there to begin with. The use made by homosexual activists of this disingenuous argument does little to dispel confusion over this issue and can mislead public opinion.

But perhaps the best case against these silly charges of discrimination, bigotry and so on come from homosexuals themselves. Not all homosexuals see the case against same-sex marriage as being discriminatory, an attack on their rights, or simply the product of bigotry and homophobia.

Irish homosexual writer Richard Waghorne, for example, puts it this way:[91]

> Explaining that you oppose gay marriage as a gay man tends to get a baffled response at first. This is understandable given how quickly the debate on gay marriage can collapse into allegations of homophobia. The message, explicit or implicit, is often that being anti-gay marriage means being in some way anti-gay.
>
> I have watched with growing irritation as principled opponents of gay marriage have put up with a stream of abuse for explaining their position. Public figures who try to do so routinely have to contend with the charge that they are bigoted or homophobic.

During the 2011 Irish general election campaign, when Fine Gael's Lucinda Creighton confirmed her opposition to same-sex marriage there were calls for party leader Enda Kenny to sack her. Waghorne continues:[92]

> David Quinn of the pro-marriage Iona Institute is regularly abused in sometimes extraordinary terms for making similar arguments. They're not the only ones. The reflex response from many gay marriage advocates is to paint all dissent as prejudice, as if the only reason for defending marriage as it has existed to date is some variety of bigotry or psychological imbalance. ...
>
> Surely it's time to have a proper conversation about gay marriage, a conversation where people are no longer made to feel that if they do not offer knee-jerk support to it, they will be branded anti-gay. Only then will the essence and the real reason for supporting traditional marriage be allowed to come to the fore again. The best interests of the children of the nation must always come first.

The race card

Indeed, another way they seek to deceive the public is to use faulty analogies. For example, many advocates of same-sex marriage use the faulty analogy of racial segregation and policies that prevented people of different races from marrying (anti-miscegenation laws). They claim that, just as we now have renounced such discriminatory laws regarding marriage between the races, so too we should stop the restriction on same-sex marriage.

For example, when former Australian Prime Minister John Howard said he wanted to block legal recognition of same-sex marriages, high-profile lesbian couple Kerryn Phelps and Jackie Stricker said this was a "form of apartheid".[93] But this is simply fallacious. There is no comparison between racist laws and defending heterosexual marriage.

> **Apartheid and laws banning inter-racial marriage are about keeping races apart. Marriage is about bringing the sexes together.**

Even black activists have rejected such a disingenuous analogy.[94] For example, Jesse Jackson told a group of Harvard Law School students in 2004 that "gays were never called three-fifths human in the Constitution, and they did not require the Voting Rights Act to have the right to vote".[95]

Apartheid and laws banning inter-racial marriage are about keeping races apart. Marriage is about bringing the sexes together. Heterosexual marriage has been around for millennia. Talk of same-sex marriage has been around for a few short decades. Marriage was thus not created to discriminate against anyone, as apartheid was.

Laws banning interracial marriages were unjust, and overturning them did not mean a redefinition of marriage but an affirmation of it. Men and women should be allowed to marry regardless of skin colour, as this does nothing to alter the one-man, one-woman aspect of marriage. Same-sex marriage however is completely different, and it is a redefinition of marriage.

As one commentator notes:[96]

Same-sex marriage and interracial marriage have nothing in common. There is no difference between a black and a white human being because skin color is morally trivial. There is an enormous difference, however, between a man and a woman. Ethnicity has no bearing on marriage. Sex is fundamental to marriage.

Or as three noted authorities argue:[97]

But the analogy fails: anti-miscegenation was about whom to allow to marry, not what marriage was essentially about; and sex, unlike race, is rationally relevant to the latter question. Because every law makes distinctions, there is nothing unjustly discriminatory in marriage law's reliance on genuinely relevant distinctions.

Francis Beckwith makes clear these distinctions. He is worth quoting at length. He argues that anti-miscegenation laws:[98]

… were attempts to eradicate the legal status of real marriages by injecting a condition – sameness of race – that had no precedent in common law. For in the common law, a necessary condition for a legitimate marriage was male-female complementarity, a condition on which race has no bearing.

It is clear then that the miscegenation/same-sex analogy does not work. For if the purpose of anti-miscegenation laws was racial purity, such a purpose only makes sense if people of different races *have the ability by nature to marry* each other. And given the fact that such marriages were a common law liberty, the anti-miscegenation laws *presuppose this truth*. But opponents of same-sex marriage ground their viewpoint in precisely the opposite belief: people of the same gender *do not have the ability by nature to marry each other* since gender complementarity is a necessary condition for marriage. Supporters of anti-miscegenation laws believed in their cause *precisely because* they understood that when male and female are joined in matrimony they may beget racially-mixed progeny, and these children, along with their parents, will participate in civil society and influence its cultural trajectory.

In other words, the fact that a man and a woman from different races were biologically and metaphysically capable of marrying each other, building families, and living among the general population is precisely why the race purists wanted to forbid such unions by the force of law. And because this view of marriage and its gender-complementary nature was firmly in place and the only understanding found in common law, the Supreme Court in *Loving* knew that racial identity was not relevant to what marriage requires of its two opposite-gender members. By injecting race into the equation, anti-miscegenation supporters were very much like contemporary same-sex marriage proponents, for in both cases they introduced a criterion other than male-female complementarity in order to promote the goals of a utopian social movement: race purity or sexual egalitarianism.

Even some homosexual activists admit that this is a bad comparison. Says one:[99]

> I am uneasy with the frequent equation of the prohibition of same-sex marriage with interracial ones: in the latter case racism prevented marriages that were indistinguishable for any other reason. Same-sex partnerships are as valid and as significant as heterosexual ones, but they are also different, and maybe we should celebrate, not deny the difference.

Racial segregation is wrong, and is an example of unjust discrimination. But the colour of one's skin is far different from sexual behaviour. Societies have good reasons not to embrace any and all types of sexual activity. While skin colour is a benign and unalterable condition, this is not true of various sexual behaviours. No black person can cease being black, but plenty of homosexuals have ceased being homosexual.

The truth is, a society can, if need be, get along without same-sex sexual relationships. But no society can get along without heterosexual marriage and family. As two family researchers put it:[100]

> There is no research saying biracial parents are developmentally harmful to children. But there are thousands of definitive studies showing motherless and fatherless families limit every important

measure of children's physical, psychological, emotional and intellectual development.

Apples and oranges

Given how important all this is, let me repeat my main arguments here: The truth is, there is no law anywhere preventing homosexuals from marrying. Anyone can marry, provided they meet the criteria for marriage. Those who do not meet these criteria are minors, blood relatives, groups, those already married, and so on. To get married you must meet the qualifications of marriage. The primary qualification, of course is to have two people, one from each gender. These restrictions apply equally to everyone, whether heterosexual or homosexual. Thus there is no discrimination here.

When homosexuals try to circumvent these rules or ignore them altogether, they are not endeavouring to get equal rights; they are attempting to get special rights. Indeed, what they claim "is a new right; the right to reconfigure the conditions of marriage in such a way as to change its very definition, while denying they are doing any such thing".[101]

Indeed, what is being attempted here is to treat unequal things equally. But a basic purpose of justice is to ensure that equals are treated equally. If equals are being treated unequally, then charges of injustice can be made. But there is no injustice in recognising the obvious differences between a same-sex relationship and a heterosexual relationship.

Sure, homosexuals, as individual human beings, are fully equal to heterosexuals. But while all people are equal, not all relationships are. The many important ways in which these two types of relationships differ have already been discussed earlier.

And love between homosexuals – or between those in other sorts of relationships – can still continue and flourish without marriage. As American professor of jurisprudence Hadley Arkes states:[102]

The most genuine love may subsist between parents and children, grandparents and grandchildren, brothers and sisters, and in the nature of things – *in the nature of things* – nothing in those loves could possibly be diminished as love because they are not attended by penetration or expressed in marriage.

Thus those arguing for same-sex marriage are mixing apples with oranges. Everyone should be entitled to the benefits of marriage so long as they meet the conditions and requirements of marriage. Homosexual relationships simply do not meet these criteria. The rule of thumb is simple: if you want the benefits of marriage, then meet the qualifications – the most basic of which is having one man and one woman. Governments have no obligation whatsoever to treat unequal things equally, or to grant the benefits of marriage to those who refuse to meet its most basic of conditions.

And of course various social goods are denied to all sorts of people for various reasons.

> **All societies, in order to survive, engage in proper acts of discrimination all the time.**

A driver who cannot meet the obligations of low insurance rates (too young, too inexperienced, too many accidents, etc) will not be eligible to receive those benefits. That is how life operates. If anything, it is a necessary and just discrimination.

All societies, in order to survive, engage in proper acts of discrimination all the time. Just as there can be bad discrimination, so there can be good discrimination. Societies have always discriminated in favour of heterosexual unions and the children they produce because of the overwhelming social good derived from them.

Procreation and the raising of children is such an overwhelmingly important social good, and the mother-father unit cemented by marriage such an overwhelmingly superior way of ensuring the best outcomes for children (and therefore society), that societies everywhere extend favours and benefits to married couples that they do not to other types of relationships.

So all this has nothing to do with unjust or arbitrary "discrimination"; it is simply about encouraging everyone to play by the rules. Since homosexuals refuse to play by the rules when it comes to marriage, it is ridiculous to pull out the violins here and moan about forgone "rights" and so on.

⋇ To argue that this is unjust discrimination or a violation of rights is simply inappropriate in this context. It is about as helpful as trying to argue that Aretha Franklin is being discriminated against since she cannot play for the Melbourne Football Club. Never mind all the ways in which she doesn't qualify here: wrong country, wrong gender, too old, too heavy, too out of shape, no skills in Australian Rules football, no knowledge of the game, and so on. There is no discrimination going on there at all.

⋎⋏ ⋈ All the homosexual lobby is doing here is seeking to fundamentally rewrite the rule books on marriage so that it can get all the benefits thereof while not meeting its obligations.

Childless heterosexual couples

Finally, when marriage is declared to be about the best interests of children, homosexuals will still object. They argue that if you deny marriage for homosexuals because they cannot reproduce, what about all the heterosexual couples who do not have children? Marriage isn't just about having children, is it?, they ask.

This seems a good argument, but it isn't really. Marriage is certainly open to the possibility of children, even though for various reasons not all marriages will result in children. One commentator offers this insight on the relationship of marriage to reproduction: just turn the question around. That is, instead of asking "whether actual reproduction is essential to marriage, ask this: If marriage *never* had *anything* to do with reproduction, would there be any reason for the government to be involved in regulating or rewarding it?"[103] Governments do not determine who your best friend should be. But when the possibility of children arises, then governments and societies are greatly concerned.

Or as another commentator puts it:[104]

Marriage's main purpose is to make sure that any child born has two responsible parents, a mother and a father who are committed to the child and committed to each other. To achieve this goal, it has never been necessary, and it would never be possible, for society to require that each and every married couple bear a child!

Sterility is the exception to the rule for heterosexual couples, while it is the norm for homosexual couples. A couple is not required to have babies when getting married, but it remains the generally expected norm. Some couples cannot have children. Some don't want them. But heterosexuality makes procreation possible, while homosexuality makes it impossible.

The fact that a book can lie unread does not make it anything other than a book. The purpose or function of a book is to be read, but it does not become less than a book if it is not read. Nature's purpose or function for human sexuality is procreation. The fact that not every sexual act results in procreation does not take away this essential feature.

As one law professor notes, "Homosexual sex is never procreation; male-female sex (even in sterile couples) is always potentially and at least symbolically procreative in kind."[105] Several experts offer an analogy here which is worth quoting at length:[106]

A baseball team has its characteristic structure largely because of its orientation to winning games; it involves developing and sharing one's athletic skills in the way best suited for honorably winning (among other things, with assiduous practice and good sportsmanship). But such development and sharing are possible and inherently valuable for teammates even when they lose their games.

Just so, marriage has its characteristic structure largely because of its orientation to procreation; it involves developing and sharing one's body and whole self in the way best suited for honorable parenthood – among other things, permanently and exclusively. But such development and sharing, including the bodily union of the generative act, are possible and inherently valuable for spouses even when they do not conceive children.

Therefore, people who can unite bodily can be spouses without children, just as people who can practice baseball can be teammates without victories on the field. Although marriage is a social practice that has its basic structure by nature, whereas baseball is wholly conventional, the analogy highlights a crucial point: Infertile couples and winless baseball teams both meet the basic requirements for participating in the practice (conjugal union; practicing and playing the game) and retain their basic orientation to the fulfilment of that practice (bearing and rearing children; winning games), even if that fulfilment is never reached.

> **Even some homosexuals themselves realise how important a mother and a father are to children.**

On the other hand, same-sex partnerships, whatever their moral status, cannot be marriages because they lack any essential orientation to children: They cannot be sealed by the generative act. Indeed, in the common law tradition, only coitus (not anal or oral sex even between legally wed spouses) has been recognized as consummating a marriage.

And even some homosexuals themselves realise how important a mother and a father are to children, and therefore oppose same-sex marriage. Let me cite just one example here. I have already mentioned Irish homosexual Richard Waghorne. A big part of his argument against homosexual marriage has to do with the well-being of children. He is worth quoting at length:[107]

> Marriage is vital as a framework within which children can be brought up by a man and woman. Not all marriages, of course, involve child-raising. And there are also, for that matter, same-sex couples already raising children. But the reality is that marriages tend towards child-raising and same-sex partnerships do not.
>
> I am conscious of this when considering my own circle of friends, quite a few of whom have recently married or will soon do so in the future. Many, if not most or all of them, will raise children. If, however, I or gay friends form civil partnerships, those are much more unlikely to involve raising children. So the question that

matters is this: Why should a gay relationship be treated the same way as a marriage, despite this fundamental difference?

A wealth of research demonstrates the marriage of a man and a woman provides children with the best life outcomes, that children raised in marriages that stay together do best across a whole range of measures. This is certainly not to cast aspersions on other families, but it does underscore the importance of marriage as an institution.

This is why the demand for gay marriage goes doubly wrong. It is not a demand for marriage to be extended to gay people – it is a demand for marriage to be redefined. The understanding of marriage as an institution that exists and is supported for the sake of strong families changes to an understanding of marriage as merely the end-point of romance.

If gay couples are considered equally eligible for marriage, even though gay relationships do not tend towards child-raising and cannot by definition give a child a mother and a father, the crucial understanding of what marriage is actually mainly for has been discarded.

What that amounts to is the kind of marriage that puts adults before children. That, in my opinion, is ultimately selfish, and far too high a price to pay simply for the token gesture of treating opposite-sex relationships and same-sex relationships identically. And it is a token gesture. Isn't it common sense, after all, to treat different situations differently? To put it personally, I do not feel in the least bit discriminated against by the fact that I cannot marry someone of the same sex. I understand and accept that there are good reasons for this.

Why is homosexual marriage wanted?

Before dealing with the issue of children, one final matter should be addressed. Just why is it that some homosexuals are so insistent on marriage rights? Why the very strong push by at least some in the homosexual community to be able to marry?

As many homosexuals themselves admit, a major reason why they want marriage is not so much to be like heterosexuals, or because they want to abandon their more free and promiscuous lifestyle, but because of its symbolic value. It will give them public recognition, approval and acceptance. This has long been the overriding goal of the homosexual lobby: complete social and public endorsement and approval. Thus by getting marriage rights, and, in turn, the last hurdle for homosexuals, full adoption rights, homosexuals will have achieved their longstanding goal: legitimising the homosexual lifestyle.

As even *Time* magazine admitted in an article on same-sex marriage, the real goal is complete social acceptance and validation:[108]

> Ultimately, of course, the battle for gay marriage has always been about more than winning the second-driver discount at the Avis counter. In fact, the individual who has done most to push same-sex marriage – a brilliant 43-year-old lawyer-activist named Evan Wolfson – doesn't even have a boyfriend. He and the others who brought the marriage lawsuits of the past decade want nothing less than full social equality, total validation – not just the right to inherit a mother-in-law's Cadillac. As Andrew Sullivan, the (also persistently single) intellectual force behind gay marriage, has written, 'Including homosexuals within marriage would be a means of conferring the highest form of social approval imaginable'.

A leading American homosexual who has championed the cause of same-sex marriage, Jonathan Rauch, admits that this will be an important effect of same-sex marriage: "It will ennoble and dignify gay love and sex as it has done straight love and sex."[109] Exactly, but as I have shown above, such a dangerous threat to public health and safety should not be ennobled or dignified, certainly not by governments who have the duty and responsibility to promote the health and wellbeing of all its citizens.

Australian homosexual activists have also acknowledged that their attempt to join heterosexuals in marriage is about legitimacy and acceptance. Consider the words of Rodney Croome:[110]

This isn't about sex, it's about symbolism. Despite, or perhaps because of, an increase in de facto relationships and divorce, many Australians value marriage highly. For better or worse, it bestows on a relationship society's ultimate seal of approval. This is why social conservatives deeply loathe marriage equality and why, as the inheritors of centuries of stigma, many same-sex couples yearn for it.

That is what Mr Croome and so many others want: social approval. That is why there is such a concentrated effort to redefine marriage by the homo-sexual lobby.

Another leading Australian homosexual activist also admits that this is really just about the symbolism.

> **The bottom line of all homosexual activism is ultimately complete social acceptance and approval.**

Dennis Altman puts it this way: "The argument is quite simple: marriage is the ultimate legitimation of equality, according same-sex relationships the same status as heterosexual ones. Essentially this is a symbolic claim, for there is a whole raft of ways in which the state regulates relationships outside formal marriage."[111]

Indeed, the bottom line of all homosexual activism is ultimately just that: complete social acceptance and approval. As Kirk and Madsen put it back in 1989, "to gain straight tolerance and acceptance is not just a legitimate goal of gay activism, it must be the *principal* goal".[112]

Plenty of other homosexual activists have admitted as much. For example, same-sex marriage advocate Arthur Leonard put it this way: "Legal recogni-tion of same-sex couples would have the effect over time of 'normalizing' such relationships. ... Those who argue that the gay rights movement is out to transform society by getting people to view gay people as 'normal' are completely correct."[113]

Exactly. The activists realise that the majority will not acknowledge normal-ity concerning the homosexual lifestyle, so they must resort to bypassing the public will and the legislative process, using instead the blunt instrument of judicial activism. It is the activist courts which are forcing the homosexual lifestyle on the rest of society, whether society likes it or not.

As African-American Shelby Steele, in an article on why same-sex marriage is not a civil rights issue, rightly notes: "In the gay marriage movement, marriage is more a means than an end, a weapon against stigma. That the movement talks very little about the actual institution of marriage suggests that it is driven more by this longing to normalize homosexuality itself than by something compelling in marriage."[114]

Stanley Kurtz puts it this way:[115]

> Ultimately, it may be that what lies behind the demand for same-sex marriage, whether couched in conservative or in 'civil-rights' terms, is a bid to erase entirely the stigma of homosexuality. That bid is utopian; as radical gays like Michael Bronski acknowledge, the stigma arises from the fundamental separation between homosexuality and reproduction, which is to say from the fundamental fact that the world is, for the overwhelming part, heterosexual. Nevertheless, in pursuit of this utopian end, we are being asked to transform, at unknown cost to ourselves and to future generations, the central institution of our society.

Or as family researcher Peter Sprigg has said:[116]

> The logical answer would seem to be that this campaign is not really about marriage at all. Instead, it is about the desperate desire of homosexuals for society at large to affirm that homosexuality (not just homosexual individuals, but homosexual sex acts) is the full equivalent of heterosexuality in every way – morally, socially, and legally.

In sum, same-sex marriage is a bad idea. It is bad for society, bad for marriage and, as we shall see in a moment, bad for children. The concept is self-contradictory, and it confers no benefits to society. Indeed, as shown above, it will in fact be harmful to society. As David Coolidge summarises:[117]

> If one believes that a good society requires a critical mass of healthy male-female marriages with children, then any policies

that redefine, and thereby weaken, that basic unit are a bad idea. I believe that same-sex marriage is a bad idea, not because same-sex couples are bad people, but because same-sex marriage is not marriage. A genuinely pluralistic society must do justice to individuals. But it must also do justice to marriage.

CHAPTER 10

Homosexual Adoption Rights

A major part of the homosexual agenda has been that of homosexual adoption rights. And slowly they are getting what they want. On February 10, 2004, the Australian Capital Territory government's controversial parenting bill, which allows homosexual and lesbian couples to adopt children, was passed.[1] Other states are expected to follow suit. But is this the right direction to be taking?

Now the desire for people, especially women, to have children is of course normal, but one has to ask if homosexual or lesbian parenting is desirable. Homosexuals may claim that there is no reason why they should not raise children, that sexual preference has nothing to do with the issue of good parenting. But does the evidence bear this out? Initial research is beginning to show that children do suffer from being raised by same-sex parents. Before turning to this evidence, let me say that obviously many traditional families have poor parenting skills. But exceptions do not make the rule. The point is, in most cases, a child will do better with a mother and father, and in most cases, a child will suffer as a result of being raised by same-sex parents.

One person who has spent a lot of time looking into this question is psychologist Dr Joe Nicolosi. He argues that children raised by homosexuals are traumatised emotionally and socially.

Children, he argues, are profoundly affected by parental behaviour. For example, children of smokers often become smokers. Says Nicolosi:[2]

> Homosexuality is primarily an identity problem, not a sexual problem, and it begins in childhood. The process begins when a child realizes that the world is divided between male and female and that he is not equipped to be identified as male. His father fails to sufficiently encourage male-gender identity. Because he is not fully male-gender-identified, he is not psychologically prepared to feel heterosexual attractions. In order to be attracted to women, a male must feel sufficiently masculine. Faced with this predicament, he goes into a world of fantasy and denies the imperative of being either male or female.

The lack of a strong father figure seems to be a major factor in those who become homosexuals. Another researcher, Dr Paul Cameron, says the admittedly scant data on the subject confirm Nicolosi's findings. These studies show that between eight per cent and 33 per cent of adult respondents raised by homosexuals said they considered themselves homosexual or bisexual, far above the national (U.S.) norm of two per cent of the adult population.[3]

The absence of role models presents other problems. How will a man raised by two men know how to relate to a woman? Or how will a man raised by two women know how to relate to men? Thus the Beatles were wrong: love is *not* all you need, at least when it comes to parenting. As two family experts point out: "The two most loving mothers in the world can't be a father to a little boy. Love can't equip mothers to teach a little boy how to be a man. Likewise, the two most loving men can't be a mother to a child."[4]

They continue:[5]

> Love does little to help a man teach a little girl how to be a woman. Can you imagine two men guiding a young girl through her first menstrual cycle or helping her through the awkwardness of picking out her first bra? Such a situation might make for a funny television sitcom but not a very good real-life situation for a young girl.

133

One woman who was raised by lesbians now runs a support and recovery program for those coming out of the homosexual lifestyle and their families. She put it this way:[6]

> I realise that homosexuals feel they can give a child love and support that even many straight families can't provide, but I've been there. I know the finger-pointing and the shame one carries. For years, you struggle with the thought that you might be a homosexual. People say 'like mother, like daughter.' Most of us become promiscuous to prove we're straight.

Another woman says this of her upbringing by two homosexuals:[7]

> From 40 years of experience, I can tell you that, even though my father loved me, his homosexual orientation handicapped my ability to learn to relate to life in a healthy way. My homosexual home stunted my growth as a person and as a woman, not to mention the damaging effect of 16 years of drugs and alcohol abuse on my early childhood development. I spent the first 20 years of my life in a family that nearly destroyed me and the last 20 years analyzing and being analyzed in order to make sense of it. The bottom line is: I was dearly loved by my father. His love alone was not enough to give me the foundation that I needed to grow into a secure young woman. ... My father and I have looked back through the past and discussed the issue of homosexual parenting. With great remorse, he agrees the homosexual lifestyle, no matter how conservative, is not healthy for children. My father and I agree: homosexuality and raising healthy children exclude each other.

Or consider the tragic case of a 12-year-old Melbourne boy who has run away from home five times. The reason? He refuses to live with his mother and her lesbian partner. The boy's father has repeatedly been denied access to the child, and the boy has threatened to kill himself as a result.[8]

And, finally, someone who can speak from experience in this area: a lesbian mother has publicly expressed her regret at bearing three children through artificial insemination. The New Zealand woman, who says she is "now in the process of becoming a heterosexual", had a stormy relationship, which eventually broke down, with her lesbian lover. Her comments are worth noting: "I realise now that I deprived my kids of their right to a father, and I see the hurt in their faces every day. ... I believe children should have the best opportunities in life. The best way they can have a balanced view of what is normal is with heterosexual parents."[9]

> **Children need to see how men and women interact together.**

Children need to see how men and women interact together. A homosexual or lesbian union cannot provide that role model. Children deserve better. But the interests of the child are the last thing being considered in this debate. Indeed, today everyone is demanding rights to do this and that, but very few seem to realise that rights must be balanced by responsibilities. The right to have a child must be balanced by the rights of the child. Children should be given the first priority, and not be allowed to be used as a political football by the homosexual lobby in their efforts to seek legitimacy for their lifestyle. If the data are still not all in yet then, for the sake of children, we should not rush headlong into homosexual adoption and same-sex marriage.

However, some will argue that the data are coming in. In the last few years studies have appeared that claim children raised in same-sex households suffer no ill-effects, and may even do better than children raised in heterosexual families. How are we to assess such studies?

Several points can be made. First, there are many studies that have arrived at the opposite conclusion. For example, a study of Australian primary school children from three family types (married heterosexual couples, cohabiting heterosexual couples and homosexual couples) found that in every area of educational endeavour (language, mathematics, social studies, sport, class work, sociability and popularity, and attitudes to learning), children from married heterosexual couples performed the best, while children from homosexual couples performed the worst. The study concludes with these words: "[M]arried couples seem to offer the best environment for a child's social and educational development."[10]

135

And a major American study arrived at these conclusions:[11]

> Children of homosexuals will 1) be more frequently subjected to parental instability (of residence and sexual partners) and 2) have poorer peer and adult relationships. Also, as is held to be true of their parents, homosexuals' children will be more apt to 3) become homosexual, 4) be unstable (have emotional problems and difficulty forming lasting bonds) with reduced interest in natality, and 5) be sexually precocious and promiscuous.

Second, most of these studies purporting to show that children raised in same-sex households do as well as other children have been roundly criticised for methodological shortcomings. One meta-analysis of 49 such studies found a number of methodological flaws. These include the lack of any proper hypothesis statement, the problem of affirming the null hypothesis, the lack of proper comparison groups, the problem of measurement error and probability, neglect of extraneous variables, and so on.[12] On a less technical level, these studies suffer from small sample sizes, lack of a proper control group, inadequacy of self-reporting, and lack of proper timeframe (longitudinal analysis).

Two U.S. researchers, after examining the available data, said that "studies on same-sex parenting are plagued with persistent limitation[s]". They conclude their study with these words: "we cannot be confident concerning the generalizability of many of the findings".[13]

Another expert, sociologist Steven Nock of the University of Virginia, who claims to be agnostic on the question of same-sex marriage and the like, has also analysed the literature on homosexual parenting. He came up with these conclusions: "1) all of the studies I reviewed contained at least one flaw of design or execution; and 2) not a single one of those studies was conducted according to general accepted standards of scientific research."[14]

Consider self-reporting. Most of these studies simply ask the children how they enjoy their same-sex parents. Not surprisingly, they don't find any problems. But what child is going to bag his or her own parents? Indeed, if that is all they have known, it is even more difficult to criticise it. Thus scientific objectivity is sorely lacking in these types of studies. And since homosexual parenting is relatively recent, most children in same-sex households are relatively young. So asking 10-year-olds about their social, mental and psychological well-being may not result in very reliable data.

But many of the children in same-sex households originally came from heterosexual families, making measurement more difficult. How much of their well-being or lack of it is attributable to heterosexual upbringing, and how much is attributable to homosexual upbringing?

As but one example, pro-homosexual researchers have admitted that their study used "volunteers obtained though gay and single-parent magazines and associations. Obviously these do not constitute random samples, and it is not possible to know what biases are involved in the method of sample selection."[15] Obviously, indeed.

A further problem with many of these studies is the political agenda being promoted. That is, most of these studies are conducted by those who are homosexual or support the homosexual agenda. To confirm this point, one study examined all the major studies on same-sex marriage and homosexual parenting published in law review publications in the 1990s:[16]

> Only one of the seventy-two pieces published in the nineties unequivocally supports the rule of exclusive heterosexual marriage, while sixty-seven pieces advocate or support same-sex marriage. ... Likewise, virtually all of the law review literature addressing homosexual parenting advocates the politically progressive position favoring legalization or expansion of legal status, benefits, and privileges for homosexual parenting.

Interestingly, two American sociologists who are openly supportive of the homosexual agenda have recently admitted that bias is a real factor in these studies. They declare that "heterosexism" has "hampered the intellectual progress in the field" and show that in these studies the researchers "frequently downplay findings indicating difference regarding children's gender and sexual preferences and behavior that could stimulate important theoretical questions". After examining the findings of 21 psychological studies published between 1981 and 1998, they "identified conceptual, methodological, and theoretical limitations in the psychological research on the effects of parental sexual orientation and ... challenged the predominant claim that the sexual orientation of parents does not matter at all". Indeed, they "recognise the political dangers" of pointing out the truth that "children with lesbigay [*sic*] parents are themselves apt to engage in homosexual activity".[17]

Thus, the so-called evidence that homosexual parenting is just as beneficial as heterosexual parenting has been examined and found wanting. The remarks of one group of researchers who reviewed 14 of these homosexual parenting studies are worth noting. Their "most impressive finding" was that "all of the studies lacked external validity. The conclusion that there are no significant differences in children raised by lesbian mothers versus heterosexual mothers is not supported by the published data base".[18]

Finally, one must recall why adoption laws have been established in the first place. Because young children are so vulnerable, the aim of adoption has been to provide the child in question with a secure, permanent, legal family. The paramount concern in adoption has been the best interests of the child. Thus only the best families have been allowed to adopt, not just "good enough" families. The issue of homosexual fostering is really all about homosexual rights, not the interests and needs of children.

The simple truth is, there exists a mountain of social science research that demonstrates that children do best when raised in a biological, two-parent household, cemented by marriage.

Can a homosexual couple love and nurture a child? Undoubtedly many can. But that is not the issue. As the former vice-president of the National Council for Adoption in the U.S., Mary Beth Style, has put it:[19]

> ... [P]roviding a nurturing environment is not enough. A homosexual parent cannot provide the parental experience of a parent of the opposite sex, and this is as critical to the child as anything else. When discussing a child's needs, it is not just a discussion of what a particular parent can provide – it is just as important to consider what a parent cannot provide and, in this case, it is half of a child's needed parenting experience.

138

The simple truth is, there exists a mountain of social science research that demonstrates that children do best when raised in a biological, two-parent household, cemented by marriage. The evidence is so overwhelming that the reader is advised to look at recent summaries of the data.[20] However, several recent academic studies can be mentioned here, which demonstrate the importance of children growing up with their married biological mother and father.

One American study of 19,000 young people conducted by the Bowling Green State University (Ohio) found that teens fare best when living with two married biological parents:[21]

> Adolescents in married, two-biological-parent families generally fare better than children in any of the family types examined here, including single-mother, cohabiting stepfather, and married stepfather families. The advantage of marriage appears to exist primarily when the child is the biological offspring of both parents. Our findings are consistent with previous work, which demonstrates children in cohabiting stepparent families fare worse than children living with two married, biological parents.

Another large-scale American study found that there are "overall disadvantages" in not living with both biological parents.[22] The author concludes:[23]

> My analyses have clearly demonstrated some overall disadvantages of living with neither parent. Among adolescents from all six family types, those in non-biological-parent families appear to rank the lowest in academic performance, educational aspiration, and locus of control. Further, they appear to fare less well in the remaining outcome areas (self-esteem, behavior problems, and cigarette smoking).

The evidence then is quite plain. Children deserve a biological mother and father, preferably cemented by marriage. The emotional appeals of homosexuals and their own selfish adult demands must be balanced by the interests of the child, and the right of every child to be raised by a mother and a father.

Yet critics might argue that in many other situations children are already being raised without a mother or a father. True, but there is a big difference in dealing with an existing crisis and the creation of a new crisis. That is, when one parent dies or is deserted by his or her spouse, society does all it can to help the children get through such difficult periods. But it is another matter altogether to deliberately create those sorts of situations.

As two family experts and child psychologists put it:[24]

> While a compassionate and caring society *always* comes to the aid of motherless and fatherless families, a wise and loving society *never* intentionally creates fatherless or motherless families. But that is exactly what every same-sex family does and for no other reason than adults desire such families. No child-development theory says children *need* parents of the same gender – as loving as they might be – but rather that children *need* their mother and father.

But too often the well-being of children is not at the forefront of homosexual concerns. For many homosexuals, the demand for adoption rights, like the demand for marriage rights, is really about seeking legitimacy and acceptance. That is, these are symbolic demands, as much as anything. They are part of the attempt to seek the complete public acceptance and normalisation of their lifestyle, something many societies are rightly hesitant about. Mary Beth Style writes:[25]

> For the homosexual rights movement the right to adopt is a symbol – a goal which must be achieved in order to achieve broader victory. ... Clearly, adoption as a political statement does not take into account a child's needs at all. And an individual parent, whether heterosexual or homosexual, who is seeking to adopt principally to meet narcissistic needs is also not concerned about the best interests of the child.

And the desire for children may even spring from more sinister motives. Consider this revealing quote from someone who should know. Tammy Bruce is the former president of the Los Angeles chapter of the National Organisation for Women. She is also a pro-abortion feminist and a lesbian. But she is greatly alarmed by homosexual activism. This is what she says about the issue of children and the homosexual agenda:[26]

Today's gay activists have carried the campaign a step further, invading children's lives by wrapping themselves in the banner of tolerance. It is literally the equivalent of the wolf coming to your door dressed as your grandmother.

The radicals in control of the gay establishment want children in their world of moral decay, lack of self-restraint, and moral relativism. Why? How better to

> **Now that enough time has passed to see some of the negative impacts of homosexual parenting, the results are starting to come in.**

truly belong to the majority (when you're really on the fringe) than by taking possession of the next generation? By targeting children, you can start indoctrinating the next generation with the false construct that gay people deserve special treatment and special laws. How else can the gay establishment actually get society to believe, borrowing from George Orwell, that gay people are indeed more equal than others? Of course, the only way to get that idea accepted is to condition people into accepting nihilism that forbids morality and judgment.

Now that enough time has passed to see some of the negative impacts of homosexual parenting, the results are starting to come in. Some book-length treatments of what it is like to be raised in a homosexual household are now appearing. These provide real-life stories of what the studies are telling us: children suffer greatly in these alternative lifestyle families.

One very important new book in this regard is *Out From Under* by Dawn Stefanowicz.[27] It is a shocking story of a child thrust into the world of male homosexuality. It is a story of abuse, betrayal, loneliness and suffering. The book tells it all: her dad's multiple male lovers and sexual escapades; the abuse she suffered at the hands of her dad; the string of boyfriends her dad had at the house; the emotional, psychological and physical dangers she experienced growing up.

No one can read this moving story and not see how destructive homosexual parenting is to a child. It is an important book, but because it speaks the truth about homosexuality, do not expect it to be featured in the mainstream media, except to be dismissed.

Finally, it needs to be stressed that homosexuals themselves are quite divided on the issue of same-sex parenting. While it appears that lesbians want to have children more than do homosexual men, it seems that in general most homosexuals do not even want to have children. As two homosexual "parents" admitted, "We have to be careful sometimes that we don't give the appearance of crusaders trying to convert gay men into breeders. And we do totally understand that probably most gay men don't aspire to parenthood."[28]

And a recent major article in the homosexual press admitted that there were deep divisions in the homosexual community over both marriage and parenting issues. As one long-time homosexual activist admitted: "There is little point in chasing access to IVF, ART [Assisted Reproductive Technology] and getting parenting reforms if the vast majority of us are never going to have children. These issues are important but they are not the whole game."[29]

But the media are quite happy to pick up the cause of a very small percentage of homosexuals who make up a very small percentage of all adults who do want children, and turn it into a major campaign. But the well-being of children should be our first concern. As psychologist Bill Maier puts it:[30]

> A just, compassionate society should always come to the aid of motherless or fatherless families. But a just, compassionate society should never, ever, intentionally create motherless and fatherless families. And that's exactly what same-sex marriage means.

More on homosexual parenting

Because this issue has been getting considerable media treatment of late, it is worth devoting more attention to the topic. Indeed, the media have made much of several new studies that purport to show no adverse effects on children raised in same-sex households. One of the newest and most extensive critiques of such studies is that by British sociologist Patricia Morgan. In her

160-page book she does a thorough job of documenting the evidence for the
advantages of the two-parent family and revealing how studies purporting
to show the benefits of being raised in a same-sex family are deeply flawed.[31]

She begins her analysis by noting a common tactic used by those who support same-sex parenting: the observation that there are so many dysfunc-
tional heterosexual families. But, "no amount of decrying or demonstrating
the disadvantages of one situation is, in itself, proof of the advantages of
another. Deficiencies or condemnations of heterosexual parenting are not,
in themselves, valid evidence for the superiority of homosexual parenting."[32]
Moreover, as she points out, most children who go into government care
because of abuse or other problems come from homes other than where a
mum and dad are present, committed by marriage.[33]

And as politically incorrect as it may be, "the evidence is that around a third
of all molestations of children are homosexual molestations, and the same
applies to the proportion of paedophiles who are homosexual".[34]

The bulk of her book is a review of 144 academic papers on homosexual
parenting. She demonstrates that the overwhelming majority of these studies
are quite worthless. They are so poorly done that the "results" prove nothing. The methodological shortcomings include: failure to design the study
properly; failure to properly measure the relevant variables; failure to control
for extraneous variables; and failure to use proper statistical tests. These and
other shortcomings mean that most of the studies and reports are invalid.

Many of the studies, for example, are little more than anecdotal. People offer gushing praise for their lifestyle choice, and report that everything is just
fine in the family. Says Morgan: "While anecdotes may illustrate conclusions
drawn from well-conducted research, in themselves they prove nothing."[35]
Using self-congratulatory testimonials is hardly objective science. "It is astonishing how collections of anecdotes are reverentially accepted by public
bodies, academics and research institutes, who would immediately laugh
away the use of similar material as 'evidence' elsewhere."[36]

Plenty of other problems are found in the so-called studies. Small-sample
groups are a frequent drawback. Often just several dozen are featured in

a study, making any reliable and informative statistical conclusions almost impossible to achieve.

* Another problem is where the samples come from. The truth is, in most cases the study is advertised in a homosexual newspaper, and people with a vested interest (those who want to promote the homosexual agenda) are thereby recruited. Self-selected volunteers with vested interests are hardly scientific sample groups. Proper studies of child development based on randomly selected, representative sample groups seem not to exist.

* And that leads to a further problem. Self-reporting is not a basis for an objective, neutral study. What homosexual is going to say he or she is a lousy parent, and what young child raised in a same-sex household is going to badmouth his or her parents? Self-reporting leads to no useful objective evidence.

* Also, the volunteers involved in such "research" already "know the purpose of the research and have an interest in the outcome. So have the researchers, who are overwhelmingly sympathetic to the homosexual movement".[37]

Another point that can be raised is what the studies actually say. Often the media give them a spin that is not so accurate. Some of the better studies, for example, are much more qualified and nuanced than the popular press would have us believe. That is, some of the studies really offer a mixed message, and call for further research in the area. And some of the studies actually make admissions that the pro-homosexual side does not want too widely publicised. For example, "many studies actually indicate significant differences between homosexual and heterosexual parenting outcomes for children, particularly the likelihood that children of homosexuals may become involved in homosexual behaviour themselves".[38]

Also, we know that family behaviour tends to be intergenerational. Thus children of divorce or single motherhood are proportionally far more likely to repeat cycles of divorce and non-marriage than those born to married couples who stay in intact families. Says Morgan, all this "seems even more likely to be the case with homosexual parents and their children".[39]

Moreover, surveys of post-adolescent offspring of same-sex parents show large proportions living a homosexual lifestyle. The figures range from eight to 24 per cent, which is four or five times higher than the general population (of British males). Morgan offers the interesting insight that if "it were true that there was any genetic or biological basis or predisposition for homosexuality, a greater frequency among the children of homosexuals would be expected".[40]

Speaking of the so-called genetic basis of homosexuality, Morgan points out some other arguments against the thesis. Studies on identical twins show that often one is and one is not homosexual, which belies any genetic basis, since identical (monozygotic) twins have the same genes. Also, we know that homosexuality is not distributed in the population either randomly or uniformly like left-handedness or intelligence.[41]

> **The welfare of children, not the preferences of adults, should be our major concern.**

Furthermore, research on outcomes for sexually-abused young males, found that early homosexual contact with an adult was highly related to homosexual outcomes.[42] All of which suggests that social and cultural factors are as, or more, important than biological factors.

If it is true that children of same-sex couples are more likely to become homosexuals themselves, some might reply, "So what?" The answer is, the welfare of children, not the preferences of adults, should be our major concern. And we know that the homosexual lifestyle is a dangerous, high-risk lifestyle. Homosexuals "suffer disproportionately from a range of morbid conditions compared to heterosexuals, particularly sexually transmitted diseases, like gonorrhoea, syphilis, hepatitis A and B, anorectal warts and AIDS", with 70 per cent of the cases of HIV in Britain due to homosexual intercourse.[43] (The figure is about 85 per cent in Australia.) And the average lifespan of a homosexual is much shorter than that of a heterosexual.

Also we know that homosexual relationships (especially among men) are less stable and more transient than heterosexual relationships. Homosexuals also tend to be much more promiscuous. According to Morgan's study:[44]

The most 'stable' of 'gay partnerships' are ones where there is an arrangement between the two to have sex with third parties on the side, while maintaining a permanent living arrangement.

This all suggests that children living with homosexuals – particularly male homosexuals – are more likely to face high prospects of repeated family disruption, or multiple family transitions and exposure to high stranger levels in the home, compared to those living with heterosexuals.

In the light of all this, Morgan asks this pointed question. If we tend not to allow children to be adopted into situations where there is obesity, smoking, old age and other factors that may result in shorter life spans, thus leaving vulnerable children at risk of being prematurely orphaned, why do we not also consider homosexuality a similar risk factor?[45]

Concludes Morgan: "From the perspective of the 'best interests of the child', if homosexual activity – like intravenous drug use – is life shortening, and morbidity attracting, then children should be placed with parents who, at very least, will not steer them towards this."[46]

If the evidence presented above is correct, we should not be talking so cavalierly about homosexual adoption rights. We should not be treating children as trophies. Nor should we be treating children as guinea-pigs in a radical social experiment. The rights of children, not the desires of adults, should be our primary concern.

And if it be thought that the concept of children as trophies is overstating things a bit, there are in fact many examples of this. A recent example in Australia clearly demonstrates the dangers of how children are being treated as commodities and lifestyle accessories by some homosexuals. A lesbian couple has sued a doctor over what they consider to be a botched IVF case. The couple ended up with twin girls, instead of just the one child that they were hoping for. They are demanding financial payment for "wrongful birth".[47] They complained that the extra child interfered with their careers and relationship. But just imagine how the children must feel, knowing that at least one of them is publicly unwanted. This commodification of children seems to be an inherent feature of the homosexual lifestyle.

CHAPTER 11

Homosexuality and Children

Mention has already been made of the issue of pedophilia. However, the issue of children needs to be examined more closely. It is of course obvious that homosexuals cannot multiply by reproduction.[1] Therefore recruitment is the only way to increase their numbers. An unfortunate aspect of this is the tendency to recruit among young people.

Many homosexuals speak of being introduced to the homosexual lifestyle by someone older, while they were still in their teens. Consider this representative quote: "Nobody is fooled when we proclaim that the gay movement has nothing to do with kids and their sexuality. ... Many of us – both women and men – had our first homosexual experience with partners who were older than ourselves".[2] Indeed, one study found that 75 per cent of homosexual men report their first homosexual experience before the age of sixteen. This compares to 22 per cent of heterosexual men reporting their first heterosexual experience.[3]

A well-known saying states that the hand that rocks the cradle rules the world. Homosexual activists know this all too well. As one lesbian put it, "Whoever captures the kids owns the future."[4] Hence the constant attempts by homosexual activists to influence children.

147

There have been many attempts lately to get access to young people. For example, in the United States the New Jersey Supreme Court has ordered the Boy Scouts to admit homosexuals.[5] The Girl Scouts have also caved into political correctness. Indeed, according to some Scout staffers, one in three of the Girl Scouts' paid professional staff is lesbian.[6] And in the United Kingdom, the English Scout Association recently lifted the ban on homosexuals becoming troop leaders.[7]

In Australia a number of homosexual activities have made many conclude that children are indeed being targeted by older homosexuals. Several years ago a major outcry arose over the discovery of homosexual swap cards. The cards, which featured sexually explicit photos, pictures and cartoons, were part of a safe-sex campaign.[8]

Also, in a recent edition of a Melbourne homosexual newspaper, there was a large article entitled "Comics come out".[9] The article described how mainstream as well as underground comic-book makers are increasingly using homosexual characters and themes in their comics. Homosexual superheroes have been featured, along with graphic homosexual scenes and dialogue. Indeed, one comic, *The Authority*, features two main characters who are homosexual superheroes.[10]

Another article in the homosexual press on the same issue reported that there are "probably around a hundred gay characters out there" in comics right now.[11] Given that children are usually the main readers of comics, one has to ask if recruitment is not part of the strategy.

And we also have homosexual cartoon characters in both TV series and in the movies. Consider *Utena, Revolutionary Girl*, an anime character who is a lesbian. Anime, or Japanese animation, is of course hugely popular with children – (*Pokemon* being but one example). Advertisements for Utena the movie feature in homosexual newspapers.[12]

Along the same lines, what is one to make of the world's first talking homosexual dolls? The dolls, which have been sold in the U.S. and Europe, were made available in shops for Christmas 2003 in Australia. Openly homosexual Elton the Biker (complete with nipple rings), and his plastic counterpart

Marshall, evidently have sold well overseas.[13] Given that dolls are usually the kind of thing that children, not adults, play with, one has to ask if this is another recruiting attempt.

In the U.S. pro-homosexual books such as *Heather Has Two Mommies* are found in many schools and libraries.[14] And in Australia, similar books can be found, for example, in Sydney school libraries. Another example is *Daddy's Roommate*.[15] One book entitled *My House* has this as part of its story line: "I've got a cat and two dogs. I've got two mums."[16]

In similar fashion, the producers of the much-loved Australian children's program *Playschool* decided to push the boundaries of political correctness by featuring a segment where a young girl goes to the park with her "two mummies".[17] Such indoctrination of two and three-year olds is reprehensible. And their lame explanation that they were just trying to reflect life in the real world simply does not stand up. Do they also feature segments on crack cocaine use, prostitution, child pornography and rape? These are all parts of the real world as well, after all.

Interestingly, the same lesbian who appeared on the Playschool episode has produced two children's books. Entitled *The Rainbow Cubby House* and *Koalas on Parade*, the books, about homosexual families, are funded by the New South Wales Government and available in public schools and libraries.[18] This is another example of promoting the homosexual lifestyle to primary school students at taxpayers' expense.

Moreover, homosexual pornography sites have been featuring pictures of school boys, taken without their knowledge or permission. A number of Melbourne private schools discovered that hundreds of their male students aged 12 to 18 had their photos taken while at sports events. The semi-clad boys appeared in hardcore homosexual sites.[19] As far as I am aware, such exploitation of young people was nowhere denounced or disowned by the homosexual community.

In a similar vein, a homosexual magazine managed to take sexually suggestive photos of male models posing as school boys at an elite Melbourne high school and publish them. They include pictures of boys pulling down the pants of other boys, and pictures of nude boys in locker and shower-room scenes. The photographers told the high school that they were doing a photo shoot for a fashion magazine.[20] The homosexual magazine, *DNA*,[21] ran the photos without comment, but told journalists that it was harmless "fun". However, it was not just conservatives or religious types who were outraged; even other homosexuals failed to see the humour. One rightly asked, "What were *DNA Magazine* doing at Melbourne High School anyway? If they were intending to end up with a photo spread that looks like it was catering to paedophiles, they've succeeded."[22]

> There has been the long-standing push to make pro-homosexual classes compulsory in Australian schools.

Many other attempts to reach young people can be mentioned. Many of our state and federal anti-discrimination and equal opportunity boards have pro-homosexual activities and programs aimed at young people. For example, the Australian Human Rights Commission (AHRC) is a Commonwealth (taxpayer-funded) body that has a very active homosexual component. One such program is called Outlink. It is described in these terms: "Towards a national rural lesbian, gay and bisexual youth network. The commission, with funding from the Australian Youth Foundation, has engaged prominent Tasmanian homosexual activist Rodney Croome to begin the network building process." One of its publications is *Not Round Here: Affirming Diversity, Challenging Homophobia*.[23] The commission's website says this is "a training manual produced under the auspices of Outlink, a project of the Human Rights and Equal Opportunity Commission and the Australian Youth Foundation."[24]

In addition, there has been the long-standing push to make pro-homosexual classes compulsory in Australian schools. As but one example, Rodney Croome claims that to stamp out "homophobia" we must have mandatory pro-homosexual kits in classrooms.[25] And in a related matter, former High Court judge, Justice Michael Kirby, who is homosexual, was reported to have said to school students that homosexuality is normal.[26]

This is already happening quite extensively overseas. For example, in the UK, children "are to be taught about homosexuality in maths, geography and science lessons as part of a Government-backed drive to 'celebrate the gay community'".[27] A London newspaper article reports on just how far-reaching this is.

The article continues:[28]

> Lesson plans have been drawn up for pupils as young as four, in a scheme funded with a £35,000 grant from an education quango, the Training and Development Agency for Schools. The initiative will be officially launched next month at the start of 'LGBT History Month' – an initiative to encourage teaching about lesbian, gay, bisexual and transsexual issues. The lesson plans, spread across the curriculum, will be offered to all schools.

One quite well-known homosexual blog site openly admits to just how intent the activists are in targeting young children in our schools. He says in an article entitled, "Can We Please Just Start Admitting That We *Do* Actually Want To Indoctrinate Kids?":[29]

> 'NOOO! We're not gonna make kids learn about homosexuality, we swear! It's not like we're trying to recruit your children or anything.' But let's face it – that's a lie. We want educators to teach future generations of children to accept queer sexuality. In fact, our very future depends on it.

He continues, (and pardon his crude language):[30]

> I for one certainly want tons of school children to learn that it's OK to be gay, that people of the same sex should be allowed to legally marry each other, and that anyone can kiss a person of the same sex without feeling like a freak. And I would very much like for many of these young boys to grow up and start f**king men. I want lots of young ladies to develop into young women who voraciously munch box. I want this just as badly as many parents want their own kids to grow up and rub urinary tracts together to trade proteins and forcefully excrete a baby. I and a lot of other people want to indoctrinate, recruit, teach, and expose children to queer sexuality AND THERE'S NOTHING WRONG WITH THAT.

In addition to schools, homosexual activists are also targeting daycare centres. For example in a Sydney suburb the council-funded childcare centres are teaching a homosexual-"friendly" curriculum to the toddlers there. The centres are teaching the very young children that gay, lesbian, transgender and inter-sex parents are normal in a bid to "challenge the perception" of young children about sexuality.[31]

One wonders if there will be other changes to the teaching done at day-care centres, to further let the toddlers learn about the "real world". Will the taxpayer-funded councils also teach about how some parents are heroin addicts? Maybe the little kiddies need to know that some parents are spending time in prison. Or perhaps little Johnny should know that some parents are arsonists, cross-dressers or bank robbers. After all, we do want to be inclusive and reflect all of the social realities out there, don't we?

Then there is the propaganda role of popular culture. Indeed, a whole book could be written on how popular culture is doing its best to normalise homosexuality, seeking to make it look cool. Just one of many examples will here suffice. One of Australia's longest-running and most popular television soap operas has recently added a homosexual character. A 19-year-old actress is playing a lesbian to spice things up on *Neighbours*.[32] The problem is, this is a G-rated program, shown every week night at 6:30pm, and has a large audience of children and young people. We do not need the force-feeding of homosexuality on programs not aimed at adults and not aired at adult time-slots.

Yet this is not an isolated incident. On any night of the week, Australian TV offers a whole host of homosexual characters, programs and themes. Even the homosexual press has run a number of stories lately discussing the proliferation of homosexuality on prime-time television. One can only suspect that indoctrination is as much at work here as is entertainment.

And this constant barrage of pro-homosexual imagery, especially in film and on television, is beginning to pay off. A recent study conducted by the University of Minnesota in the U.S. found that those exposed to homosexual programs on television were more likely to accept homosexuality. A homosexual activist commented, "The study reinforces that visibility leads to understanding, and understanding leads to acceptance."[33]

Pro-homosexual activities in schools

The issue of homosexuality and children is worth looking at in more detail. A major way in which the homosexual lobby can reach children is, of course, through school curricula, especially in sex education programs. There are many such programs around the country, taught in many schools, all designed to instil in young children the idea that homosexuality is natural, normal and to be accepted and embraced.

Such programs, and/or proposals for them, have been around for years. These programs have often been justified as part of AIDS education, or more recently, as a means of dealing with bullying. As an example, back in 1987 the Australian Teachers' Federation called on teachers to educate students on male and female homosexuality as part of basic sex education.[34]

Much more recently we find this: "A government program to tackle homophobia in high schools is set to be rolled out across New South Wales. The $250,000 dollar pilot program aims to fight abuse and negative attitudes faced by gay teens, and will be implemented at 12 schools in Sydney, the Hunter and on the Central Coast."[35] The truth is, probably most kids have been bullied for a variety of reasons, but courses like this will simply be used to push the homosexual agenda.

Consider some other examples. In 1992 an AIDS study commissioned by the University of Queensland recommended that explicit sex education courses be taught in the first three years of primary school. The study said that students should become experts in contraception techniques and sexually-transmitted diseases before they enter secondary school.[36]

In January of 1995 the Australian Education Union called for mandatory AIDS and sex education for all students, beginning in primary school. The course should include "positive information about gays and lesbians", the union said.[37] The union argued that not only should these classes be mandatory for even primary school children, but that parents who ban their children from attending such courses for religious and cultural reasons should be prosecuted by the law![38]

At an October 1995 conference on Schooling and Sexualities at Victoria's Deakin University, yet more such proposals were made. Speakers told the delegates that homosexuality should be taught as accepta-ble to primary and secondary students, and gay relation-ships should be recognised through school projects.[39]

> **Pro-homosexual indoctrination is not limited to sex education classes.**

And pro-homosexual indoctrination is not limited to sex education classes. In 1995 the Victorian Association for the Teachers of English said that AIDS and homosexuality studies should be incorporated into mainstream English studies. It said that the study of English must embrace "the burgeoning field of lesbian and gay studies", and that teachers need to "promote awareness of homosexual issues".[40]

And the Australian Education Union called for pro-homosexual education to be integrated into all parts of the curriculum. It spoke of the "rights of all teachers to influence curricula in ways that will enhance understanding and acceptance of lesbians, bisexuals and gay men".[41]

In mid-2002 a pro-homosexual booklet was distributed to every second-ary school in Victoria. The 72-page booklet, *Alsorts*, was jointly published by the Alternative Lifestyle Organisation (ALSO Foundation) and Deakin University.[42] The book, filled with a number of statements that many would consider inaccurate and misleading, is just one of many attempts by the homosexual lobby to convince young people that homosexuality is an ac-ceptable and positive lifestyle.

Also, in New South Wales a recommended reading list of fiction and non-fiction books providing positive images of homosexuals and lesbians has been distributed to NSW schools. The lists have been distributed by the De-partment of School Education as a response to perceived anti-homosexual attitudes.[43]

The push continues today. Consider several recent examples. In a newspaper article entitled, "Sex survey shocks", there was a story about a Wodonga

(Victoria) High School course for 14-year-olds.[44] Year 9 students were forced to answer a blatantly pro-homosexual questionnaire. The mandatory questionnaire, which students had to sign their names to, was part of a compulsory health class. The survey asked these sorts of questions:

- If you have never slept with a person of the same sex, is it possible that all you need is a lesbian/gay lover?
- How can you become a whole person if you limit yourself to compulsive and exclusive heterosexual behaviour?
- Is it possible that your heterosexuality stems from a neurotic fear of others of the same sex?

The students then had to discuss these questions in class. It is designed to show that homosexuality is just the same as heterosexuality, that the two are interchangeable. But they are not, of course. This appears to be nothing but propaganda: forcing students to feel guilty about being heterosexual. This is just a blatant attempt to force the homosexual agenda upon impressionable young people.

Most 14-year-olds are too young to be questioned about explicit details in sexuality. Indeed, some 14-year-olds can't even handle questions about what they want for breakfast! Thus our public schools, with our tax dollars, are pushing the homosexual agenda on to our children.

The following day there was a follow-up article about the questionnaire.[45] It seems that as a result of a loud public outcry, Victoria's state government had to go into damage control. The article said that the premier had ordered an inquiry to find out what was happening. It also said that the survey has been scrapped from the class. The school authorities claimed that the adult-only survey was actually meant for teachers, not for students.

However, in an article in another newspaper, a much different slant was put on the affair.[46] According to that report, the principal of Wodonga High School was standing by the decision of the teacher to hand out the survey. He said the survey had been handed out at a professional development course run by the federally-funded Family Planning Victoria (FPV). A spokesperson for FPV in turn said the questionnaire was designed by the

Australian Research Centre in Sexual Health and Society at La Trobe University to develop teachers' sex education skills, and was "not a classroom tool".

Whatever the actual facts and explanations are, many questions still remain: Why are our tax dollars being used to indoctrinate teachers, who are then in turn expected to indoctrinate their students with pro-homosexual propaganda?

Simply swap the word tobacco for homosexuality and see how this plays out. Every class has some smoking students. We need to respect this diversity. We do not want them to feel stigmatised. We need to embrace them in their lifestyle choices. We should let all students know that smoking is as normal as non-smoking. The important thing is for all students to be tolerant and non-judgmental. We do not want the smoking students to feel alienated or vilified for his behaviour. No one lifestyle choice is better than another.

Does anyone really believe such an approach would get very far in our school systems? Homosexuality is a very dangerous and high-risk lifestyle, just as smoking is. Why do we have such double standards in these areas? Why do we protect our children against tobacco while forcing them to embrace homosexuality?

This questionnaire is part of a Commonwealth-funded national teacher development package that has been adopted by more than 250 Victorian schools, and presumably by schools across the nation. I have seen several versions of this kit, and it is one big exercise in pushing the homosexual agenda onto our nation's children, via their teachers.

In another example of pro-homosexual activities in Australian schools, the Tasmanian Committee for Human Rights Education gave three Tasmanian schools prizes for their "anti-homophobia" programs. In December of 2003, the schools were given the awards after they trialled the six-week Pride and Prejudice courses. The schools are now planning to make the courses compulsory, and the Education Department plans to run the program state-wide. Homosexual activist Rodney Croome praised the program, saying that challenging homophobia must be "put in a human rights context".[47]

More recently in Victoria there was another push to indoctrinate our children, while also aiming to see the traditional family defined out of existence. Schools are being urged by a taxpayer-funded booklet to never allow the children to call their parents mum or dad. Parent, yes, or guardian, But not the words "mummy" and "daddy".

The idea is that we don't want to offend any homosexuals or lesbians out there. Lesbian activist Vicki Harding has written a book for teachers entitled *Learn to Include*. This teachers' manual also urges schools to put up posters of homosexuals and lesbians, and also not to use gender-specific toys. Children as young as five are also urged to act out homosexual scenarios.

> **All of this is an exercise in social engineering, seeking to convince very young children that there is no such thing as family, or mum and dad.**

The teachers' manual is meant for students from the first year of primary school to Level 3, and is already in use in dozens of Victorian schools. But not content to stop there, Victoria's Department of Education and Early Childhood Development (its present title) has invited Ms Harding to promote the manual to principals and teachers.[48]

While the teachers' manual does not actually say that the words "mum' and "dad" should be banned, what it does say is nearly identical: "Use inclusive spoken and written language (e.g., 'parent' or 'carer' rather than 'mother' and 'father'; 'dominant' or 'widespread' rather than 'normal') whenever possible."[49]

And the whole tenor of the book is to argue that there is no such thing as mum and dad, or family, anyway. For example, when it discusses one group activity, it proposes this question for students: "What is a family?" In the Teaching Notes it says that one should "accept all answers". Another question listed is, "Who makes up a family?" In the Teaching Notes, teachers are encouraged to "Lead students to various configurations".[50]

All of which is an exercise in social engineering, seeking to convince very young children that there is no such thing as family, or mum and dad.

Instead, they can mean whatever anyone wants them to mean. In which case they mean exactly nothing.

And in Sydney the same lesbian activist has been involved in another case of homosexual propaganda wars. A council-funded childcare centre there is teaching a homosexual and lesbian-"friendly" curriculum. Story-books promoting homosexuality are used in the centre, and the infants, aged from six months to six years, are taught about gay, lesbian and transgender "parenting".[51]

Vicki Harding, who has written a series of pro-homosexual books for toddlers, said that the books used in the child-care centre and other places were "not about sex, but about things families do together".[52]

The constant push by homosexual activists to get access to all school children, from the earliest of ages, is a part of the larger attempt to coerce mainstream society not only to accept but to welcome homosexuality. The progress they have made has been quite alarming, and all parents should be aware of the pro-homosexual agenda being pushed in our schools.

As mentioned earlier, increasingly the concept of bullying is being used to promote the homosexual agenda. Bullying, of course, should not be tolerated, and one can counter bullying without pushing the homosexual agenda. But homosexual activists are linking the two together.

In 2004, the then Victorian Education Services Minister told a homosexual interviewer that more needs to be done in this area, and she spoke of a recent conference on the issue, and that the department was "ensuring all schools have a code of conduct" on the issue. In the same interview she took a swipe at the Catholic Church, saying their abstinence approach was misguided: "The zero tolerance approach to young people and sexuality is not the best".[53] Thus she was lining herself up with homosexual activists, and against parents who might have religious concerns about homosexuality and condom use.

CHAPTER 12

Conclusion

It is clear that the homosexual lobby is on a roll. It has made tremendous advances in very short time, and looks to make more gains in the near future. The effect this is having, and will have, on families, faith communities and other groups is of great concern.

For centuries the family has been the bedrock and safeguard of society. As the homosexual juggernaut continues, the influence and viability of the family will be lessened. At stake is nothing less than the survival of the family unit, and the fundamental institution of marriage.

In addition, as the above documentation makes clear, also at risk are basic freedoms such as freedom of speech, freedom of conscience and freedom of religion. All concerned citizens need to become informed on these issues and take a stand on behalf of the family, faith and freedom.

The institution of the family has survived many assaults. But the homosexual assault on the family may be the most severe and the most important thus far. With these considerations in mind, I offer the following recommendations concerning the issue of homosexuality and public policy.

Negatively,

- Homosexual relationships should not be viewed as equal to or of the same natural order as heterosexual marriage.
- Homosexual couples should not be allowed access to artificial insemination or to IVF procedures.
- Homosexual marriage and adoption should not be allowed.
- Public schools should not be used as a channel for the promotion of the homosexual lifestyle.
- Public monies should not be used to promote the homosexual lifestyle (be it the Gay and Lesbian Mardi Gras, school sex-education programs, and the like).

Positively,

- Traditional marriage and family life should be promoted by government and society as both the norm and the ideal. Other relationships are just that, types of relationships, which share no moral or social reciprocity with heterosexual marriage and family arrangements.
- Conscious social policy should affirm and support marriage and family. Legal, taxation and other policies should prioritise marriage and family life.
- Australia should never allow marriage to become anything other than the voluntary union of one man and one woman for life, to the exclusion of all others.
- Family benefits should be restricted to actual families, not to alternative lifestyles. Family benefits should be seen for what they are, not as penalties to homosexuals, but as incentives for the glue that holds society together.

PART 2

Biblical and Theological Concerns

Introduction to Part Two

"The debate over homosexuality and the Bible – specifically, whether or not the Bible condemns homosexual acts in all cases – will do no less than rip the body of Christ apart within the next decade. It will force believers to declare, in black and white terms, where they stand on issues of sexuality and biblical interpretation."[1]

This quote, by a former homosexual, had a prophetic air about it when uttered in 1991. Time has indeed born out the author's fears. Today there is a determined effort being made by some in the church to undermine the scriptural position on homosexuality. A number of theological revisionists have appeared over the past several decades, arguing for a radically different understanding of the biblical prohibition against homosexuality.[2] A small but growing group of theologians, clerics and lay people are suggesting that the traditional understanding of the issue must be jettisoned for a more contemporary approach. Many are charging that the usual understanding of the issue is homophobic and incompatible with Christ's love and acceptance. And, sadly, some evangelicals are becoming fellow-travellers in this type of revisionism.[3]

This paper will examine the claims being made by the theological revisionists in the light of biblical Christianity and the traditional understanding of the issue. The various ploys or attempts to undermine or challenge the orthodox position will be assessed. Then the relevant biblical texts will be examined in more detail. Taken together, it is hoped that the traditional understanding of homosexuality will be vindicated and upheld.

CHAPTER 1

Ten Ploys of the Revisionists

Ploy # 1: An old book, an old culture

One very common criticism of the revisionists is to argue how different the culture of today is from that of biblical times. Many argue that we have to move on with the times, and that we need to realise how different our culture is from the cultures of the biblical world. Even as I pen these words, American radical Episcopal Bishop John Shelby Spong (in yet another tour of Australia) was opining on television about how old and dated the Bible is. "The Bible was written between 1000 BC and 135 AD," he said. "Would we take medical advice that was so ancient?" I heard another critic say, "It is very difficult to decide how much of these texts should be taken literally today."

> **Since when is truth determined by a calendar?**

Melbourne Anglican layperson and radical revisionist Muriel Porter takes a similar line. She speaks of those who uphold the biblical teaching on homosexuality as "still captive to an outdated understanding of human sexuality".[1]

There are several problems with such complaints. First, they show what a low view of Scripture the revisionists hold. Do they really suggest that we have so "progressed" in our understanding that old truths must be "reinterpreted" to fit in with modern secular thinking? Either Scripture is the eternal word of God or it is not. Of course each new generation must grapple with the text and apply it to new situations; but we are to interpret a changing world by the unchanging Word, not the other way around.

Second, since when is truth determined by a calendar? If something is true, it is true now, a thousand years ago, and a thousand years from now. C.S. Lewis called this unhelpful tendency "chronological snobbery": the idea that the new-fangled is necessarily truer. G.K. Chesterton also commented on this practice:[2]

> An imbecile habit has arisen in modern controversy of saying that such and such a creed can be held in one age but cannot be held in another. Some dogma, we are told, was credible in the twelfth century, but is not credible in the twentieth. You might as well say that a certain philosophy can be believed on Mondays, but cannot be believed on Tuesdays. You might as well say of a view of the cosmos that it was suitable to half past three, but not suitable for half-past four. What a man believes depends upon his philosophy, not upon the clock or the century.

Third, the revisionists assume that whatever is new is progress. However, what is new might equally be a sign of regress, not progress. Why are ancient peoples and cultures to be regarded as somehow inferior to ours? In many ways they in fact seem to be superior. Newer is simply not necessarily better.

Ploy # 2: Misunderstanding cleanliness and holiness laws

It is quite common for homosexual activists, as well as atheists (who are often one and the same!), to throw out the challenge that the laws forbidding homosexuality in the Old Testament also forbid things like eating animals which do not chew the cud, or fish without scales.

These critics who think they are quite clever argue, if it is now okay to eat all foods, why forbid homosexuality? As but one example, I recently received this comment: "Bill, it's not just the homosexual Christians we should be worried about. What about the crayfish-eating Christians, or indeed the mixed fabric-wearing Christians. Both these 'Christian' types distort God's holy directions as laid out in his Bible. What do you suggest we do, Bill?"

While this fellow thought he was being cute, all he did was reveal that secular homosexual activists know nothing about biblical theology or Old Testament legislation. Sadly, of course, many believers do not know much more either, so it is worth looking at this whole issue in some detail.

To keep this discussion from blowing out, let me just interpose what we find in the book of Leviticus. In Lev. 11-15 we find laws concerning the clean and unclean. In Lev. 17-26 we find what is known as the "Holiness Code". These are the main chapters dealing with holy and unholy, pure and impure, clean and unclean.

Admittedly, much has been written about these laws, and how they are to be understood today. Briefly, this legislation primarily had to do with the proviso found in Lev. 19:2: "Be holy because I, the Lord your God, am holy." Israel was to be a holy and clean people before the Lord.

It was also to be clearly distinguished from the surrounding cultures. That in part explains the various laws about distinction, division, and separation. Holiness always implies separation, being set apart from that which is unholy, and devoted to that which is holy.

As Bruce Waltke explains: "The Israelites were commanded not to mix seeds or crops and not to mix different types of cloth in sewing. Therefore, the theme of purity was worked into the everyday life of the Israelites and safeguarded them from mixing their human seed with pagans. These purity laws inculcated the notion of holiness so that Israel would learn that they were to be a pure people, set apart for God."[3]

Or as John Goldingay puts it: "Israel's holiness lies in distinctively belonging to Yhwh. Distinguishing holy and ordinary, and also pure and taboo, then contributes to its manifesting its distinctiveness over against other people. ... Israel's observance of these distinctions is an expression of its accepting its position as a people that God has distinguished from the rest of the world."[4]

> **While it is true that we are no longer under the ceremonial and civil laws of ancient Israel, the moral laws remain.**

And one must bear in mind the differences between the realm of the clean/unclean, and the realm of the holy/profane. Ceremonial uncleanness was particularly associated with Israel in Old Testament times, while moral holiness is forever enjoined upon all peoples.

Thus, while it is true that we are no longer under the ceremonial and civil laws of ancient Israel, the moral laws remain. As Allen Ross explains: "To be free from the regulations of the law is not a license to be free from obeying what the law revealed." He continues:[5]

> The New Testament makes this very clear: moral imperfections and impurities – that is, the sinful activities that rendered a person unclean in the Old Testament – are still sinful in the new covenant and still require repentance and confession and forgiveness in order to comply with God's standard of holiness. It is folly – it is dishonest – to argue that because the purification regulations of Old Testament Israel were fulfilled by the death of Christ, the sins listed in Leviticus are no longer sins.

Goldingay ties this all together concerning the issue of homosexuality:[6]

> Leviticus 18:22 and Leviticus 20:13 explicitly disallow homosexual acts. Yet it also disallows many other practices (such as sex with a woman during her period) on the basis of a concern with purity and taboo, and in general such prohibitions are withdrawn in Christ.

> It has also been argued that the Levitical ban on homosexual acts also ceases to apply once Christ has made all things clean. But the context of these regulations in Leviticus implies that they are not simply concerned with purity and taboo.

And Ross reminds us of the differences between the ceremonial and moral when we consider the means of absolution: "Homosexuality was never merely part of the purity problem that sanctuary ritual covered; it was a major offense for which there was no ritual law – it required forgiveness because it violated the moral code."[7]

Please note that much more remains to be said about this, and I look specifically at Lev. 18-19 below, and there go into much more detail about this form of theological revisionism.

Ploy # 3: Arguing from silence

This is one of the major tactics used by the revisionists. The claim is often made that the Bible says very little about homosexuality in general, and Jesus said nothing about it in particular. Concerning Scripture as a whole, let me cite a quite recent example, from an article that appeared in a major Melbourne daily by a well-known revisionist. Speaking of the debate over the issue in the Anglican church, she said, "the Bible, in a few much-disputed verses, seems to condemn certain homosexual practices".[8] There are more than a few passages which deal with this issue, as we shall see in a moment. And, of course, they are only "much disputed" by the theological revisionists. Almost everyone else throughout church history thought they were pretty clear and straightforward.

> Jesus, as a good Jew of his day, shared the common Jewish understanding of homosexuality, which was to utterly oppose it.

As to the claim that Jesus said nothing about homosexuality, that is quite true, in one sense,[9] just as it is true that he never said a word about rape, incest, child abuse, arson or pollution. Are we to argue therefore that these behaviours are acceptable? Is anything okay if Jesus did not specifically condemn it or mention it? The truth is, arguing from silence is always poor logic. Did Jesus approve of rape because he did not explicitly condemn it? Hardly. In the same way, Paul never once explicitly mentions the virgin birth. Did he therefore not believe in it?

The answer to this objection is quite simple. Jesus, as a good Jew of his day, shared the common Jewish understanding of homosexuality, which was to utterly oppose it. There was very little need for Jesus to proscribe homosexuality. It was a given in Jewish culture that it was an abomination to God and was not to be practised among the Jews.

Indeed, "the reason for Jesus' silence on this matter is most likely the fact that homosexuality was virtually unknown in Jewish Palestine (it was considered *the* Gentile vice) and, therefore, unlikely to have come to Jesus' attention."[10]

Moreover, what Jesus did do throughout his ministry was to affirm the authority of the Old Testament, where the sin of homosexuality is, of course, clearly spelled out. We see this, for example in such places as John 17:17 and Matthew 19:4-5.

But the argument that Jesus never condemned homosexuality needs to be considered from an even wider perspective. God's plans for human sexuality have always been limited to that of male/female married sex. No other sexuality is allowed in the Bible. And married heterosexual sexuality was established by God in the opening chapters of Genesis. That has always been, and forever will be, the divine intention for sex.

Indeed, this is one of the most important considerations to bear on this subject. The negative prohibitions against homosexuality must be seen in the light of the positive teaching about heterosexual marriage as elaborated in Genesis 1 and 2, and reaffirmed throughout Scripture. As De Young puts it: "[T]he creation of humans as male and female (Genesis 1) and the heterosexual union that constitutes marriage (Genesis 2) lie at the basis of the rest of Scripture and its comments about sexuality and marriage."[11]

God's intention for human sexuality is made clear in the early chapters of Genesis. John Stott says three fundamental truths emerge from the creation account of Genesis 1 and 2: a) the human need for companionship; b) the divine provision to meet this human need; and c) the resulting institution of marriage.[12]

Genesis 2:24 makes it clear that one man and one woman only can constitute a marriage bond:[13]

Thus Scripture defines the marriage God instituted in terms of heterosexual monogamy. It is the union of one man with one woman, which must be publicly acknowledged (the leaving of parents), permanently sealed (he will 'cleave to his wife'), and physically consummated ('one flesh'). And Scripture envisages no other kind of marriage or sexual intercourse, for God provided no alternative.

As one Old Testament scholar says: "Without question 2:24 serves as the bedrock for Hebrew understanding of the centrality of the nuclear family for the survival of society. Monogamous heterosexual marriage was always viewed as the divine norm from the outset of creation."[14]

Or as Dr J.J. Davis says: "Human sexuality is reflected in the differentiation of two, not three or four, sexual genders, nor some androgynous combination of the two."[15] Homosexual couples cannot fulfil the command to be fruitful and multiply (Gen 1:28).

Says another commentator: "It was God's ordained design for sexual relations to be in the form of male-female union, man and wife becoming 'one flesh,' and God created the distinction between the sexes to that end. This creation of sexual differentiation by God from the beginning established heterosexuality as the normative direction for the sexual impulse and act."[16] Moreover, this creation ordinance "is continually reaffirmed by the interpretations of the creation account in the New Testament."[17] Jesus affirms it in Mark 10:6-9 (= Matt. 19:4-6) for example, while Paul affirms it in I Cor 6:16 and Eph. 5:31. As ex-gay Bob Davies of Exodus International says: "Any alternative of this pattern is a distortion of God's original plan."[18]

The words of Jesus in Matthew 19 need to be spelled out here. In verses 4-6 we find this very strong affirmation of the Genesis ideal: "'Haven't you read,' he replied, 'that at the beginning the Creator "made them male and female," and said, "For this reason a man will leave his father and mother and be united to his wife, and the two will become one flesh"? So they are no longer two, but one. Therefore what God has joined together, let man not separate'."

As theologian and ethicist Stanley Grenz remarks: "Christians maintain that this radical teaching of Jesus forms the heart of the biblical understanding of marriage and as such constitutes the ideal in all eras."[19]

Says Robert Gagnon:[20]

> Jesus shows no awareness, much less acceptance, of any other pattern – even though no Jew in antiquity could have been oblivious to homosexual relationships among many Gentiles.

> There was no need for him to comment on whether homosexual unions should be permitted and, if so, whether his stance on divorce and remarriage should apply to them too. The creation texts authorized only one type of sexual union. It would have been a foregone conclusion for him that homoerotic relationships and human-animal unions, both proscribed in Leviticus, were unacceptable.

Thus heterosexual marriage as intended by God is the measuring rod by which we judge homosexuality or any other sexual expression. As Schmidt reminds us: "Every sexual act that the Bible calls sin is essentially a violation of marriage, whether existing or potential."[21]

Finally, it can be said that perhaps Jesus did refer to homosexuality, albeit indirectly. That is, on a number of occasions in the gospels we read about Jesus mentioning the destruction of Sodom and Gomorrah as an example of the judgment of God (Matt 10:14-16, 11:23-25; Luke 10:11-13 and 17:28-30).

Ploy # 4: Finding same-sex couples in Scripture

Another even more radical revisionist ruse is to argue that there are many same-sex couples mentioned in Scripture. David and Jonathan are frequently cited.[22] Sometimes Ruth and Naomi are held up as an example of a lesbian relationship. And some even go so far as to suggest that Jesus may have had a same-sex relationship with John!

The appeal to Jonathan and David as an example is based on passages found in 1 Samuel 18 – 2 Samuel 1. This portion of scripture speaks of the close relationship they had. For example, in 1 Sam. 18:3 we read that Jonathan made a covenant with David, "because he loved him as himself". And in 20:41 we read of how David and Jonathan wept together and kissed each other upon David's departure.

Concerning the first passage, men can obviously have a deep love for one another without any sexual overtones. One would have to read into the text any supposed hints of homosexuality. And the same with the other passage. Anyone familiar with social customs of the ancient Middle East (or even many modern Middle Eastern cultures, for that matter) will see nothing unusual in this practice. As Gagnon remarks, "There is nothing inherently homosexual about two men kissing each other" in ancient Middle Eastern society. "These were not erotic kisses but kisses of sorrow that conveyed the deep emotional pain of a committed friendship and alliance cleft by circumstances beyond their control."[23]

It just takes too much of an out-of-control imagination to see these two men as anything other than normal, virile males. As Stanley Grenz reminds us: "Whatever feelings David and Jonathan had for one another, both were definitely heterosexual in behavior, for both were married and fathered children."[24]

Norman Geisler puts it this way:[25]

> There is no indication in Scripture that David and Jonathan were homosexual. On the contrary, there is strong evidence that they were not. David's attraction to Bathsheba (2 Sam. 11) reveals that his sexual orientation was heterosexual, not homosexual. In fact, judging by the number of wives he had, David seemed to have too much heterosexuality!

Claims that Jesus and his disciples may have been gay are even more outrageous. But such claims are increasingly being made. A somewhat amazing example of these claims appeared in a letter to a national newspaper written by a man with the title, "Research Associate, Department of Modern Greek, University of Sydney". His letter was an attempt to show that Jesus was a homosexual, and that the four gospels "implicitly approve" of homosexuality.[26]

The academic informs us that when Jesus said we are to "love one another as I have loved you", this is clear proof of his approval of homosexuality. He claims Jesus uses the Greek word *agapeo*, and that this word can mean physical love. He even insists that this term does not mean "spiritual love". He then asserts that Greek was the spoken language of the Jews back then, and that Greek customs did not prohibit homosexuality.

Considering that this fellow is meant to be a research associate in Modern Greek, one is appalled at his misleading and/or uninformed claims. First, as this man should know, there are major differences between Modern Greek and Koine, or New Testament, Greek. The Greek of today has experienced many changes and

If Jesus had meant physical love, that is the term he would have chosen.

gone through a gradual evolution over the past two millennia. Second, as any layman knows, Jesus spoke Aramaic, not Greek. More sophisticated (better educated) Jews of Jesus' day may have spoken Latin and Greek as well, but Aramaic was the lingua franca (common language) of the day.

The assertion that *agapeo* can mean physical love and really does not mean spiritual love is just plain wrong. There are a number of Greek words for love, of course, and *eros* was the common term for passionate, physical love. If Jesus had meant physical love, that is the term he would have chosen.

Back then *agapeo* almost always referred to the love of God. Any standard lexicon of New Testament Greek will make this clear. If he wanted to speak of another kind of love, he could have used either *eros* or *philos* (these are the nouns; the verbal forms are *erao* and *phileo*). The latter means more of a brotherly love, or love between friends. Not that this term is always clearly distinguished from *agapeo*, but there were nonetheless differences.

Not only the terminology, but the context of the passage in question (John 15:12) makes it quite clear that physical love is nowhere to be found in the thinking of Jesus. The context is the impending death of Jesus, and the need of the disciples to be willing to lay down their lives one for another. To cheapen this injunction to mean carnal relationships is not only to do injustice to both New Testament Greek and the Gospel writer's clear intention, but it is to speak sacrilegiously of the atoning work of Christ.

172

Jesus here was hours away from going to a horrible death on our behalf. He was not making a pro-homosexual speech. Such an interpretation indicates confused thinking at best, or a deliberate misreading of the text in order to push a foreign (and quite recent) agenda on to the biblical text.

This academic then seeks to further strengthen his case by telling us that Jesus reclined on the disciple whom he loved. Well, that must prove the case, mustn't it! One is amazed at either the academic's woeful ignorance of the cultural world of first century Palestine or his incredible attempt to twist Scripture. It was, of course, the custom of the day to recline at table while sharing a meal together. And as God incarnate, of course Jesus loved his disciple. Indeed, he loved all his disciples, even the whole world. But by the academic's perverted logic, perhaps he had (or desired) sex with all mankind (and womankind as well?).

Actually, that last thought may be in his mind as well, since he also speaks of the "close relationship with his mother". It seems a son cannot even have love for his own mother without the academic putting a kinky spin on things.

The eunuch of Matthew 19:12

Another attempt to find homosexuality in Scripture is to radically abuse and misuse the passage about eunuchs in Matthew 19. The claim is made that part of this text is actually about homosexuality. Thus it is worth looking at in some detail. Every text needs to be examined in the light of its context, so we must look at Matt. 19:1-12 to properly understand and interpret this passage.

In this pericope Jesus answers a question about marriage and divorce, and he reinforces God's desire for permanence in marriage. This text is also about those who have the gift of celibacy and do not follow the norm of hetero-sexual marriage. That is the idea as set out in verses 4-9.

After giving a strong and restrictive word against divorce and remarriage, his disciples reply in verse 10 with these words: "If this is the situation between a husband and wife, it is better not to marry." The reply found in the next two verses comprises the difficult passage:

Jesus replied, 'Not everyone can accept this word, but only those to whom it has been given. For some are eunuchs because they were born that way; others were made that way by men; and others have renounced marriage because of the kingdom of heaven. The one who can accept this should accept it'.

Homosexual activists want to claim that the eunuchs who "were born that way" were in fact homosexuals. They want to argue that Jesus meant some people are born with a same-sex attraction, and therefore heterosexual marriage is not for them.

> **Jesus is simply stating that celibacy is an option for some of his followers.**

But is that what Jesus intended here? The short answer is no. Jesus is simply stating that celibacy is an option for some of his followers. There is nothing here to suggest that Jesus is talking about some people being born homosexual.

Of course, in first century Jewish culture celibacy was a fairly radical concept. Jews back then considered marriage and the bearing of children to be a duty. The unmarried Jesus would have been a rare exception in that culture. Marriage is certainly God's norm, but as Paul explains in 1 Corinthians 7, both marriage and singleness are gifts of God.[27]

Indeed, John the Baptist, Jesus and Paul were all single and celibate for the sake of the kingdom, as have been numerous other people. While celibacy may be the exception to the rule, it is nonetheless a valid gift and calling of God.

As D.A. Carson comments, we must recognise that "neither Jesus nor the apostles see celibacy as an intrinsically holier state than marriage (cf. 1 Tim 4:1-3; Heb 13:4), nor as a condition for the top level of ministry (Matt 8:14; 1 Cor 9:5), but as a special calling granted for greater usefulness in the kingdom".[28]

Thus talk of singleness and celibacy need not be seen in the least as somehow referring to or implying homosexuality. To refrain from sexual relations with a woman does not at all indicate that having sex with another male is in mind.

As to the three categories of eunuchs which Jesus mentions, the first two are to be understood in a literal sense, while the third is evidently metaphorical in intent. The first category has to do with those who are born without the physical capability – in other words, those who are, for various reasons, impotent.

As R. T. France states, it is of course anachronistic to read back modern Western notions of homosexual orientation into this passage. No first-century Middle Easterner would have thought in those terms. Also, as France reminds us, back then homosexuality most often meant what we today call bi-sexuality: primarily men who had sex with both women and other men. There was no thought of people being born with some inherent, unalterable homosexual orientation.[29]

Says France: "Such a choice [of bisexuality] could hardly be described as being 'born a eunuch,' and the idea of an innate and irreversible homosexual orientation belongs to modern Western psychology rather than to the world in which Jesus lived."[30]

The second category would have to do with castration and the like, a common practice for those who worked in harems. Those men who worked with women in high positions in the royal court were usually castrated. We have an example of this in Acts 8:27: the Ethiopian eunuch.

The third category has to do with an individual's choice. While self-castration may be a very slight possibility here (something that would have been abhorrent to Jews), it most likely should be understood in a figurative sense: it has to do with choosing celibacy over marriage.

That is, some people are willing to remain single for the sake of the kingdom. That is why Jesus could say it would not be accepted by all, and only those to whom it has been given (i.e., the gift of celibacy) would be able to receive it.

Looked at in this light, Matthew 19:11-12 is not very difficult to understand. The passage, following on from a section about marriage and divorce, has absolutely nothing whatsoever to do with homosexuality. All that Jesus is teaching here is two paths for the disciple: marriage without the option of divorce, or celibacy.

Homosexuality was everywhere seen as abhorrent in first century Judaism – indeed, in all of ancient Judaism. That anyone during this time would have understood Jesus as referring to homosexuality is patently absurd.

Paul's thorn

Perhaps the most bizarre and perverse attempt to find approval for homo-sexuality in Scripture has to do with the apostle Paul. Some of these homo-sexual activists who seek to hide under the cloak of Christianity have actually claimed that they know something that theologians have been dumbfound-ed by for two millennia. They actually claim to know what Paul's thorn in the flesh was! You guessed it: a struggle with homosexual tendencies!

You will remember this famous passage in 2 Corinthians 12:1-10. Paul says that he prayed three times to have this removed, but God informed him that his grace was sufficient for him, and the thorn was not removed. Of course, a lot of speculation has gone into seeking to determine the exact nature of this thorn that Paul wanted to have removed.[31]

Some think of external things such as persecution. Many have suggested some sort of physical illness, such as malaria or bad eyesight (cf. Gal 4:15; 6:11). For example, Gordon Fee states that while we cannot know with cer-tainty what it was, it must have been "some form of physical infirmity".[32]

Many commentators simply say we just cannot know for sure what it was. Some wits, seeking to throw a bit of light relief into the issue, suggest the thorn was Paul's mother-in-law! But the idea that this was a struggle with homosexual feelings or actions is simply preposterous, and no serious New Testament scholar or theologian has ever offered such a suggestion.

Indeed, we might as well say that Jesus had struggles with sex addiction, or that Peter had a major gambling problem, or that James was a closet paedo-phile, or that John the Baptist secretly viewed child porn on the Internet. These claims make just as much sense as this idiotic and bizarre suggestion about Paul and his thorn.

And recall what Paul says about this thorn: it is "a messenger of Satan" (v.7). Ralph Martin rightly says that "the thorn was inherently evil. Nowhere does

Paul imply that this thorn was good. It was used to buffet Paul and caused him great consternation and pain."[33]

So even if this were a struggle with homosexual desire – which it clearly is not – Paul tells us its origins are satanic, and that it is not something he ever countenanced embracing or submitting to. While God may have allowed it to afflict Paul, it was not itself from God, but from Satan.

Ploy # 5: Misreading Acts 10

Another approach taken by the revisionists is to say that just as God told the Jews that he now accepts Gentiles, so now we should accept homosexuals. An appeal is made to Acts 10 and the story of Peter's rethink on the issue of eating unclean foods and accepting Gentiles into the Christian faith.[34]

The attempted analogy from Acts 10 is really quite surprising, given that some who make these claims are presumably educated and biblically literate. There is no way that the justification of homosexuality can ever be deduced from this passage.

The whole point of Acts 10 (or more accurately, 9:32-11:18), is to teach Peter (and other Jewish Christians) that salvation is no longer the sole domain of the Jews, but is made available to all people. It has nothing to do with continuing in known sin. It has nothing to do with overriding universal and timeless moral prohibitions. Thus this revision is simply comparing apples and oranges, and the analogy just does not hold up. Indeed, to argue that this passage means that God somehow accepts everyone just as they are, with no repentance necessary, is "an exceedingly childish error", to use Calvin's phrase.

As Grenz reminds us:[35]

> [The] apostles did not urge the new converts to bring their old
> Gentile ideas and ways with them into the church. ... The early
> church leaders instructed Gentile converts to leave behind their
> former 'ignorance.' They were to park their pagan religious

177

practices and immoral activities outside the door of the church. All Christians – whether Jew or Gentile – were to live out the same ethical calling, namely, to be holy (1 Peter 1:13-16).

We should not withdraw the offer of salvation to anyone. That is the message of Acts 10. But once a person has accepted the gracious good news, that is when a major house-cleaning takes place. Again, it does not occur overnight but, as Paul says in Ephesians 4, let those who steal, steal no more. Or as he says in 1 Corinthians 6:9-11, "such were some of you". Yes, some of you were adulterers, thieves, homosexuals and other sorts of sinners. But that has been put aside once salvation is at hand. Now is the time to pursue holiness and renounce sin.

We do not become perfect, or try to become perfect, in order to obtain salvation. We can't do it. That is why it is all of grace. But once that acceptance of God's gracious gift has taken place, there is then the lifelong process of sanctification: renouncing and forsaking all known sin by God's grace and the enabling of the Holy Spirit.

Ploy # 6: God made me that way

Another common line heard is that "Homosexuality is a gift from God" or "God made me this way, so how can it be wrong?" As one example, a group of leaders and lecturers at one Melbourne theological institution wrote: "We believe God has made some people homosexual."[36]

A simple response to this is that God has not made anyone to be sinful. But because we live in a fallen world, everyone is born with a depraved and fallen nature. So even if certain people feel a same-sex attraction from a very young age, this does not make God the author of that attraction. It is a result of living in a fallen world.

> **If God made people to be sinners (be it homosexuality or any other kind of sin), how can God then condemn such sin?**

Moreover, if God made people to be sinners (be it homosexuality or any other kind of sin), how can God then condemn such sin? It is simply not fair for God to condemn homosexuals or murderers or adulterers if God made them that way.

But people tend to argue from their experience back to Scripture, instead of letting Scripture be the judge of experience. Thus, even if we concede with some that they may have felt same-sex desire for as long as they can remember, that still does not mean God made them that way. Nor does it mean that such desires are therefore acceptable. As psychologists Jones and Yarhouse put it:[37]

> The Christian church has never taught that all our desires come from God, has never taught that all our desires are good, and has never taught that every desire, even every good desire, ought to be fulfilled. A heterosexual man's lust for a woman who is not his wife does not come from God and is not a good desire, and should not be indulged.

The issue of a supposed genetic basis of homosexuality has already been extensively explored in the first part of this book, so I direct readers to go back there for the full documentation on this.[38] But even if a small element of the homosexual condition can be attributed to a genetic factor,[39] that still speaks of living in a sin-stained world. And it still does not excuse people of not availing themselves of the saving and healing power of Christ to set them free from that situation. I again cite Jones and Yarhouse:[40]

> At the broadest level all humans are heirs to a predisposition that we have not chosen and that propels us toward self-destruction and evil – our sinful nature. The plight of the homosexual who has desires and passions that he or she did not choose is in fact the common plight of humanity. We all face the same challenge: how are we to live when what we want is out of accord with what God tells us we should want in this life?

And even if we are born with various desires which seem to be so real and so natural, we still have the ability to say no to desires that are not in our best interest, or that are clearly contrary for God's design for us. We are not robots; nor are we animals. We can say no to harmful desires and tendencies, and say yes to what is right.

> **That we should say no to passion and desire that are not in accordance with God's purposes for us should be obvious to every Bible-believing Christian.**

Indeed, that is how civilisation works. As William F. Buckley once put it, "Civilization is about curbing appetites." No society can last long if it simply says we should give in to every appetite, passion and desire that comes our way.

Christians, of all people, should know this. That we should say no to passion and desire that are not in accordance with God's purposes for us should be obvious to every Bible-believing Christian. Sure, in a fallen world we will all be born with proclivities, desires and tendencies that are not of God. But we certainly do not need to just give in to every passion and inclination.

In fact, even with this fallen and sinful orientation, we can still determine whether or not we act out those inclinations and desires. We are not so utterly fallen that we have absolutely no say in the matter. We still enjoy God's common grace.

Believers should never excuse sin just because we have a leaning toward something, or a desire for something. The Christian life is all about saying no to bad desires, and doing that which is right. Even a non-believer does not excuse evil by appealing to desire. We certainly do not excuse a child-molester and say, "Well, he was just acting out his natural orientation."

Former homosexual Alan Chambers does not believe that homosexuality is genetic. But even if there were a genetic basis for it, he argues, that "doesn't make it healthy, optimal, desirable, or right. No group would ever advocate for the special rights of alcoholics. And who in their right mind would encourage others to become alcoholics or to celebrate their alcoholism? Genetics aren't meant to be used as justification for sin."[41]

Frank Turek puts it this way:[42]

Let's suppose that scientists someday discover a genetic contribution to homosexual desires. Would that give license to behavior? No, all of us have desires that we ought not to act on. In other words, we were all born with an 'orientation' to bad behavior, but desires don't justify the behavior. For example, some may have a genetic predisposition to alcohol, but who would advocate alcoholism? If someone has a genetic attraction to children, does that justify pedophilia? What homosexual activist would say that a genetic predisposition to violence justifies gay-bashing? (Born gay? What if the gay-basher was born mean?). Desires do not justify behaviour. In fact, there is a word we use to describe the disciplined restraint of destructive desires – it's called 'civilisation'.

Because of the Fall, we all come into this world as sinful, selfish beings. But the good news of the Gospel is that God has come to deal with the sin question and to set us free from our addiction to self, to selfishness, and to every sinful desire. We are clearly instructed to resist and overcome sinful desires, not simply give in to them.

Turek is worth quoting some more here:[43]

But let's suppose that some homosexuals cannot change their orientation. Does that mean they cannot control their behavior? Why do we expect pedophiles to resist their desires but not homosexuals? Because we know pedophiles are human beings who can choose not to act on their sexual desires just like anyone else. We also demand them to resist their desires because our children will not be safe if they don't … .

The truth is, sexual behaviour is not compulsory. It is always a choice. We all must resist our sexual urges at times. And while it's not desirable, some do so for their entire lives and never have sex. That's possible for people with any sexual desire. After all, if I honestly believe that I've been born with heterosexual desires, am I required to engage in heterosexual acts? Am I not capable of controlling my sexual desires and remaining celibate? If you claim that I am not, then you have also made the absurd contention that no one in the history of the world has ever been morally responsible for any sexual crime, including rape, incest, and child molestation.

Finally, the biblical language makes it clear that genuine choice is involved here. While I will look at the biblical data much more thoroughly in the next chapter, let me here just briefly focus on Romans 1:24-32. Here the textual data will not allow for the excuse, "But I was born that way". As New Testament scholar Linda Belleville rightly states:[44]

> It is sometimes said that homosexuality is not freely chosen and therefore is unavoidable. Yet, Paul goes on to say just the opposite. His language is active rather than passive. Both genders are described as free agents. Men wilfully abandoned (active voice) natural relations with women and opted for unnatural sexual activity with men (vv. 26-27). The language is that of consenting adults. It is not a case of 'my hormones made me do it'.

Ploy # 7: Committed, loving same-sex relationships are not condemned

Revisionists will sometimes agree that some types of homosexuality are wrong, but only the promiscuous variety. They argue that homosexuals in a monogamous and long-term, loving relationship can and do receive God's blessing. But from everything the Bible *does* say about homosexuality (see below), we can safely assume that there is no such thing as "loving and loyal" same-sex relationships. If homosexuality is a sin, full stop, then there are no respectable versions of it, just as there are no respectable versions of rape or murder.

Biblical love is always about willing the highest good for the other person.

As John Stott once said: "I do not deny the claim that homosexual relationships can be loving. ... [but] they are incompatible with true love because they are incompatible with God's law. Love is concerned for the highest welfare of the beloved. And our highest human welfare is found in obedience to God's law and purpose, not in a revolt against them."[45]

Indeed, biblical love is always about willing the highest good for the other person. If you really love someone with God's love, you will want the very best for them. Thus the most loving thing any Christian can do to the homosexual is tell him the truth about his condition: that it is a sinful and dangerous lifestyle; that he does not have to be homosexual; and that God in Christ offers genuine change for those seeking it.

Christ came to set the captives free (Luke 4:18) and to deliver those ensnared by the devil (2 Timothy 2:26). He did not come so that people could remain in their sinful and high-risk addictions. There is nothing loving about letting people remain in their oppressive bondage and sinful conditions. Setting people free to love God, as they were created to do, should always be our aim.

Moreover, as I demonstrated earlier in this book, long-term, monogamous homosexual relationships are quite rare. And even where longer-term relationships exist, they typically still tend to involve outside sexual flings.[46]

And finally, as mentioned above, all relationships need to be judged in the light of God's standard, of God's ideal. Walton, commenting on the Sodom episode, makes these pertinent remarks:[47]

> The Bible is clear that homosexual practice is wrong and sinful. It is not just wrong insofar as it is promiscuous. Rather, as with adultery, incest, and bestiality, it is wrong because of the nature of the sexual partner. An illicit sexual partner may be married to someone else (adultery), may be a close relative (incest), may be an animal (bestiality), and may be someone of the same gender (homosexuality). Monogamous homosexual relationships are no more acceptable than committing adultery with only one person.

Ploy # 8: Homosexual orientation is okay

Even if critics concede that homosexual activity is wrong, they still want to argue that same-sex orientation is okay. As an example, back in 1994

183

the then-Uniting Church minister and Australian Democrat Senator John Woodley made this distinction: "Nearly all of the biblical references are to sodomy rather to homosexuality as such." He said that homosexuality today refers to an orientation, and heterosexuals can commit sodomy.[48] But again, Scripture takes a different stance. It seems to regard the desire itself as wrong, whether or not expressed in acts (Rom 1:24, 26, 27). And not just one, but eight different terms are used in Romans 1:24-27 to express the wrongness, the sinfulness, of homosexuality.[49]

As one New Testament scholar has mentioned: "While it is true that homosexual *acts* are the specific focus in the Pauline prohibitions, this does not mean that he would have considered 'celibate' homosexual relationships to be within the scope of the divine creative will; this would be to exchange a man's 'natural' function for what is 'unnatural'."[50]

> **Elsewhere Jesus stressed that outward evil actions come from an inner evil heart.**

And as White and Niell point out concerning the Sodom episode, "though these men did not actually *accomplish* their desires, they are still identified as wicked. The distinction between act and desire that is so often a part of modern discussions is not to be found in the ancient text."[51]

Although Christians differ on this issue, it may well be that homosexual orientation (desire, lust, attraction), not just homosexual activity, is also sinful, just as is heterosexual lust and desire. As an indication of this, throughout Scripture, the condition of the inner man is intimately connected with outward actions. When Jesus spoke of lust as adultery in Matthew 5:28, he was making it perfectly clear that it is not only the act, but the thought, which is sinful, and in need of transformation.

Elsewhere Jesus stressed that outward evil actions come from an inner evil heart: "For from within, out of men's hearts, come evil thoughts, sexual immorality, theft, murder, adultery, greed, malice, deceit, lewdness, envy, slander, arrogance and folly. All these evils come from inside and make a man 'unclean'." (Mark 7:21-23).

184

When Paul speaks of homosexuality he uses terms like "thoughts", "desires" and "lusts", as in Romans 1: 24, 26, and 27. When David prayed his great prayer in Psalm 51, he didn't ask that he would no longer commit acts of adultery. Instead, he pleaded with God for a clean heart and pure thoughts (v.10). A person's disposition (or what the Bible often calls our 'heart'), is the ultimate driving force behind our actions. As Proverbs 4:23 put it: "Out of the heart are the issues of life."

Two passages from James also speak of sinful desires. "When tempted, no one should say, 'God is tempting me.' For God cannot be tempted by evil, nor does he tempt anyone; but each one is tempted when, by his own evil desire, he is dragged away and enticed. Then, after desire has conceived, it gives birth to sin; and sin, when it is full-grown, gives birth to death" (James 1:13-15). And James 4:1-3 also connects wrong desires with wrong actions:

> What causes fights and quarrels among you? Don't they come from your desires that battle within you? You want something but don't get it. You kill and covet, but you cannot have what you want. You quarrel and fight. You do not have, because you do not ask God. When you ask, you do not receive, because you ask with wrong motives, that you may spend what you get on your pleasures.

The tenth commandment especially highlights this point: "You shall not covet your neighbour's house. You shall not covet your neighbour's wife, or his manservant or maidservant, his ox or donkey, or anything that belongs to your neighbour" (Exodus 20:17). Coveting is here clearly condemned, regardless of any outward actions taken. (The actual action of adultery is covered in the seventh commandment – Exodus 20:14.) Thus, the desires, the lusts, the longings (which may or may not translate into action), are a violation of God's law.

The second chapter of Peter also makes this point quite clear when he speaks of God one day judging those who "have eyes full of adultery." (2 Peter 2:14) In contrast to this Paul tells us to keep our thoughts and desires pure (Phil 4:8). Timothy is told to "flee youthful passions" (2 Tim. 2:22) and Roman believers are admonished to "make no provision for the flesh, to gratify its desires" (Rom 13:14).

185

Other texts speak of sinfulness of wrong desires and thoughts. One very clear passage is found in Proverbs:

> Do not lust in your heart after her beauty or let her captivate you with her eyes, for the prostitute reduces you to a loaf of bread, and the adulteress preys upon your very life. Can a man scoop fire into his lap without his clothes being burned? Can a man walk on hot coals without his feet being scorched? So is he who sleeps with another man's wife; no one who touches her will go unpunished. (Proverbs 6:25-29)

Thus the lustful desire is sinful already, regardless of whether it results in overt action or not. The first sin is the lust, the wrong and sinful desires. And of course all people are born with perverted desires, twisted inclinations and depraved natures, which include a depraved sexuality. This depraved sexual nature can be expressed in various ways, be it homosexuality, adultery, voyeurism, rape or bestiality. But "our physical inclinations are to be subordinated to God's moral direction, not used as an excuse for transgressing it".[52]

Former Senator Woodley emphasises the distinction, saying "homosexuality is not a lifestyle choice but an orientation which for many is impossible to change. ... [S]uch a change is impossible because that is who they are".[53] But of course if this is true, then many thousands of ex-gays are either liars or lunatics. Indeed, why, if gays cannot change, are there more than 200 centres in North America alone devoted to helping them go straight?

I concede that some people may have a homosexual orientation, just as some have an orientation or predisposition to over-eating or anger. But what separates us from animals is the ability to choose how we act out those inclinations. As Timothy Dailey remarks:[54]

> While Scripture teaches that we are born with fallen natures that incline us toward any number of vices, it does not permit us to excuse any particular inclination as inevitable or uncontrollable. While we all have 'tendencies' or weaknesses, each of us has at least the capacity to strive against wrong or harmful urges.

Even some homosexuals take this position. As gay activist and La Trobe University lecturer Dennis Altman put it:[55]

To be Haitian or a hemophiliac is determined at birth, but being gay is an identity that is socially determined and involves personal choice. Even if, as many want to argue, one has no choice in experiencing homosexual desire, there is a wide choice of possible ways of acting out these feelings, from celibacy and denial ... to self-affirmation and the adoption of a gay identity.

"Being gay," says Altman, "is a choice".[56]

Woodley goes on to reinterpret the sin of Sodom and Gomorrah in terms of breaking the holy code of hospitality, an argument we have already examined. He concludes by saying that homosexuals can be at peace with themselves only if they accept their homosexuality as "part of God's gift of life to them, an integral part of our inner being". Such people, he argues, cannot be regarded as being "outside the salvation offered in Jesus Christ".[57] Well, there you have it: gays are born that way, their homosexuality is a gift of God, and Jesus will accept them just as they are.

> **Why, in the name of compassion, should the revisionists deny homosexuals the chance to escape from their bondage and misery?**

Not only is Woodley at odds with Christian tradition and doctrine, he is also at odds even with secular authorities. The decidedly non-religious Masters and Johnson Clinic in St Louis has treated hundreds of homosexuals and bisexuals. Masters reports that they have successfully "changed" more than half of their homosexual clients, and more than 75 per cent of bisexuals.[58]

Why, in the name of compassion, should the revisionists deny homosexuals the chance to escape from their bondage and misery, and to experience the life-changing power of the Gospel? As Roger Magnuson says, such revisionist theology is far from compassionate: "It is cruel to homosexuals themselves. The sodomite is trapped in a lust that is destroying him by inches and yards. To tell him he cannot help himself, to tell him to rejoice in his fatal disease, is to consign him forever to unhappiness. Much better the simple message of Christian grace."[59]

Plenty of ex-homosexuals have testified to how God changed not only their actions but their same-sex attractions. Of course it is not easy, but it is possible for those who want to change and will allow God to help them in the process. As one former homosexual put it:[60]

> The Good News of Jesus is that God loves us, accepts us, and promises to transform us if we let Him into our lives. It's not like God is demanding anything more of homosexually attracted people than everyone else – He wants the same thing: our love and obedience. And He promises to change us so we can love and obey Him. *All* Christians can experience deep changes in who they are through God's power.

Still, some will say that they tried to change, even with God's help, but just could not do it. Another former homosexual, Joe Dallas, responds to this objection:[61]

> That doesn't make it right. I know it's hard to change. I know some Christians who have to resist homosexual temptations nearly every day.

> But then, doesn't every Christian have to resist temptations every day? That's what sanctification is all about – growing daily to become more like Him! When we're born again, our sinful feelings don't just vanish. Some of them, in fact, stay with us our whole lives.

No one said the Christian life would be easy. And seeking to overcome any deep-seated sexual addiction can be a time-consuming and difficult process. But God is in the business of changing lives, so we should never call him a liar and refuse to believe that he can indeed do as he has promised. As Paul said in 2 Corinthians 5:17, "If anyone be in Christ, he is a new creation."

Ploy # 9. Love is all that matters

This is a common fall-back position. "God is love", we are told. "We need to love and accept people just as God loved and accepted all people." This is of course a half-truth. And as with all half-truths, it contains enough truth to sound convincing, but it also contains enough falsehood to seriously lead one astray.

Of course, God is loving and gracious. He is also holy, just and pure. All the attributes together make up the Godhead. His various attributes are never set at odds with one another, and all are fully present at all times. God always loves, but he always hates sin. He is always ready to forgive, but is always set to judge those who reject his love and forgiveness.

The loving Christ of the Gospels was also the person who spoke more about hell and judgment to come than any other person in the Bible. The same Christ who drew children in his arms will also come back with a sword to judge the earth, as the Book of Revelation makes clear.

> **If we really love someone, we will want the best for them.**

Yes, love matters. But so too do holiness, righteousness and justice. When we come to God, we come under his terms, not our own. His holiness has not been lessened one iota. Christ's death at Calvary was an act of supreme love and supreme justice combined. He has paid the penalty for our sins. But when we come to Christ and receive his forgiveness, we must, like the accepted adulterer, "go and sin no more" (John 8:11).

And as I already mentioned, if we really love someone, we will want the best for them. The best for a person never comes by violating God's laws, which are for our good. "God has already declared what love is and is not by the commands He had given. Love is the fulfilment of the law (Rom. 13:10), so any breaking of the law is an unloving act."[62]

As one theologian points out, love is undoubtedly the central biblical principle of Christian ethics, but without further guidelines "we transform 'love' into a self-regarding relativistic individualism".[63] And as former homosexual Joe Dallas rightly comments: "The love between two homosexuals cannot make homosexuality normal or legitimate, any more than the love of two people committing adultery justifies the breaking of marital vows."[64]

An example of twisted thinking on this issue can be seen in the debate over American Episcopalian Bishop Gene Robinson. He left his wife and two children and took up a homosexual relationship. The Anglican communion worldwide is split over his being made a bishop. He told his New Hampshire congregation just prior to becoming bishop, "I pray about this every day" and "I do feel called by God to move forward in this".[65] Of course, God never calls anyone to sin, to disobedience, or to defy his holy standards.

Loving God means keeping his commandments. The entire Bible is clear about this. In the Old Testament the connection between loving God and keeping his commandments is repeatedly made. Consider just a few such passages as found in the book of Deuteronomy:

> – Deut 6:5-6 – Love the Lord your God with all your heart and with all your soul and with all your strength. These commandments that I give you today are to be on your hearts.

> – Deut 10:12-13 – And now, O Israel, what does the Lord your God ask of you but to fear the Lord your God, to walk in all his ways, to love him, to serve the Lord your God with all your heart and with all your soul, and to observe the Lord's commands and decrees that I am giving you today for your own good?

> – Deut 11:1 – Love the Lord your God and keep his requirements, his decrees, his laws and his commands always.

> – Deut 30:16 – For I command you today to love the Lord your God, to walk in his ways, and to keep his commands, decrees and laws.

In the New Testament we find the very same teaching. There is simply no understanding of relationship with Christ as some sort of antinomian experience, free of any laws or commands. Jesus made this perfectly clear. Indeed, Jesus said exactly the same thing as Moses did. Consider just a few quotes as given to us by John in his Gospel:

> – John 14:15 – If you love me, you will obey what I command.

> – John 14:21 – Whoever has my commands and obeys them, he is the one who loves me. He who loves me will be loved by my

Father, and I too will love him and show myself to him.

– John 14:23 – Jesus replied, "If anyone loves me, he will obey my teaching. My Father will love him, and we will come to him and make our home with him."

– John 15: 10 – If you obey my commands, you will remain in my love, just as I have obeyed my Father's commands and remain in his love.

– John 15:14 – You are my friends if you do what I command.

And consider these words from John's epistles:

– 1 John 2:3 – We know that we have come to know him if we obey his commands.

– 1 John 3:24 –Those who obey his commands live in him, and he in them. And this is how we know that he lives in us: We know it by the Spirit he gave us.

– 1 John 5:2-3 –This is how we know that we love the children of God: by loving God and carrying out his commands. This is love for God: to obey his commands. And his commands are not burdensome.

– 2 John 6 – And this is love: that we walk in obedience to his commands. As you have heard from the beginning, his command is that you walk in love.

There are plenty more such passages that could be mentioned in this regard. So if we are going to talk about love here, it must be in the context of obedience to his Word, including his commands about human sexuality. Biblical love is never to be divorced from obedience to God and his clearly-stated commands.

Ploy # 10. Misusing texts on equality

The Bible says much about our equal worth and value as image-bearers of God, and the New Testament makes much of our oneness and equal footing in Christ. In a world where huge social inequalities existed, Christianity came along and said that we were all equal in God's eyes, and that in Christ there were to be no distinctions.

However, many homosexual activists have sought to argue that this biblical truth means, therefore, that homosexuality is to be regarded as equal to heterosexuality. They seek to use such biblical language on equality and apply it to their own sexuality. They want to argue that in Christ their sexual lifestyle is on a par with that of non-homosexuals.

One of the key passages on our equality and oneness in Christ – and one quite often appealed to by the theological revisionists – is Galatians 3:28. This passage reads as follows: "There is neither Jew nor Gentile, neither slave nor free, nor is there male and female, for you are all one in Christ Jesus".

As mentioned, such a concept was quite revolutionary in Paul's day. Society was highly stratified and divided back then, and the idea that all people were to be regarded as equal would have been widely dismissed. But Christian unity transcends these various distinctions.

Gordon Fee explains the revolutionary impact of this passage: "What is seldom seen clearly in contemporary western and westernized cultures is the truly radical nature of this sentence with regard to the context in which it was written. ... In Paul's day the top of the ladder belonged exclusively to a 'free gentile male,' while a 'Jewish female slave' would be at the bottom." Hence the shocking effect "of Paul's words in a culture where position and status preserved order through basically uncrossable boundaries".[66]

This is not to suggest, of course, that all distinctions somehow magically disappear in Christ. It is not as if men and women lose their distinctive genitalia for example. Very real differences still exist, but our oneness in Christ becomes paramount. As Ben Witherington comments:[67]

> Gal. 3:28 has sometimes been called the Magna Carta of Humanity and there is a sense in which that label is apt, but it is also well to be aware that Paul is not suggesting here the obliteration of the distinctions he mentions in this verse, but rather their redemption and transformation in Christ. The new creation is the

old one transformed and transfigured. These ethnic, social, and sexual distinctions continue to exist but in Christ they are not to determine one's soteriological or spiritual or social standing in the body of Christ.

It is clear that Paul here says nothing about sexual lifestyles. He could have if he so chose, but he did not. As Paul Copan remarks: "Scripture clearly affirms the equality of all *individuals* – blacks, women, slaves – because they are God's image-bearers. The same doesn't hold true for *sexual relationships*."[68]

William Webb has written an entire volume on the issue of slaves, women and homosexuals. He carefully demonstrates how biblical texts concerning the first two groups "move in a less restrictive or freeing direction relative to their original culture. ... On the other hand, homosexual texts move in a conservative or restrictive direction relative to the original culture."[69]

As to the Galatians passage, an examination of it shows that it "has nothing to do with the breaking down of social stigma concerning homosexuals, on either an exegetical level or in terms of extrapolated implications for subsequent generations".[70]

The revisionists are simply mixing apples and oranges here.

Indeed, Webb says that modern additions to Paul's threefold list would include such things as:[71]

In Christ there is neither:

– rich nor poor

– blue-collar nor white-collar

– black nor white

– baby-boomer nor generation X-er

– single nor married.

But if we followed the thinking of the theological revisionists and add "neither gay nor straight" to Paul's original list, then we would also have to extend our list today this way:[72]

In Christ there is neither:

– erotic lover of animals nor erotic lover of humans

– adulterer nor faithfully married

– sexually active single nor waiting virgin

– incestuous person nor non-incestuous person.

This is the inescapable logic of the revisionists' position; but they are simply mixing apples and oranges here, and they have absolutely no biblical or theological warrant for doing so.

There are many other ploys raised by the theological revisionists that could be mentioned here. Suffice it to say that every trick in the book seems to have been dug out. The revisionists are a good example of the warnings found in Scripture about how in the last days, deceit, deception and false prophets will abound.

In sum, the various theological ploys attempted by the activists have been examined and found wanting. Their case has been found to be weak, unbiblical, illogical, and disingenuous. They are straining at gnats and swallowing camels (along with clutching at straws) in their attempts to rewrite biblical morality to suit their own radical homosexualist agenda.

CHAPTER 2

Challenging the Biblical Texts

A number of texts found both in the Old and New Testaments clearly condemn homosexuality. However, all of these texts have been challenged by the revisionists, with any number of bizarre and twisted approaches taken. Consider just one general remark made by a Melbourne pastor of the homosexual Metropolitan Community Church. He said that the passages that condemn homosexuality "were probably mistranslated by the mainstream churches to make gay men second-class citizens"![1]

Since all of the biblical texts on homosexuality have been radically reinterpreted by the revisionists, they will here be examined in more detail. Altogether nine major texts will be examined.

The fact that the Old Testament is just that, old, does not make it less reliable or less truthful. All Christians who are committed to a high view of Scripture recognise the authority and importance of the Old Testament. And the Old Testament is quite clear in its condemnation of homosexuality. The four main texts bearing on the issue are: Genesis 18:20-19:29; Leviticus 18:22, 20:13; and Judges 19:1-21:25.

Sodom and Gomorrah

The story of Sodom and Gomorrah (Gen 18:20-19:29) has been understood as a clear denunciation of homosexuality for most of Christian history. However, a new spin on this event has recently come into vogue, with revisionists arguing that these cities were judged because of a lack of hospitality, not because of homosexuality. They deny, therefore, 3,500 years of Jewish, and 2,000 years of Christian, tradition on this verse. Actually, it wasn't until 1955 that this interpretation was first put forward by D.S. Bailey.[2]

This interpretation, which many have followed since Bailey, states that the people of Sodom violated the important codes of hospitality, so prominent in the ancient Middle East, in the way they treated the visitors. This interpretation is not altogether off the mark, as hospitality was indeed a very important social custom of the day in the ancient Orient, and to not be hospitable was a serious matter indeed. This view, however, has some major drawbacks.

First, totally destroying four cities (the cities of the plain were in fact five in total, according to Gen 14:2, 8; 19:20-22, 29-30; Deut. 29:23; Hosea 11:8; Admah and Zeboim were destroyed along with Sodom and Gomorrah, while Zoar was spared, because of Lot) merely for the sin of not showing proper hospitality seems a bit rich. As John Feinberg and Paul Feinberg state, this "would be a huge case of divine overkill! God simply doesn't do that. The only interpretation that makes sense of the judgment meted out is that the men of Sodom wanted same-sex sexual relations that evening, even as they had habitually engaged in homosexual sex acts before."[3]

Second, according to Jude 7, Sodom and Gomorrah fell because of "fornication and going after strange flesh". And 2 Peter 2:7-10 refers to the "sensual conduct of unprincipled men" at Sodom and Gomorrah. Third, the word "sodomy" to this day refers to male homosexual activity. Surely one has to perform linguistic and logical somersaults to get away from the obvious meaning of the text here.

The liberal interpretation tries to avoid these issues by saying that the citizens simply wanted to get acquainted with the two visitors. The word "to know" in Hebrew is *yadah*. It is used 943 times in the Old Testament. True, the verb usually means to become acquainted with. But about ten or twelve times it means "to have sex with" *(New International Version* NIV).[4] The context here makes it clear how the word is to be used. Lot described the citizens' desire to know the two visitors as a great wickedness (v.7), and shut the door behind him. And when he offered his own two daughters, he said they had not known a man. Surely this does not mean they had never met, nor were acquainted with, men. The parallel story in Judges 19 also makes it clear that the desire of the men of Gibeah to "know" their victim was not a mere acquaintance, but a sexual encounter. What they proposed is described as "wicked, vile and disgraceful".

As Victor Hamilton puts it: "When Lot responds by offering his daughters 'who have never known a man' (v.8), it becomes clear that the issue is intercourse and not friendship. Lot would never have made such an unusual suggestion if the request was only for a handshake and moments of chitchat."[5]

Some seek to argue that it is homosexual rape that is condemned here, not just homosexuality in itself. Hamilton offers four compelling reasons why this cannot be the case, and then concludes, "Clearly, then, the incident frowns on homosexual relations for whatever reason."[6]

> **The revisionist account of this story may be appealing to some, but it is not one that can be derived from proper exegesis or hermeneutics.**

The revisionist account of this story may be appealing to some, but it is not one that can be derived from proper exegesis or hermeneutics. As Hamilton puts it, this "interpretation can only be evaluated as wild and fanciful".[7]

The mainstream understanding of this text has always seen homosexuality as being clearly in view. As Robert Gagnon reminds us, "the two most prominent Jewish writers of the first century C.E., Philo and Josephus, interpreted Gen 19:4-11 to refer explicitly to homosexual acts. ... For Philo and Josephus homosexual conduct was merely the most outrageous example of a much wider range of sinful excess."[8]

Leviticus and the holiness code

It is quite typical of the revisionists to especially attack the passages on homo-sexuality found in Leviticus. The way they do this is to say that in the same passages are verses which also forbid men from cutting the corner of their beards, (19:27) or warn of menstrual uncleanness (20:18), and so on. They say that we obviously no longer obey passages on beard trimming and the like, so why not ignore the ones on homosexuality as well?

Most evangelical scholars recognise that the passages in question (18:22; 20:13) are both prohibitive of homosexuality and normative for today. The holiness code, of which these passages are a part (Chapters 17-26), was a clear reminder to Israel to maintain distinct ethical practices from the sur-rounding Canaanite nations. "Seven times [in Chapter 18] it is repeated that the Israelites are not to behave like the nations who inhabited Canaan before them (vv. 3 [2x], 24, 26, 27, 29, 30)."[9] As such it contains numerous prohibitions, some of which are still normative for today, and some of which are not. The whole of Scripture offers the context in which we make such distinctions.

How do we decide which are still normative? De Young is worth quoting at length here:[10]

> Although some instructions and prohibitions of chapters 18 and 20 are limited to Israel (distinguishing clean and unclean animals and having sexual relations with one's wife during her menstrual period), most are not. The context itself distinguishes limited, cultic prohibitions from universal prohibitions. The reader is able to discern which laws are universal. In addition, the similarity of these chapters to the Ten Commandments and the New Testament's applications of this section warrant consideration of most of these rules as valid. Prohibitions of homosexuality elsewhere in the Old Testament, ancient Judaism, the Apocrypha and Pseudepigrapha, and in the New Testament also justify the interpretation that the prohibition is universal.

Moreover, there are other interpretive clues. For God to assign the death penalty to homosexuality obviously means that he takes it very seriously indeed. However, there is no death penalty for a women's monthly period. Instead, the woman was considered ceremonially unclean for a seven-day period (Lev 15:19). Most of the other ceremonial purity laws also have much lighter penalties. As Grenz remarks, "under the Old Covenant the severity of the penalty was an indication of the importance of the precept."[11] Thus the penalties imposed tell us something of the nature of the various laws in the Holiness Code.

Of interest, it should be noted that bestiality is also condemned here (Lev 20:15-16), and it also carries the death penalty. The same reasoning applies to bestiality as to homosexuality: In both cases God's original intention for human sexuality is being violated. "With bestiality, as with homosexuality, one is breaking the 'boundaries' of biological design and sexual order. Reproduction of species does not take place between an animal and a human; nor does it take place between humans of the same sex."[12]

As Norman Geisler explains:[13]

> The prohibition against homosexuality is moral, not merely ceremonial. Simply because the Mosaic prohibition against homosexuality is mentioned in Leviticus does not mean that it was part of the ceremonial law that has passed away. If this were so, then neither would rape, incest, and bestiality be morally wrong, since they are condemned in the same chapter with homosexual sins (Lev. 18:6-14, 22-23).
>
> Homosexual sins among Gentiles, who did not have the ceremonial law, were also condemned by God. It was for this very reason that God brought judgment on the Canaanites (18:1-3, 25). Even in the Levitical law for the Jews, there was a difference in punishment for violating the ceremonial law by eating pork or shrimp, which was a few days' isolation, and that for homosexuality, which was capital punishment (18:29). Jesus changed the dietary laws of the Old Testament (Mark 7:18; Acts 10:12-15), but moral prohibitions against homosexuality are repeated in the New Testament (Rom 1:26-27; 1 Cor 6:9; 1 Tim 1:10; Jude 7).

Old Testament scholar Walter Kaiser also examines the argument that says the law against homosexuality is a part of the ceremonial law, and so is done away with the coming of Christ: "Nothing in its proscription points to or anticipates Christ, and the death penalty demanded for its violation places it in the moral realm and not in temporary ceremonial legislation."[14]

Also, we must understand how the New Testament appropriates these portions of the Old Testament. Most Christians understand that the Old Testament laws can be divided into civil law (pertaining to the civic culture of ancient Israel), ceremonial law (ritual cleanness and dietary laws, for example), and moral law (timeless and universal moral truths). Civil laws, relating to Israel as a nation, are not applicable today, as the nation of Israel no longer exists as God's sole covenant people. The ceremonial laws, too, have been rescinded in the New Testament. But transcultural moral laws remain in force.

Admittedly, confusion can arise at times when all three types of laws are found in the same passage. But again, the context often determines how to proceed. Scripture usually tells us what are timeless moral truths and what are cultural and temporal regulations. As Webb remarks, the "homosexual prohibition is not tied to mere ceremonial impurity. ... The homosexuality laws are not part of ceremonial law, as can be seen from its severe penalty and the New Testament handling of homosexuality, in contrast to its treatment of ceremonial law."[15]

As to the specific passages, the revisionists want to argue that only certain types of homosexuality are being proscribed, such as cultic prostitution or idolatrous practices. But as Wold summarises, after a detailed examination of the terms and the texts, "all same-gender sexual relations are categorically forbidden by

God's unchanging purposes for human sexuality have to be taken into account here.

the Hebrew terms. The biblical writer leaves no room for compromise. The language is emphatic. ... The inference is clear: only heterosexual intercourse is normal and normative."[16]

And as one Old Testament scholar points out, what is being condemned here is not just outward actions but inward lusts. Nobuyoshi Kiuchi is worth quoting at length here in this regard:[17]

> It is not just that the fate of one's soul is seriously affected by his conduct, but verse 29b explicitly states that the souls who do ('violate') them will be cut off. Herein lies the deepest cause of the abominations: the desire to violate a prohibition springs from the innermost part of the human, which is why the soul is said to be cut off. Despite the chapter's apparent emphasis on outward but hidden acts, an inner desire such as lust is assumed to be the source of the misconduct. Furthermore, the phrase 'the souls that do' stresses the inseparable bond between one's inner motives and outward conduct. And this opens up the possibility that all the acts prohibited in this chapter are merely manifestations of the human soul: the prohibitions assume no room to exist between what a person desires in the heart and how he or she behaves. It is only a small step towards Jesus' words in the Sermon on the Mount, 'But I say to you that everyone who looks at a woman with lust has already committed adultery with her in his heart' (Matt.5:28, *New Revised Standard Version* RSV).

Finally, as mentioned previously, God's unchanging purposes for human sexuality have to be taken into account here. Many commentators highlight the creation account and how homosexuality is a violation of God's fundamental purposes for mankind. As Radner says, homosexual coupling is a "rejection of the created and creative purposes of God by which life is received, nurtured, and passed on".[18]

Or, as Goldingay notes: "If we again consider how things were 'at the beginning of creation,' then Genesis 1-2 note that 'God made them male and female' (Mk 10:6) and envisage sexual relationships only between a man and a woman. It seems likely that the Torah's ban on homosexual acts is based not just in rules about cleanness and taboo, but on the purpose of creation."[19]

Veteran Old Testament scholar Kenneth Mathews connects this passage with the New Testament: "We have the reasoning of why homosexuality is unlawful provided in Romans 1 when the apostle Paul addressed the universality of human sin and guilt (vv. 18-30, esp. 26, 27). The Gentiles had rejected the testimony of nature and chose sinful idolatry and sexual perversions to honor their gods. The sexual practices of the Gentiles were a great affront to God because they were a rejection of God as Creator.

Mathew says:[20]

> He made men and women to play their appropriate sexual roles whereby they would propagate and dominate the world as stewards of the Lord's creation (Genesis 1:28). Heterosexuality outside the bounds of marriage is no less a sin, but the nature of homosexuality has more serious repercussions since it is a repudiation of the Lord's claim on his created order.

Judges

In Judges 19 and onwards we have a story which in many ways parallels the Sodom and Gomorrah account. Again we have a tragic episode where the local men want to sexually attack a visitor to town – this time a Levite. As in the Genesis account, the host offered the mob other people by whom to satisfy their lusts. And, as in the other account, revisionists argue that homosexuality is not the issue, but violation of ancient hospitality codes.

But as with the Sodom and Gomorrah account, the text here is quite plain. The men wanted to have sex with the visiting man. As Arthur Cundall comments: "Their request to the old man (22) revealed the extent of their sexual perversion, whilst his answer to them (23, 24) showed his immediate and horrified recoil at such conduct."[21]

That Judges 19 depicts homosexual gang rape is clear. But as Younger says:[22]

> [I]t is important not to judge the sin of Gibeah as simply homosexual rape, since while this was the intent of these wicked individuals, it did not in fact occur. But this in no way removes the initial homosexual intent and its condemnation in the narrative, nor does this remove the clear condemnation in the rest of Scripture concerning homosexual men.

This tragic homosexual lust is but one example of the decline of Israel, which the book of Judges is concerned to highlight. Or, as Block puts it, the broader goal of the book is "to chronicle the increasing Canaanization of Israelite society".[23] Or, as we would put it in today's context, the issue of homosexuality and its acceptance is but one of many examples of moral decline and the increasing secularisation of the Christian church.

Block comments on the close connection between Judges 19 and Genesis 19: "The echo of Genesis 19 in this text is intentional. By patterning this account after the earlier story, the narrator serves notice that, whereas these travelers had thought they had come home, finding safety with their own countrymen, they have actually arrived in Sodom. The nation has come full circle. The Canaanization of Israel is complete."[24]

Wolf concurs: "Gibeah had imbibed the morals of Canaan and had become another Sodom. Just as the worship of Baal had brought about a near catastrophe in the plains of Moab (Num 25:1-9), so the Baal cult was probably responsible for subverting the Benjamites."[25]

And he is certainly right to note that this passage "relates one of the most shocking episodes in Israel's history".[26]

Other Old Testament passages could also be appealed to. For example, some scholars believe that the sin for which Ham was judged so severely was homosexual incest (Gen 9:20-29). That is, he not only discovered his father Noah naked, but had sexual relations with him as well. This helps to explain the severity of Noah's curse on him and his descendants.

Geisler makes the case this way:[27]

> For several reasons, homosexuality seems to be implied here. First, surely, inadvertently seeing a nude parent was insufficient grounds for such a severe punishment of all his posterity for generations to come (v. 25). Second, to 'uncover the nakedness' of another is a way of expressing illicit sexual relations in the Mosaic law (see Lev. 18). Third, since the punishment was on Ham's son Canaan and descendants, and not on Ham himself, it seems to imply a continuation of perverse activity from father to son. Finally, it

was because of this kind of perverse sexual activity that God later judged Canaan's descendants, 'the Canaanites,' when Israel came into the land. It was so bad that the land had to 'vomit out' its inhabitants (see Lev 18:28).

Other indirect passages could be mentioned. For example, we have a clear warning against cross-dressing (and possibly also transvestitism) in Deut. 22:5: "A woman must not wear men's clothing, nor a man wear women's clothing, for the Lord your God detests anyone who does this."

In sum, every reference to homosexuality in the Old Testament is negative, "whether in narrative or law – and carry heavy sanctions in the form of death or the threat of extinction".[28] Or as James Dunn writes:[29]

> Jewish reaction to it as a perversion, a pagan abomination, is consistent throughout the OT. ... [A]ntipathy to homosexuality remains a consistent and distinctive feature of Jewish understanding of what man's createdness involves and requires. That homosexuality is of a piece with idolatry is taken for granted (as several of the same passages show), both understood as a demeaning of the people who indulge in them.

New Testament texts

The five major New Testament passages dealing with homosexuality are Romans 1:18-32; 1 Corinthians 6:9-11; 1 Timothy 1:9-10; 2 Peter 2:4-10; Jude 1:4-8. The first three will be dealt with in some detail, while the last two, mainly dealing with the Sodom story, will only briefly be discussed, as they have already been referred to in passing earlier.

Taken together, the passages clearly condemn homosexuality, just as the Old Testament passages do. "When one comes to the New Testament, there is no softening of Scripture's negative assessment of homosexuality found in the Old Testament."[30] Thus we find a continuity of thought between the two Testaments on this issue.

Romans 1

One of the most significant passages on homosexuality is Romans 1:18-32. Here Paul tells us why the wrath of God falls on the Gentiles. He will later do the same concerning the Jews (2:1-3:8). In verses 18-23, Paul argues that God's judgment comes down on those who suppress the truth of God and turn to idolatry. In verses 24-32, the consequences of this rebellion against God are spelled out in

Paul views homosexuality as a major example of the rejection of God.

detail, with homosexuality a main example of such idolatry and rejection of God. Verses 26-27 specifically refer to homosexuality: "Because of this, God gave them over to shameful lusts. Even their women exchanged natural relations for unnatural ones. In the same way the men also abandoned natural relations with women and were inflamed with lust for one another. Men committed indecent acts with other men, and received in themselves the due penalty for their perversion."

Thus Paul views homosexuality as a major example of the rejection of God. Indeed, as Joseph Fitzmyer comments, "Paul [singles out] homosexual conduct as an example of moral perversion. ... Paul sees homosexual conduct as a symbol of the perversion stemming from idolatry".[31]

And as Paul argues in verse 27, the penalty for rejecting God is the handing over to the sin of homosexuality. That is, Paul seems to suggest that "the sexual perversion itself is the punishment".[32] Or as Morris puts it: "The punishment for the conduct involved in idolatry was their being given over to shameful lusts."[33]

Paul argues that homosexuality goes against the natural order as God created it. Many commentators focus on this aspect of Paul's argument. Says Schreiner: "Paul rejects homosexuality as contrary to the created order – homosexual activity is a violation of what God intended when he created men and women."[34] Or as Stott remarks, "to act 'against nature' means to violate the order which God had established".[35]

Or as Ben Witherington comments: "Paul certainly believes there is a natural order of things that God put into creation which ought to be followed. In verse 27 he speaks of a corresponding penalty for such 'unnatural behavior.' ... In Paul's view homosexual behavior flows naturally from idolatry in that it is a rejection of the creation order that the Creator God set up in the first place."[36]

C.K. Barrett reminds us of just how pronounced this sin was: "No feature of pagan society filled the Jews with greater loathing than the toleration, or rather admiration, of homosexual practices. Paul is utterly at one here with his compatriots; but his disgust is more than instinctive. In the obscene pleasures to which he refers is to be seen precisely that perversion of the created order which may be expected when men put the creation in place of the Creator. That idolatry has such consequences is to Paul a plain mark of God's wrath."[37]

R.C. Sproul cuts to the quick here:[38]

> When we become involved in homosexual practices, we are not only sinning against God but against the nature of things. All the debates today about whether homosexual behaviour is acquired or inherently genetic can be answered here in this text. The Word of God says that such behaviour is not normal. It is against nature as God created it.

And it is not just homosexual acts that Paul condemns. He speaks of those who were "inflamed with lust for one another" (v. 27). The desires are just as evil as the acts, Paul says. But some revisionists claim that Paul simply warns against pederasty (having sex with boys) here. But the bulk of New Testament scholarship rejects such views.

As Dunn notes: "Paul's indictment seems to include all kinds of homosexual practice, female as well as male, and was not directed against one kind of homosexual practice in distinction from another".[39] Or, as Morris puts it, "Paul is saying in strong terms that the men were burned up with a powerful but unnatural passion."[40]

As another commentator put it:[41]

There is no more a Christian form of homosexuality than there is a Christian form of adultery or bestiality or rape, etc. Romans 1 makes no room for any kind of homosexuality whatsoever, for it is plainly and simply 'error' and wrong lifestyle. If Paul's words can be twisted to allow for homosexuality under certain conditions, the same line of thought can be taken with all of the sins elaborated in verses 28-31 – indeed, with any sin whatsoever!

It is also significant that this passage includes lesbianism. It is "the only passage in the Bible that refers to lesbian sexual relations".[42] Thus male homosexuality and female lesbianism are both subject to the wrath of God.

Also, this passage is not condemning merely the abuse or perversion of same-sex relations, as some revisionists seek to argue. As Belleville explains:[43]

It is important to notice that what is shameful is not same-sex perversions but same-sex activities per se. Paul states in the first part of verse 26 that God 'gave humanity over to dishonorable passions.' He then goes on to identify these dishonorable passions with the exchange – not the abuse – of natural sexual relations for unnatural ones."

Also, the creation language of 'masculine' (*arsen*) and 'feminine' (*thely*) shows that Paul is concerned with a reversal of the created order of male and female, and not with perversions or abuses of same-sex relations. It is men and women acting against their universally created nature as heterosexuals that marks the activity as 'shameful' and 'indecent'.

This entire passage teaches in unmistakable clarity that homosexuality is a prime example of the rebellion and idolatry of which fallen mankind is a part. As Fitzmyer puts it: "Homosexual behavior is the sign of human rebellion against God, an outward manifestation of the inward spiritual rebellion. It illustrates human degradation and provides a vivid image of humanity's rejection of the sovereignty of God."[44]

Sproul concurs:[45]

When the apostle Paul describes the radical corruption of the human race, he sees the sin of homosexual behavior as the sin most representative of the radical nature of our fall. It is seen here not simply as a sin, nor even as a serious sin or a gross sin, but as the clearest expression of the depths of our perversity.

Or as Dr J.J. Davis has said: "In Romans 1, homosexuality is seen not merely as a violation of some Jewish or Christian sectarian code, but as a transgression of the basic moral law of God known in all cultures."[46]

1 Corinthians 6

Another important passage is 1 Cor 6:9-11:

> Do you not know that the wicked will not inherit the kingdom of God? Do not be deceived: Neither the sexually immoral nor idolaters nor adulterers nor male prostitutes nor homosexual offenders nor thieves nor the greedy nor drunkards nor slanderers nor swindlers will inherit the kingdom of God. And that is what some of you were. But you were washed, you were sanctified, you were justified in the name of the Lord Jesus Christ and by the Spirit of our God.

Two Greek words are used here: *malakoi*, for "male prostitutes" and *arsenokoitai* for "homosexual offenders". Some revisionists claim that this passage refers to male prostitution, not homosexuality. But the context says nothing of such a distinction. And the literal meaning of the second word *arsenokoitai* is "a male who [sexually] lies with a male".

The etymology and immediate context make it clear that homosexuality is in view.[47] As Barrett remarks, the second term should be translated "sodomites" and it refers to "the passive and active partners respectively in male homosexual relations".[48] Or as one Greek scholar has said, "arsenokoites is a broad term that cannot be confined to specific instances of homosexual activity such as male prostitution or pederasty."[49] See more on this term below.

The first term, *malakoi*, literally means soft, and can be translated as effeminate. In Greek literature the term can mean a number of things. Here in context the term can mean the passive homosexual partner. Thus both words, in the context of the vice list, refer to unacceptable sexual practices, specifically homosexual practices.

Of course the theological revisionists "seek to water down any condemnation in the NT of homo-erotic acts", as David Garland notes. But much "of this attempt to recast the traditional link of these words to male same-sex eroticism appears to be driven by special pleading and riddled with obfuscation".[50]

After an extensive examination of the terms in question, Anthony Thiselton offers this summation: "What is clear from the connection between 1 Cor 6:9 and Rom 1:26-29 and their OT backgrounds is Paul's endorsement of the view that idolatry, i.e., placing human autonomy to construct one's values above covenant commitments to God, leads to a collapse of moral values in a kind of domino effect."[51]

Ciampa and Rosner concur:[52]

> Paul's opposition to all homosexual behavior (clearly targeting those who engaged in it freely and willingly) seems to derive from Leviticus 18:22 and 20:13, which represent absolute bans. Paul's opposition to homosexual acts was not because he had not thought about the subject or had simply taken over a conventional list of vices from Hellenistic authors, whether Jewish or secular ... Paul opposed homosexual behavior on the basis of creation theology and because it is marked as a vice in the Torah and was stressed as a vice by Jews.

1 Timothy

The relevant verses here are in chapter one: "We also know that law is made not for the righteous but for lawbreakers and rebels, the ungodly and sinful, the unholy and irreligious; for those who kill their fathers or mothers, for murderers, for adulterers and perverts, for slave traders and liars and perjurers – and for whatever else is contrary to the sound doctrine" (1:9-10).

The term rendered by the New International Version (NIV) as 'perverts' is *arsenokoitai*, which, as we have already seen, means males who take other males to bed. As scholars point out, it is a rare word. It "does not appear to have existed before the time of Paul".[53]

After examining some contemporary Greek and Roman usages of the term, New Testament scholar Ben Witherington says this: "This word literally and graphically refers to a male copulator, a man who has intercourse with another man."[54]

The compound word is made of two terms, *arsenos* (= male) and *koitain* (= sleep with, lie in bed, have sexual relations with, from which we get the word coitus, i.e., intercourse). "Male bedders" would be a literal, if somewhat wooden, translation. Sex between men, or homosexuality, is clearly in view here.

Both of these two terms come directly from the Septuagint (the Greek translation of the Old Testament) version of the two Leviticus passages. Lev. 18:22 contains both terms, as does 20:13. So Paul clearly has the Holiness

The term clearly covers all aspects of homosexuality, not just some.

Code in view when he used this term.[55] Scholars such as David Wright in fact believe that Paul coined this term from the two Leviticus texts.[56]

The term clearly covers all aspects of homosexuality, not just some. As George Knight comments, the "word does not refer, as some writers have alleged, only to sex with young boys or to male homosexual prostitutes, but simply to homosexuality itself (so Paul explicitly in Rom. 1:26, 27)."[57] Or as Quinn and Wacker argue, "the *arsenokoitai* are ... understood to be all homosexuals, active or passive, old or young".[58]

One leading expert on the Pastorals (the epistles of Paul to Timothy and Titus), Philip Towner, says this about the term in question: "It denotes, unequivocally, the activity of male homosexuality, and the view of this practice adopted in this text corresponds to that of Paul elsewhere (Rom. 1:27)."[59]

He goes on to rightly note: "Contemporary arguments that advocate the legitimacy of homosexuality cannot resort successfully to the biblical texts and etymology. The exegesis of these passages is not in question, and the fate of the current debate about homosexuality will rest on hermeneutics."[60]

One interesting aspect of this passage is the close connection between false doctrine and wrong living. Paul stresses the need for right living (orthopraxis) along with right doctrine (orthodoxy). Both feed off each other. Indeed, idolatry and immorality are often associated in the Old Testament. When we believe the wrong things, we start doing the wrong things. Also, when we act improperly, we start to believe improperly (e.g., try to rationalise our behaviour). The two are closely bound up with each other. Thus Paul here shows that false teaching is closely connected with immoral and ungodly living.

2 Peter 2

In 2 Peter 2:4-10 Peter gives three examples of God's judgment on sinful activity, including the Sodom account. He refers to the judgment on Sodom and Gomorrah and says this is an example of what God will do with the ungodly. While homosexuality is not directly mentioned here, it is pretty clear that Peter has it firmly in mind.

As Thomas Schreiner remarks: "Peter did not identify the sin of the cities but directed attention to their judgment. Probably there was no need to highlight the sin since it was well known both from the Scriptures and post-biblical tradition."[61]

Also, verse 10 speaks of "those who follow the corrupt desire of the flesh and despise authority". But as Douglas Moo points out: "The NIV rendering of this first description is too mild. Peter piles up some very strong words; a literal rendering is 'going after flesh in a passionate longing for defilement.' The reference is to sexual sin, probably including, in light of Peter's reference to Sodom and Gomorrah in verse 6, homosexuality."[62]

And the sexual sin is compounded by a despising and rejection of authority. As Witherington notes: "Judgment is especially reserved for those who commit grievous sexual sins (as at Sodom and Gomorrah) and despise dominion."[63]

Jude

This passage (Jude 1:4-8) is also about the Sodom story. And it is even more explicit as to why God's judgment broke forth: because of "sexual immorality and perversion". The Greek term, translated "perversion" in the New International Version, literally means "going after other flesh", as the New American Standard Bible, for example, renders it.

Schreiner notes how not only the biblical testimony is clear as to the nature of their sin, but so too are the extra-biblical references to Sodom and Gomorrah. For example, he cites writers such as Josephus and Philo, and notes various writings, such as *Testament of Naphtali*, *Testament of Levi*, and *Jubilees*.[64]

> **All in all, the New Testament witness is quite clear: homosexuality is not permissible in any form.**

Notice also that both Peter and Jude tie in the rejection of authority and appropriate (divine) structure as part of the reason for God's judgment. Jerome Neyrey speaks of the "symbolic universe of the ancients":[65]

> Ancient Jews and Greeks alike thought of the universe and all in it as a *kosmos*, an organised and structured whole. ... Something is 'pure' or 'clean' when it is in accord with the social expectation of order and propriety; conversely, things are 'polluted' or 'unclean' when they violate the common assumptions of the way the world is structured. ...
>
> [Therefore] Sodom and Gomorrah violate the biblical purity code by going after 'other flesh,' and so become polluted. ... Sodom and Gomorrah cause pollution by crossing the lines of acceptable sexual partners. Paul reflects the same pollution code in Rom

1:26-37, where he labels this pollution as 'shameful'.

Gene Green concurs: "The sexual aspect of their sin is the vehicle by which they had violated the order established by God."[66]

All in all, the New Testament witness is quite clear: homosexuality is not permissible in any form. Hays makes this summarising comment:[67]

> The New Testament offers no loopholes or exception clauses that might allow for the acceptance of homosexual practices under certain circumstances. Despite the efforts of some recent interpreters to explain away the evidence, the New Testament remains unambiguous and univocal in its condemnation of homosexual conduct.

Other biblical texts

In addition to the above clear and explicit texts, there are a number of other texts which could be appealed to here. For example, there are a number of other texts which refer to Sodom and its sins, such as Is 1:9-10; Is 3:9; Jer 23:14; Lam 4:6; Ezek 16:43-58; Matt 10:14-15; and Matt 11:22-24.

There are also the various passages which speak of "shrine prostitutes", as in the New International Version. These include: Deut 23:17-18; 1 Kings 14:24; 1 Kings 15:12; 1 Kings 22:46; and 2 Kings 23:7. The King James Version and the American Standard Version, for example, render the relevant term as "sodomite" or "catamite" (a boy kept for the purposes of pederasty).[68]

If we gather together the evidence from both Testaments, and the inter- and extra-testamental literature, the message is overwhelmingly clear: homosexuality is simply a no-go zone. As one biblical ethicist has put it, the entire scriptural revelation rules out homosexuality "for absolutely everyone *without mentioning any exception or condition*". He says:[69]

> The prohibition is stated in terms that are universal, absolute, and unconditional and that simply leave no room for restrictions based on anything at all, including speculations arising from

(future) theories regarding human psychology or biology. ... No one is excused, no matter what.

And even some of those arguing the homosexual revisionist case will concede this point. For example, the homosexual writer and theologian Pim Pronk said this: "To sum up, wherever homosexual intercourse is mentioned in Scripture, it is

> **In sum, the message of the revisionists is neither biblical, nor Christian, nor compassionate.**

condemned."[70] But he nonetheless wrote an entire book seeking to show that Scripture is wrong.

Conclusion

In sum, the message of the revisionists is neither biblical, nor Christian, nor compassionate. There is no biblical warrant for their twisted theology. There is no Christian case to embrace the homosexual lifestyle. And, given what an unhealthy and dead-end lifestyle this is, there is nothing compassionate about refusing to stand on Scripture here.

We must expose the error that is misleading the church and entrapping homosexuals who desperately need to be delivered from their oppressive and harmful lifestyle. And we need to resist those who seek to rewrite Scripture to justify their own immoral lifestyles.

Finally, we need to keep re-affirming the importance of sound doctrine along with godly living. In an atmosphere of loose living and loose doctrine, Christians need to remain vigilant and committed to the authority and truthfulness of Scripture, both in faith and in practice.

POSTSCRIPT

People's Journeys out of Homosexuality

One Man's Story
by Ron Brookman (Australia)

It certainly felt that I had no choice over my homosexuality. Bathed aged five years with other boys, I was attracted to them. Somehow I connected to them through their nakedness, etching something deep into my developing sexuality. Six years later I was invited to a sleepover at a male friend's home. I welcomed his friendship. Having recently moved, I missed my friends in Adelaide. That night my friend seduced me. Initially I did not realise what was happening, but enjoyed the experience. It was sharp relief to the batterings my dad handed out. Hidings were the only experience of touch I had from him. The sleepovers became regular. I even lived with that family for six weeks.

At the end of that year our family moved again, this time to Sydney, so over four years I made at least two trips a year back to Melbourne. I was a young teenager, desperately in search of intimacy. During latter high school years I thought I should try to have relationships with girls, but my awkwardness, their rejection, probably due to my lack of interest, and my desire to spend time with the mates I was attracted to undermined that.

Spending my early 20s as a teacher in a country city, I again tried to have relationships with girls. I even became unofficially engaged to two! My relationships were not remotely sexual. Passion with women was something I could not engender. My constant fantasies of having a life-long relationship with a man, emptied my friendships with women of any sincerity. Being intuitive of that, they gently said "goodbye". In turn, my habit of putting myself to sleep at night by dreaming of being in the arms of whatever man I was attracted to at the time, grew stronger. In the 1970s homosexuality was still considered odd. There being no evidence of it in my country town, same-sex attraction remained a consuming passion in my mind.

In my mid-20s, lust and fantasy brimmed over to pornography when I discovered a source, enabling me to gaze on airbrushed photos of naked men. Thrills of childhood bath times returned in glossy photos! Pornography made me all the

> **I knew innately that my sexuality was not according to human anatomy.**

more aware of the physical frame of men, so I became the taskmaster of the surreptitious stare. Fantasies became more complex, and my yearning for that lifelong male partner all the more intense. I needed him to complete me, and hold me. I needed his strength, his powerful masculine form, his deep but tender voice whispering in my ear, and his constant company until death parted us. I needed his affirmation, presence and delight. To have him standing by my side, so that others could see that we were one in thought, activity and domesticity, inseparable through life, would make my life complete. I couldn't write the word *"love"* there, because to my Christian friends that was unthinkable. Somehow in my naïveté I thought that I could have all that, and others not suspect what lay beneath!

Did I have a choice, simply to renounce homosexuality and convert to heterosexuality? By no means! Attraction to men lay deep in every fibre of my being, as though it was part of my DNA. Yet I was also ambivalent. I knew innately that my sexuality was not according to human anatomy. From a Christian viewpoint, I knew that it countered the straightforward teaching of the Scriptures. I asked God to change me, but only ever half-heartedly, because homosexual desire was my only real passion.

An attempt at marriage

The desire to try to conform in part led to my being married in 1978. Mistaking compassion for love, and an ecstatic experience for God's voice, I asked a Christian lady a few years younger, to marry me. Narcissism rang through my proposal. She was to marry me to help me realise the greatness God had called me to. Three months later, on our wedding day, I desperately wanted not to go ahead, but could not call our marriage off, for fear of being seen to be unstable, and for not wanting to let down my bride.

Our marriage was disastrous. It was not consummated for at least four days, and then under duress. Somehow we conceived during the six years we were married and gave birth to two great kids. Frankly I hated hetero sex, and was unable to participate.

The breakdown of my marriage, and the loss of my kids, led to my allowing myself to be seduced by my gay neighbours. In my pain, I ran back to the joy of my adolescence. Sexually active again, I sought the man of my dreams. I spent the next six years leading a clandestine life in the gay precincts of Newtown, Darlinghurst, and whatever city I travelled to. My search for my lifelong companion, seemed doomed to fail. Unless he was absolutely *Mr Right*, I would not be able to take him because such a lifestyle would be a repudiation of my evangelical ministry. I would lose everything.

Could I make a compromise and shift my theological stance to accommodate my sexuality? Being a minister of the Uniting Church meant that was a possibility. However, my conviction remained that both Scripture and human anatomy point to heterosexuality as God's plan for sexuality. Because both his Word and design testify to heterosexuality, who was I to challenge it, regardless of the apparent unchangeable intensity of my sexual feelings and drive? I could not find peace. I could neither fully embrace homosexuality, nor turn from it. My frustration was immense. My anger, shame and sense of self-hatred grew by the month. Why couldn't God just change me? But then, change me to what? I didn't want to be hetero. I could be attracted only to men. How could I expect God to change that?

The power of the Gospel

Deeper down I was convinced that he could. My spirit testified to something greater than that powerful desire of my soul and drive of my flesh. I had meditated long and deep on the death of Jesus. I saw how he became sin in its entirety, to enable us to cast it off in its entirety, to become the righteousness of God. He suffered so that we could be made whole. His resurrection revealed his power over sin, death and the powers of darkness. The fruit of his resurrection, the gift of the Holy Spirit, work in us to change us by degree into his glory and image. As powerful as my homosexual drive was, as natural as it seemed, as desperately as I wanted lifelong union with a man, I knew that these did not conform to God's Word or design, and therefore, to his image or righteousness. If Jesus' death was effective to remove our brokenness, defects and non-conformity to his purpose, to any extent at all, it needed to be to every extent, including our sexuality. This conviction, coming from my spirit, was deeper than my soul's desire. Our spirit connects to God. Our soul to others.

After six years of active homosexuality, tempered by times of seeking God for an answer and of serving him in my church (albeit hypocritically), I was burnt out. Keeping up the deceitfulness of my secret life, the emotional rollercoaster of on-and-off-again relationships with prospective men, and the guilt of participating in the raunchy promiscuity of the lifestyle, took its toll. I was trapped, powerless to change, and still ambivalent. Only God's grace could save me. In his kindness, God responded to my cry. He proved the power of his Cross, and my confidence in it.

Slowly does it!

The process was gradual. He changed me as I contemplated him and saw his beauty. My desire for men was superseded by a greater desire for him. As I waited upon him, communion with him was a two-way exchange. His love and wholeness flowed into my soul, while my brokenness was slowly assumed by him. As I found security in him I no longer needed to look for it in a male companion.

I met fortnightly with a pastor friend to whom I was accountable for any dalliance I might take back into my sin. There were many. Over the first 18 months I struggled with my need for bodily connection. Any time I made an encounter I confessed it to David. He would speak the promise of God's forgiveness over me, and pray that God would release his healing into the wounded recesses of my soul. Finally I was healed enough, and sufficiently responsive to God's command to be able to finally repent and break free from my need for sexual contact with men. Over the following 12 months I similarly cut ties with pornography, then in the next six months broke the habit pattern of lust and fantasy.

The dawning of true love

Towards the end of that time I found a new attraction. Ruth was a younger lady in my congregation and "some chemistry" flowed between us. I had never experienced attraction and the desire to know a woman before. We submitted our relationship to our elders. I could not bring myself to share with her the homosexuality from which I was extricating myself. Because I was too "raw" in heterosexual masculinity to make Ruth feel safe, our friendship floundered. Ruth moved away.

But my attraction for her did not go away, nor hers for me, gratefully! Some 12 months later we expressed our care for each other and resumed exploring where our relationship would lead. There was something about Ruth. She had such a tender heart of compassion, a purity, a zeal for justice, and a deep love for the Lord. She was tall (I am only 5 foot 6 inches), beautiful, walked with dignity and brimmed with a smile that effervesced from her heart. Her flowing black hair crowned her beauty. She was astonishing! There was no thought of the need for a man when I looked at her! She complemented me wonderfully! I was still quite broken, though not same-sex attracted. The deeper issues that had enabled homosexuality to embed in my soul were still to be dealt with. I somehow knew that Ruth's exquisite beauty, her stunning looks delightfully displaying the depths of her inner charm, brought a rich complement to my life. Only I knew how shameful I felt. She had dignity. Only I knew how broken I was (and then not the half!), she seemed so whole. I was man, she was woman! I lacked integrity, she had it all! I was a *"just do it"* person. Ruth was a *"let's think about the implications"* person. Writing this, I feel sad that I could not offer myself to her as a good gift. I was still becoming that good gift. Love is not to take from the other, but in the giving of self, to receive the good gift of the other. Though I didn't disclose to Ruth my broken life, she trusted me and grew to love me. My attraction for her grew into love, and our mutual love, into marriage! In 1994 we were married at Newtown Mission, where I was still senior pastor.

Our marriage has passed through many challenges that we have turned to growth opportunities. When I finally disclosed to Ruth my past, 18 months into our marriage, she initially dealt with it with immediate forgiveness, and ongoing trust. It wasn't until two years later, when I finally also disclosed to my church my past, that she was alerted to the deeper issues which her love for me had glossed over. She came to realise that I duped her in presenting myself to her as one person, in asking her to marry me, but in fact being a very different person. Still, she stood by me as I underwent the shame of discipline, and ultimate resignation. That led to a Living Waters internship, where the course, and personal counsel, enabled us to work through our issues.

I recognised and repented of the false self I had presented to her, and to all around me. Ruth's gentle but non-negotiable insistence that I deal with, and strip away, my layers of dishonesty, defence, pride, survival, driven-ness and insecurity enabled me to grow into the integrity and self-appreciation that had always eluded me. Indeed, the qualities that I first perceived in Ruth stimulated me to yield the chrysalis of my false self, to emerge into the freedom and beauty that God meant me to have.

Our marriage continues to cross-stimulate us to grow as people, individually and together, the good of both genders complementing and stretching one another, to bring out the best in each, and both. Though it sometimes seems too hard, once I embrace the process, the change and maturing it stimulates bring an exhilaration and greater fullness to life! Moving from the safety, familiarity and myopia of limiting my vulnerable relationships to the masculine, has realised a new man! Our marriage has been life-giving in another significant way too! Our love for each other has conceived and given birth to three wonderful children, now 15, 13 and 12. Raising them together is a great delight – again, bringing out gender differences in approach, and requiring mutual growth to nurture them well. I am able to address issues with my younger three which I couldn't with my older two, because I didn't have the insight, skill and matured love. This is the fruit that healthy encounter in marriage has brought.

APPENDIX 2

One Woman's Story
by "Sarah" (Australia)

I grew up going to various churches, so I know what it is to discover I was homosexual in a church environment. The internal conflict about what I believed and how others would judge me was overwhelming. In the end, my desire to be with another woman won and I left the church.

Having tossed my faith in, I now totally embraced life as a lesbian. My first relationship was so compelling and obsessive that I thought I had found my soul mate. Never had I experienced such an all-consuming connection with anyone. It overrode any intent I had to live as person of faith, even though I had enough evidence to believe that God existed and that the Bible was his Word. Now I had the confusion of trying to understand what I saw as divine cruelty in creating me lesbian and yet condemning me to rejection.

When my "soul mate" left me for someone else, I was crushed. However, now I had no doubt that I was homosexual. I had a repulsion toward men and had found where I fitted amongst my lesbian friends. I now lived with the hope of finding my "Miss Right". However, after a number of relationships, some longer-term than others, I had come to a point where I didn't dare to love, as it led to too much pain. I had lost all illusions that I was going to find life with a woman, but now I was truly trapped by my orientation.

I felt that there had been some biological mix-up and I was really a male soul in a woman's body. I would have certainly had physical reassignment, except that I was far more afraid of my mother than I was of God. God did not seem fearsome to me, but rather remote, like my philosophical father.

At the age of 28 I had reached a stalemate. I was so ingrained in the belief that I had been "born that way and couldn't change" that I was contemplating suicide. If I couldn't reconnect in a real way with my God, then I could only see one alternative. The future alone and ageing as a lesbian and now an alcoholic, looked bleak to me.

Because I had been fully indoctrinated by popular cultural messages, I did not believe that I could change. However, a dim flicker of light remained, urging me to consider that perhaps I could find the God I had turned from. I asked him if he could somehow show me if this might be possible. If God really did exist and if he reached out to me, then I was ready to toss all hope of finding any good human love relationship. I hadn't succeeded in this area very well at all. I would be content to be single and sort my life out with God alone.

If God was willing, then I would leave every premise I had and simply follow him, trusting that in his goodness he could redefine me any way he wanted. If God didn't answer, then the only logical action for me was to end it all. If gay rhetoric was absolute, then I was trapped and the belief that I couldn't change held me in despair.

> **I simply walked away from the life I had been leading and sought my help from God.**

However, God did reach out to me in a rather amazing way, answering my one last desperate prayer by sending someone on that evening to talk with me and help me back to a life of faith. He was a gentle, loving Christian that I had known years before. I was able to talk to him about all the underlying pain as well as admitting my own wrongs – many of these issues were not about my homosexuality but were more about my rebellion against God.

I had no reparative therapy. No one counselled me. I simply walked away from the life I had been leading and sought my help from God. It was like "cold turkey". It was an extreme leap of faith. Going back to church where I had no friends and abandoning the places where I knew all my good friends hung out, was like a death and extremely difficult. But it became a new, magnificently fresh and life-breathing new start.

I did not come back to God to become "straight". I came back to follow Jesus. I wanted to be directed or changed by the Bible and by what I sensed God wanted from me, rather than any other opinion. I had lost my faith in cultural messages that had led me to the brink of despair. And I was wary of simply taking everything I heard from churches as well. As I had stopped partying and going to my favourite drinking spots, I saw few of my friends, although some did come to see me – it was a huge puzzle to them that any-one would even attempt to leave. I had been very involved in the life that I led and was very open about my orientation.

Now I had a lot of time alone and it was a valuable time of relearning and prayer. One of the first things God showed me was that I no longer needed to be identified as lesbian. My identity was in Christ. And that was all I needed.

I needed to learn how to be the woman that God had created. He had not made a mistake with my gender, and

> **The greatest help for me was reconstructing why I was as I was.**

he could show me how to be the person he had intended me to be. Later, I married, but this certainly was not my aim and I was as astonished as anyone that I could have come to such a decision.

The greatest help for me was reconstructing why I was as I was. I started to see a pattern of detachment with nearly all of my friends for one reason or another. For me it had been because I was the last of three children. The eld-est was a boy who was at the lowest functioning level of autism. He required

24-hour care. My mother often said she was glad I was a quiet baby as she only had time to feed and clothe me. A baby needs more contact than this to wire the brain for healthy connections later, and for a girl it can mean looking for connection with a woman, since this initial function never began well.

When my brother drowned at the age of 12, my family became a dark and grieving place in which to grow up. I began to think that if I were a boy I would be able to take my brother's place and perhaps find the love from my parents that I so craved. There were many other factors in my developing childhood. As I looked back, I could see that my affections had been for women from as early as I could remember. This was one of the self-assessments that made me believe that I must surely have been "born that way". I now do not believe that and can see clearly how my orientation was formed from the earliest years, becoming active in adulthood.

I had to come to terms with my mother's damaged personality and as an adult I was able to see her illness for what it had been. Forgiveness for her verbal and emotional abuse came slowly. My father had coped with the family dramas by simply not being around. I had barely any relationship with my remote father and certainly no endorsement from him of who I was as a female.

I am not saying that this is a complete pattern for everyone, as everyone has a different journey and there is no one pattern. But I could now understand and unravel my own story. At 28, I finally realised that no human can complete us. Now, I no longer wanted to identify my life around my sexuality. My plan was to live celibate and be a follower of Jesus, doing whatever he gave me to do. However, God's plan for me included marriage and a wonderful, and now decades-long, union.

Some of my gay friends led short lives and this is very sad, as I knew those who self-destructed were not ones that felt unaccepted by society, but were those who like me, wanted "out of out". Unfortunately, because it is considered bad to let people self-identify, these friends never knew that perhaps there was hope of a different life for them too.

Today it is considered, even by some misguided churches, harmful to try to attempt living by biblical truth. So, truth is now cramped and reinterpreted into current culture. But because of my story and finding that God is greater than any labels or orientation that I had, I hope that others can find this too. I feel it is harmful and unloving to not give people the right to make their own choices, find help, and hope in a God who is able to change anyone.

Forcing people to have only one option, to accept their homosexuality, hurts the many that are like me: we are now seen as the enemy, even by some churches. Silencing post-gay voices will be a sad day, as it denies freedom from what human feelings may dictate and freedom to be who God intended, within his design and will.

I have used a pseudonym, because in telling my story I have found that I have come under a lot of attack.

REFERENCES AND ENDNOTES

Chapter 1.   Strategies of the Homosexual Lobby

1   Daniel Patrick Moynihan, "Defining deviancy down", *The American Scholar*, Winter 1993, pp. 17-30.

2   Roger Magnuson, *Are Gay Rights Right?* (Portland, Oregon: Multnomah Press, 1990), p. 23.

3   Paul Rondeau, "Selling homosexuality to America", *Regent University Law Review*, vol. 14, no. 2, 2001-2002, pp. 443-485.

4   Adam Cresswell, "Lesbian kisses raise tolerance", *The Australian*, April 20, 2007, p. 8.

5   Marshall Kirk and Erastes Pill, "The overhauling of straight America", *The Guide*, November 1987.

6   Marshall Kirk and Hunter Madsen [the real name of Erastes Pill], *After the Ball: How America Will Conquer Its Hatred and Fear of Homosexuals in the 90s* (New York: Plume, 1990), pp. 186-187.

7   Ibid., p. 275.

8   Dennis Altman, *The Homosexualization of America* (New York: St. Martin's Press, 1982), p. 9.

Chapter 2.   Homosexual Practices and Behaviour

1   Charles Silverstein and Edmund White, *Joy of Gay Sex* (New York: Crown Pub., 1977), cited in Cal Thomas, "Behavior does not deserve special protection", *Los Angeles Times*, February 4, 1993.

2   Dan Savage, as cited in Jesse Monteagudo, "Much ado about Dan Savage", *GayToday*, March 6, 2000. URL: http://gaytoday.badpuppy.com/garchive/people/030600pe.htm

3   Kirk and Madsen, *After the Ball, op. cit.*, p. 47.

4   Ibid., p. 48.

5   Silverstein and White, *op. cit.*

6   Ibid.

7 Cited in Roger Magnuson, *Are Gay Rights Right?, op.cit.,* p. 44.

8 An anonymous respondent, cited in Karla Jay and Allen Young, *The Gay Report* (New York: Summit, 1979), p. 250.

9 Alan Bell and Martin Weinberg, *Homosexualities. A Study of Diversity Among Men and Women* (New York: Simon and Schuster, 1978), pp. 85, 86, 308, 312.

10 Thomas Schmidt, *Straight & Narrow: Compassion & Clarity in the Homosexuality Debate* (Downers Grove, Illinois: InterVarsity Press, 1995), p. 101.

11 Ibid., p. 108.

12 San Francisco Men's Health Study, *Journal of the American Medical Association,* vol. 257, no. 3, January 16, 1987, p. 323.

13 Paul Van de Ven, et al., "A comparative demographic and sexual profile of older homosexually active men", *Journal of Sex Research,* 34, 1997, p. 354.

14 Guy Baldwin, cited in Doug Sadownick, "Open door policy", *Genre,* April 1994, p. 34.

15 Bill Mann (and Tim Hube), cited in Sadownick, *ibid.,* p. 35.

16 Ross Jacobs, "Is monogamy the death knell of relationships?", *MCV: Melbourne's Gay and Lesbian Community Voice,* January 9, 2004, p. 6.

17 Dennis Altman, *The Homosexualization of America,* p. 17.

18 Dennis Altman, *AIDS in the Mind of America* (New York: Anchor Press/Doubleday, 1986), p. 159.

19 *The Homosexualization of America,* p. 187.

20 Ibid., p. 188.

21 Schmidt, *op. cit.,* p. 108.

22 David McWhirter and Andrew Mattison, *The Male Couple: How Relationships Develop* (Englewood Cliffs, New Jersey: Prentice-Hall, 1984), pp. 252-253.

23 Maria Xiridou, et al., "The contribution of steady and casual partnerships to the incidence of HIV infection among homosexual men in Amsterdam", *AIDS,* vol. 17, no. 7, May 2003, pp. 1029-1038, p. 1031.

24 Ibid.

25 Bell and Weinberg, *op. cit.,* p.308.

26 Garrett Prestage, et al., *Sydney Men and Sexual Health* (Sydney: HIV AIDS & Society Publications, 1995).

27 Prestage, *ibid.,* Report C.2, "Sexual identity and sexual behaviour with both men and women in a sample of homosexuality-active men in Sydney, Australia", p. 34.

28 Garrett Prestage, et al., *Sydney Gay Community Periodic Survey* (Sydney: HIV AIDS & Society Publications, 1996), p. 16.

29 Paul Van de Ven, et al., *Melbourne Gay Community Periodic Survey: February 1998* (Sydney: National Centre in HIV Social Research, 1998), p. 14.

30 June Crawford, et al., *Male Call 96: National Telephone Survey of Men Who Have Sex With Men* (Sydney: National Centre in HIV Social Research, 1998), p. 40.

31 Clive Aspin, et al., *The Melbourne Gay Community Periodic Survey February 2000* (Sydney: National Centre in HIV Social Research, 2000), p. 19.

32 Garrett Prestage, et al., *Sydney Gay Community Periodic Survey*. Sydney: Report Series C.4.: "Changes in behaviour over time". (Sydney: National Centre in HIV Epidemiological and Clinical Research and National Centre in HIV Social Research, January 2000).

33 Ibid., p. 7.

34 Ibid., p. 9.

35 Paul Van de Ven, et al., *Queensland Gay Community Periodic Survey: June 1999* (Sydney: National Centre in HIV Social Research, 1999), p. 18.

36 Andrew Grulich, et al., "Homosexual experience and recent homosexual encounters", *Australian and New Zealand Journal of Public Health*, vol. 27, no. 2, 2003, pp. 155-163, p. 158.

37 Iryna Zablotska, et al., *Gay Community Periodic Survey* (Sydney: National Centre in HIV Social Research, 2007), pp. 14-15.

38 Lance Spurr, "Sexless in the city", *B.News*, January 3, 2002, p. 8.

39 Jonathan Rauch, *Gay Marriage: Why it is Good for Gays, Good for Straights, and Good for America* (New York: Times Books, 2004), pp. 146-147.

40 Jamie Pandaram, "Gay sex forces store to close toilets", *The Age* (Melbourne), October 30, 2006.

41 Ibid.

42 Georgina Windsor, "Gays, lesbians show support for Labor", *The Australian*, July 29, 1994.

43 Robert Michael, et al., *Sex in America: A Definitive Survey* (Boston: Brown, Little & Company, 1994), pp 101-107.

44 Ibid.

45 Michael Wiederman, "Extramarital sex: Prevalence and correlates in a national survey", *Journal of Sex Research*, 34, 1997, p. 170.

46 E.O. Laumann, et al., *The Social Organization of Sexuality: Sexual Practices in the United States* (Chicago: University of Chicage Press, 1994), p. 217.

47 Gunnar Andersson, et al., "Divorce-risk: Patterns in same-sex 'marriages' in Norway and Sweden", paper presented at the 2004 annual meeting of the Population Association of America (April 3, 2004).

48 "Lesbians at greater risk, says report", *MCV* (Melbourne), September 26, 2003, p. 4.

49 Ulrike Boehmer, Deborah Bowen and Greta Bauer, "Overweight and obesity in sexual-minority women: Evidence from population-based data", *American Journal of Public Health*, June 2007, vol. 97, issue 6, pp. 1134-1140.

50 Catherine Mercer, et al., "Women who report having sex with women: British national probability data on prevalence, sexual behaviors, and health outcomes", *American Journal of Public Health*, vol. 97, issue 6, June 2007, pp. 1126-1133.

51 Bernard Klamecki, "Medical perspective of the homosexual issue", in J. Isamu Yamamoto, ed., *The Crisis of Homosexuality* (Wheaton, Illinois.: Victor Books, 1990), p. 107.

52 These practices especially involve the use of urine and faeces.

53 Kirk Cameron and Kay Proctor, "Effect of homosexuality upon public health and social order", *Psychological Reports* 64 (1989), pp. 1167-1174.

54 Garrett Prestage, et al., *Sydney Men and Sexual Health* (Sydney: HIV AIDS & Society

Publications, 1995), Report C.2, *op. cit.*, p. 38.

55 Ibid., p. 39.

56 Garrett Prestage, et al., *Sydney Gay Community Periodic Survey.* Sydney: Report Series C.4.: "Changes in behaviour over time" (Sydney: National Centre in HIV Epidemiological and Clinical Research and National Centre in HIV Social Research, January 2000), p. 9.

57 Ibid., p. 13.

58 Ibid., p. 17.

59 Ibid., p. 17.

60 Jay and Young, *op. cit.*, p. 567.

61 Cameron and Proctor, *loc. cit.*

62 Cited in Julie Iovine, "Lipsticks and lords: Yale's new look", *Wall Street Journal*, August 4, 1987.

63 Charles Silverstein and Felice Picano, *The New Joy of Gay Sex* (New York: HarperPerennial, 1992), p. 171.

64 Edward Artnak and James Cerda, "The gay bowel syndrome", *Current Concepts in Gastroenterology*, July/Aug. 1983, p 6.

65 Ibid.

66 Jeffrey Carlisle, "Syphilis surge", *B.News*, September 9, 2004, p. 3.

67 Ibid.

68 Schmidt, *op. cit.*, p. 113.

69 Prestage, *op. cit.*, Report C.2, *op. cit.*, p. 45.

70 Juliet Richters, et al., *Sydney Gay Community Surveillance Report: Update to December 1997, Report No. 6.* Sydney: National Centre in HIV Social Research, Macquarie University, June 1998, p. 15.

71 James McKenzie, "Study finds higher drug use within the community", *Brother Sister*, July 6, 2000, p. 3.

72 Cited in Caroline Marcus, "Finely chop powder, alternate nostrils, says taxpayer-funded user guide to drugs", *Sunday Telegraph* (Sydney), January 23, 2011.
URL: www.news.com.au/national/finely-chop-powder-alternate-nostrils-says-taxpayer-funded-user-guide-to-drugs/story-e6frfkvr-1225992974162#ixzz1BqTTKIN4

73 As reported in "Up in smoke", *MCV* (Melbourne), April 23, 2004, p. 11.

74 "Gay men face eating disorders", *B.News*, April 25, 2002, p. 14.

75 Susan Cochran and Vickie Mays, "Physical health complaints among lesbians, gay men, and bisexual and homosexually experienced heterosexual individuals: Results from the California quality of life survey", *American Journal of Public Health, First Look*, April 26, 2007.
URL: www.ajph.org/cgi/content/abstract/AJPH.2006.087254v1

76 Roni Caryn Rabin, "Disparities: illness more prevalent among older gay adults", *New York Times*, April 5, 2011, p. D7.

77 Ibid.

78 AFP, "Gay men report higher cancer rates: U.S. study", *Sydney Morning Herald*, May 10, 2011.
URL: http://news.smh.com.au/breaking-news-world/gay-men-report-higher-cancer-rates--study-20110510-1eg0r.html

79   Schmidt, *op. cit.*, p. 130.

80   Robert Hogg, et al., "Modelling the impact of HIV disease on mortality in gay and bisexual men", *International Journal of Epidemiology*, vol. 26, no. 2, 1997, pp. 657–661, p. 657.

81   Vincent M.B. Silenzio, "Ten things gay men should discuss with their healthcare providers", Gay & Lesbian Medical Association (GLMA).
      URL: http://glma.org/index.cfm?fuseaction=Page.viewPage&pageID=690

82   Ibid.

83   Katherine A. O'Hanlan, "Ten things lesbians should discuss with their healthcare provider", GLMA.
      URL: www.glma.org/index.cfm?fuseaction=Page.viewPage&pageID=691

84   Dr Frank Spinelli, "Cruise control", *The Advocate*, February 18, 2011.
      URL: www.advocate.com/Health_and_Fitness/Living_Well/Cruise_Control/

85   David Island and Patrick Letellier, *Men Who Beat the Men Who Love Them: Battered Gay Men and Domestic Violence* (New York: Haworth Press, 1991), p. 14.

86   Gregory Greenwood, et al., "Battering victimization among a probability-based sample of men who have sex with men", *American Journal of Public Health*, vol. 92, no. 12, December 2002, pp. 1964-1969, p. 1964.

87   Lettie Lockhart, et al., "Letting out the secret: Violence in lesbian relationships", *Journal of Interpersonal Violence*, vol. 9, December 1994, pp. 469-492.

88   Gwat Yong Lie and Sabrina Gentlewarrier, "Intimate violence in lesbian relationships: Discussion of survey findings and practice implications", *Journal of Social Service Research*, 15, 1991, pp. 41-59.

89   Claire Renzetti, *Violent Betrayal: Partner Abuse in Lesbian Relationships* (New York: Sage Publications, 1992), p. 130.

90   "Gays threaten gays, AVP says", *MCV* (Melbourne), October 24, 2003, p. 5.

91   Letter to the editor, *MCV*, October 31, 2003, p. 7.

92   Andrew Milnes, "Hurting the one you love", *MCV*, November 7, 2003, p. 7.

93   Ibid.

94   Ibid.

95   Sherele Moody, "Games gonorrhoea, syphilis fears", *Melbourne Star*, October 17, 2002, p. 1.

96   Kirk and Madsen, *op. cit.*, pp. 177-178.

97   Cited in Magnuson, *op. cit.*, p 46.

98   Reported in George Grant and Mark Horne, *Legislating Immorality: The Homosexual Movement Comes Out of the Closet* (Chicago: Moody Press, 1993), pp 40, 42.

99   Cited in Magnuson, *op. cit.*, p 14.

100   Reported in Judith Reisman and Edward Eichel, *Kinsey, Sex and Fraud* (Lafayette, Louisiana: Huntington House Books, 1990), p. 213.

101   Andrew Lansdown, *Blatant and Proud: Homosexuals on the Offensive* (Perth, Western Australia: Perceptive Publications, 1984), p 100.

102   Ibid., p 105.

103   Dennis Altman, *AIDS in the Mind of America, op. cit.*, p. 144.

104   Sharon Sargent, "Gays cancel paedophilia workshop", *Weekend Australian*, September 1-2, 1984.

105   Judith Levine, *Harmful to Minors: The Perils of Protecting Children from Sex* (University of Minnesota Press, 2002/ New York: De Capo Press, 2003), p. 88.

106   Reported in Paul Cameron, *Exposing the AIDS Scandal* (Lafayette, Louisiana: Huntington House Publishers, 1988), p. 39.

107   Ibid.

108   K. Freund and R.I. Watson, "The proportions of heterosexual and homosexual pedophiles among sex offenders against children: an exploratory study", *Journal of Sex and Marital Therapy*, vol. 18, Spring 1992, pp. 34-43.

109   Ray Blanchard, et al., "Fraternal birth order and sexual orientation in pedophiles", *Archives of Sexual Behavior*, vol. 29, no. 5, 2002, pp. 463-478, at p. 463.

110   Ibid., p. 474.

111   Sherele Moody, "Minus 18 founder on teen sex charges", *Melbourne Star*, February 20, 2003, p. 1.

112   Peter Tatchell, "Equality is not enough", *Melbourne Star*, February 7, 2002, p. 18.

113   *Lambda Report*, August 1994, p 12.

114   Ibid.

115   Kirk and Madsen, *op. cit.*, pp.161, 170.

116   Dale O'Leary, *One Man, One Woman* (Manchester, New Hampshire: Sophia Institute Press, 2007), p. 29.

117   Cited in Trudy Hutchens, "Gay teen suicide: Myths and misconceptions", *Family Voice*, August 1996, p. 15.

118   Cited in Hutchens, *ibid.*, p. 13.

119   Cited in Delia Rios, "A bogus statistic that won't go away", *Citizen*, August 18, 1997, pp. 2-3.

120   Cited in Rios, *ibid.*, p. 3.

121   Gary Remafedi, James Farrow and Robert Deisher, "Risk factors for attempted suicide in gay and bisexual youth", *Pediatrics*, vol. 87, no. 6, June 1991, p. 873.

122   Marshall Kirk and Hunter Madsen, *After the Ball* (New York: Plume, 1990).

123   Beverley LaHaye, cited in Hutchens, *op. cit.*, p. 16.

Chapter 3.   The Politics of AIDS

1   Cited in John Ankerberg and John Weldon, *The Myth of Safe Sex* (Chicago: Moody Press, 1993), pp 148, 149.

2   Robert Hogg, et al., "Modelling the impact of HIV disease on mortality in gay and bisexual men", *International Journal of Epidemiology*, vol. 26, 1997, p. 657.

3   Darryl Fears, "Study puts HIV rate among gay men at 1 in 5", *Washington Post*, September 24, 2010.
       URL: www.washingtonpost.com/wp-dyn/content/article/2010/09/23/AR2010092306828.html

4   National Centre in HIV Epidemiology and Clinical Research, *Australian HIV Surveillance*

Update, vol. 10, no. 2, April 1994.

5   "More unsafe sex reported", *MCV: Melbourne's Gay and Lesbian Community Voice*, October 31, 2003, p. 5.

6   Adam Cresswell, "HIV cases highest in 10 years", *The Australian*, October 12, 2006, p. 2.

7   Clara Pirani, "Get AIDS sense or pay price", *The Australian*, April 2, 2007, p. 7.

8   National Centre in HIV Epidemiology and Clinical Research, *Australian HIV Surveillance Report*, vol. 23, no. 1, January 2007, p. 1.

9   Ibid., p. 7.

10   National Centre in HIV Epidemiology and Clinical Research, *Australian HIV Surveillance Update*, vol. 10, no. 2, April 1994.

11   Cited in Mary-Anne Toy, "Putting a rein on HIV", *The Age* (Melbourne), November 29, 1997.

12   Garrett Prestage, et al., *Sydney Gay Community Periodic Survey*. Sydney: Report Series C.4.: "Changes in behaviour over time" (Sydney: National Centre in HIV Epidemiological and Clinical Research and National Centre in HIV Social Research, January 2000), p. 28.

13   Robert Lusetich, "AIDS fears as gays spurn rubber", *The Australian*, September 8, 1999, p. 11.

14   Quoted in Georgina Safe, "Gay abandon", *The Australian*, September 21, 1999, p. 13.

15   Glenn Mitchell, "HIV jump as risks ignored", *Herald Sun* (Melbourne), January 5, 2001, p. 12.

16   Clive Aspin, et al., *Queensland Gay Community Periodic Survey: June 2000* (Sydney: National Centre in HIV Social Research, 2000), p. 22.

17   Steve Dow, "New HIV campaign needed", *B.News*, July 17, 2003, p. 4.

18   Ibid.

19   Jen Kelly, "HIV partners sought", *Herald Sun*, December 27, 2000, p. 20.

20   William Bennett, "For our children's sake", in Jo Ann Gasper, ed., *What You Need to Know About AIDS* (Ann Arbor, Michigan: Servant Books, 1989), p. 143.

21   Jennifer Vanasco, "It's our fault AIDS is still spreading", *Washington Blade*, February 1, 2002.

22   Adam Carr, "AIDS 2001: from gay male cancer to global epidemic", *B.News*, January 3, 2002, p. 28.

23   Lawrence McNamee and Brian McNamee, *AIDS: The Nation's First Politically Protected Disease* (La Habra, California: National Medical Legal Publishing House, 1988), p. 5.

24   Michael Fumento, *The Myth of Heterosexual AIDS* (New York: Basic Books, 1990), p. 151.

25   Ibid., p. 150.

26   McNamee and McNamee, *op. cit.*, p. 1.

27   Brendan O'Neill, "The exploitation of AIDS", *The Guardian* (UK), June 12, 2008. URL: www.guardian.co.uk/commentisfree/2008/jun/12/aids.health

28   Ibid.

29   Ibid.

30   Cited in Magnuson, *op. cit.*, p. 132.

31   Peter Papadopoulos, "Migration law and HIV/AIDS: 'A door closes but a window opens'", Australian Federation of AIDS Organisations (AFAO). URL: www.afao.org.au/view_articles.asp?pxa=ve&pxs=103&pxsc=127&pxsgc=139&id=593

32   Julie Robotham, "Drugs for HIV cost up to $59m", *The Age*, November 23, 1998, p. 8.

33   "Briefing paper for AFAO members: Federal Budget 2006-2007", AFAO, 2006. URL: www.afao.org.au/view_articles.asp?pxa=ve&pxs=170&pxsc=175&pxsgc=&id=565

34   Sue Williams, "Beyond the ordeal", *The Australian Magazine*, May 13 14, 1995, p. 12.

35   Julian Cribb, "Cancer the biggest killer for second year", *The Australian*, September 24, 1993.

36   1994-95 Budget statements.

37   Jane Fraser, "Lady killers", *The Australian*, July 5, 1993, p. 9.

38   Gene Antonio, *AIDS: Rage and Reality* (Dallas: Anchor Books, 1993), p. 2.

39   Cited in Carl Ramsey, "Clinton's homosexual bias shortchanges cancer victims", *Focus on the Family Citizen*, January 1998, p. 5.

40   Ibid.

41   Lorraine Day, *AIDS: What the Government Isn't Telling You* (Palm Desert, California: Rockford Press, 1991), p. 266.

42   Shepherd Smith, "Translating science into policy: A sound approach to AIDS and HIV", in Christopher Wolfe, ed., *Same-Sex Matters* (Dallas: Spence Publishing, 2000), pp. 128-149, p. 129.

43   Stanley Monteith, *AIDS: The Unnecessary Epidemic* (Sevierville, Tennessee: Covenant House Books, 1991), p. 21.

44   Tammy Bruce, *The Death of Right and Wrong* (Roseville, California: Prima Publishing, 2003), pp. 99-100.

45   Charles Bouley, "Time to turn in my toaster oven", *The Advocate* August 16, 2002.

46   Sharon Bernstein, "HIV ads embrace, and stun, audience", *Los Angeles Times*, September 30, 2006.

47   John Heard, "Gays are too proud to confront AIDS, still the real killer", *The Australian*, December 1, 2006.

Chapter 4.   How Many Homosexuals Are There?

1   Georgina Windsor, "Gays, lesbians show support for Labor", *The Australian*, July 29, 1994.

2   Elisabeth Tuckey, "Gays 'have strong buyer instincts'", *The Australian*, September 1, 1994.

3   Patrick Rogers, "How many gays are there?", *Newsweek*, February 15, 1993, p. 46.

4   Kirk and Madsen, *After the Ball, op. cit.*, p. 46.

5   Stuart H. Seidman and Ronald O. Rieder, "A review of sexual behavior in the United States", *American Journal of Psychiatry* 151, 1994, pp. 330-339.

6   Kinsey, A.C., W.B. Pomeroy and C.E. Martin, *Sexual Behavior in the Human Male* (Philadelphia: W.B. Saunders, 1948), pp. 650, 651.

7   John Gagnon, et al., *Science*, vol. 243, 1989, pp. 338-348.

8   Dr J. Gordon Muir, "Homosexuals and the 10% fallacy", *Wall Street Journal*, March 31, 1993.

9   John O. G. Billy, et al., "The sexual behavior of men in the United States", *Family Planning Perspectives*, 25, March/April 1993, p. 58.

10   R.T. Michael, et al., *Sex in America: A Definitive Survey* (Boston: Little, Brown and Co., 1994),

p. 35.

11   Dan Black, et al., "Demographics of the gay and lesbian population in the United States: Evidence from available systematic data sources", *Demography*, 37, May 2000, p. 141.

12   Canadian Community Health Survey 2003, released by Statistics Canada, June 2004.

13   Sarah Cassidy, "Just 1.5 per cent of Britons are gay, says pioneering survey", *The Independent* (UK), September 24, 2010.
URL: www.independent.co.uk/news/uk/home-news/just-15-per-cent-of-britons-are-gay-says-pioneering-survey-2088191.html

14   Lisa Leff, "Demographer: U.S. has 4M adults who identify as gay", Associated Press / CNS News, April 7, 2011.
URL: www.cnsnews.com/news/article/demographer-us-has-4m-adults-who-identif

15   Quoted in Patrick Rogers, *op. cit.*

16   Bob Birrell and Virginia Rapson, "How gay is Australia?", *People and Place*, vol. 10, no. 4, 2002, pp. 59-67.

17   "Snapshot of our youth", *Herald Sun* (Melbourne), July 8, 1008, p. 5.

18   Suzanne Carbone, "Concern on sex findings", *The Age* (Melbourne), April 9, 2003, p. 7.

19   Anthony Smith, et al., "Sexual identity, sexual attraction and sexual experience among a representative sample of adults", *Australian and New Zealand Journal of Public Health*, vol. 27, no. 2, 2003, pp. 138-145, at p. 141.

20   Juliet Richters and Christ Rissel, *Doing It Down Under* (Sydney: Allen & Unwin, 2005), p. 56.

21   Ibid., p. 55.

Chapter 5.   Once Homosexual, Always Homosexual?

1   Cal Thomas, *The Things That Matter Most* (New York: Harper Collins/Zondervan, 1993), pp. 34, 35.

2   Marie Tomeo, et al., "Comparative data of childhood and adolescence molestation in heterosexual and homosexual persons", *Archives of Sexual Behavior*, vol. 30, issue 15, October 2001, p. 535.

3   William Holmes and Gail Slap, "Sexual abuse of boys: Definition, prevalence, correlates, sequelae, and management", *Journal of the American Medical Association*, vol. 280, no. 21, December 2, 1998, pp. 1855-1862, at p. 1859.

4   L.S. Doll, et al., "Self-reported childhood and adolescent sexual abuse among adult homosexual bisexual men", *Child Abuse and Neglect*, vol. 16, no. 6, Nov-Dec 1992, pp. 855-864, p. 855.

5   Joseph Nicolosi, *A Parent's Guide to Preventing Homosexuality* (Downers Grove, Illinois: InterVarsity Press, 2002), p. 31.

6   Irving Bieber, et al., *Homosexuality: A Psychoanalytical Study* (New York: Vintage Books, 1962), p. 172.

7   William Byne and Bruce Parsons, "Human sexual orientation: The biologic theories reappraised", *Archives of General Psychiatry*, 50 (March 1993), p. 236.

8   Tammy Bruce, *The Death of Right and Wrong, op. cit.*, p. 99.

9   Ibid.

10 Stanton Jones and Mark Yarhouse, *Homosexuality: The Use of Scientific Research in the Church's Moral Debate* (Downers Grove, Illinois: InterVarsity Press, 2000), p. 90.

11 Elizabeth Moberly, *Homosexuality: A New Christian Ethic* (Cambridge: Clark, 2001), p. 2.

12 Nicolosi, *op. cit.*, p. 22.

13 A.P. Bell, N.S. Weinberg, and S.K. Hammersmith, *Sexual Preference: Its Development in Men and Women* (Bloomington: Indiana University Press, 1981), p. 76.

14 Victoria Gurvich, "Heterosexual advertising plan angers AIDS group", *The Age* (Melbourne), March 21, 1995.

15 David Greenberg, *The Construction of Homosexuality* (Chicago: The University of Chicago Press, 1988).

16 Don Browning, "Rethinking homosexuality", *The Christian Century*, October 11, 1989, pp. 911-16.
    URL: www.religion-online.org/showarticle.asp?title=246

17 Cited in F. LaGard Smith, *Sodom's Second Coming* (Eugene, Oregon: Harvest House Pub., 1993), p. 82.

18 Robert Kronemeyer, *Overcoming Homosexuality* (New York: Macmillan, 1980), p. 7.

19 Jeffrey Satinover, *Homosexuality and the Politics of Truth* (Grand Rapids: Baker Books, 1996), p. 114.

20 National Association for Research and Therapy of Homosexuality, "New survey says change is possible", *NARTH Bulletin*, vol. 5, no. 2, August 1997, p. 1.

21 Ibid.

22 Robert Spitzer, "Can some gay men and lesbians change their sexual orientation? 200 participants reporting a change from homosexual to heterosexual orientation", *Archives of Sexual Behavior*, vol. 32, issue 5, October 2003, pp. 403-417.

23 Robin Yapp, "Gay cure claims to reignite sex debate", *Courier-Mail* (Brisbane), October 8, 2003.

24 Ronald Bayer, *Homosexuality and American Psychiatry: The Politics of Diagnosis* (New York: Basic Books, 1981).

25 Cited in LaGard Smith, *op. cit.*, p. 84.

26 Cited in *Washington Watch* by the Family Research Council, February 21, 1995, p. 2.

27 Ibid.

28 Ibid.

29 William Byne and Bruce Parsons, "Human sexual orientation: The biologic theories reappraised", *Archives of General Psychiatry*, vol. 50, March 1993, p. 228.

30 Cited in Larry Burtoft, *The Social Significance of Homosexuality: Questions and Answers* (Denver: Focus on the Family, 1994), p. 16.

31 Dennis Altman, *AIDS and the New Puritanism* (New York: Pluto Press, 1986), p. 98.

32 Ibid., p. 188.

33 Catherine Keenan, "The bare-faced radical", *Sydney Morning Herald*, September 24-25, 2005: Spectrum, pp. 4-5, p. 5.

34 Ibid.

35   Camille Paglia, *Vamps and Tramps* (New York: Vintage Books, 1994), pp. 70-72.

36   John D'Emilio interview, "LGBT liberation: Build a broad movement", *International Socialist Review*, issue 65, May-June 2009.

37   Peter Tatchell, "Homosexuality: It isn't natural", *Spiked Online*, June 24, 2008. URL: www.spiked-online.com/index.php?/site/article/5375/

38   Ibid.

39   Ibid.

40   For example, lesbian author Vera Whisman, in *Queer By Choice* (New York: Routledge, 1996), argues that choice is certainly a factor for many homosexuals and lesbians.

41   See their site at: www.queerbychoice.com

42   Kirk and Madsen, *After the Ball, op. cit.*, p. 184.

43   Schmidt, *Straight and Narrow, op. cit.*, p. 141.

44   Pete Moore, *Babel's Shadow: Genetic Technologies in a Fracturing Society* (Oxford: Lion Publishing, 2000), p. 169.

45   William Webb, *Slaves, Women and Homosexuals: Exploring the Hermeneutics of Cultural Analysis* (Downers Grove, Illinois: InterVarsity Press, 2001), pp. 233-234.

46   John Corvino, "Nature? Nurture? It doesn't matter", *Independent Gay Forum*, August 12, 2004. URL: http://igfculturewatch.com/2004/08/12/nature-nurture-it-doesnt-matter/

47   Michael L. Brown, *A Queer Thing Happened To America* (Concord, North Carolina: EqualTime Books, 2011), p. 208.

48   Ibid., p. 214.

49   William Bennett, *The Broken Hearth* (New York: Doubleday, 2001), pp. 124-125.

50   Burtoft, *op. cit.*, pp. 13-18.
      William Byne, "The biological evidence is challenged", *Scientific American*, vol. 270, no. 5, May 1994, pp. 20-25.

51   George Rice, et al., "Male homosexuality: absence of linkage to microsatellite markers at Xq28", *Science*, vol. 284, April 23, 1999, pp. 665-667.

52   As recorded in Ziauddin Sardar, "Scientific fundamentalists preach to the converted", *Australian Financial Review*, June 4, 1999: Review, p. 7.

53   Peter Tatchell, *Spiked Online, op. cit.*

54   Neil Whitehead, "The importance of twin studies", *NARTH Bulletin*, April 2001, p. 26.

55   Satinover, *op. cit.*, p. 117.

56   Edward Stein, *The Mismeasure of Desire: The Science, Theory, and Ethics of Sexual Orientation* (New York: Oxford University Press, 1999).

57   Michael Bronski, "Blinded by science", *The Advocate*, February 1, 2000, p. 64.

58   Richard Dawkins, "It's not all in the genes", *Daily Telegraph* (UK), July 17, 1993, p. 14.

59   Ruth Hubbard, *Exploding the Gene Myth* (Boston: Beacon Press, 1993).

60   Sharon Begley, "When DNA isn't destiny", *Newsweek*, December 6, 1993, pp. 53-55.

61   As reported by Robyn Williams, "How Darwin's birthday present will change our lives", *The Age*, May 28, 2001, p. 1.

62   Charles Mann, "Genes and behaviour", *Science*, vol. 26, 1994, p. 1687.

63   Edward Stein, *The Mismeasure of Desire: The Science, Theory and Ethics of Sexual Orientation* (New York: Oxford University Press, 1999), p. 221.

64   Graham Willett in an interview with *Capital Q Weekly*, November 3, 2000, p. 17.

65   Graham Willett, letter to the *Herald Sun* (Melbourne), December 1, 2000, p. 17.

66   Michael Swift, "For the homoerotic order", *Gay Community News*, February 15-21, 1987.

67   Darrell Yates Rist, "Are homosexuals born that way?", *The Nation*, vol. 255, no. 12, October 19, 1992, p. 424.

68   F. LaGard Smith, *op. cit.*, pp. 97, 98.

69   For a collection of stories about Australian homosexuals and lesbians who left the lifestyle behind, see Christopher Keane, ed., *What Some of you Were* (Sydney: Matthias Media, 2001).

70   Bob Davies and Lori Rentzel, *Coming out of Homosexuality* (Downers Grove, Illinois: InterVarsity Press, 1993), p. 16.

71   Ibid., pp. 18-19.

72   Jeff Konrad, *You Don't Have to be Gay* (Tunbridge Wells, Kent, UK: Monarch Publications, 1993), pp. 9, 11.

73   Jeannette Howard, *Out of Egypt: One Woman's Journey Out of Lesbianism* (London: Monarch Books, 1991), p. 241.

74   Robert Knight, "Opposing homosexual advocacy", in Christopher Wolfe, ed., *Same-Sex Matters* (Dallas: Spence Publishing, 2000), pp. 169-179, p. 178.

75   George Rekers, "The development of a homosexual orientation", in Christopher Wolfe, ed., *Homosexuality and American Public Life* (Dallas: Spence Publishing, 1999), pp. 62-84, p. 84.

76   Ibid., pp. 82-83.

Chapter 6.   Homosexual Rights and Discrimination

1   Andrew Grulich, et al., "Homosexual experience and recent homosexual encounters", *Australian and New Zealand Journal of Public Health*, vol. 27, no. 2, 2003, p. 162.

2   Adam Carr, "Looking for gay liberation: finding wealth and marriage", *Melbourne Star*, November 29, 2001, pp. 20-21.

3   Ibid., p. 21.

4   Cited in David Burrelli, "Homosexuals and US military personnel policy", *Current Issues*, January 14, 1993, pp. 25-26.

5   Roger Magnuson, *Informed Answers to Gay Rights Questions* (Sisters, Oregon: Multnomah Books, 1994), p. 107.

6   Ibid., pp. 107, 108.

7   For full documentation of this claim, see the author's paper, *The Historicity And Universality of the Natural Family*.

8   Anthony Butcher, "Human rights and the vulnerable in our midst", *Quadrant*, January-February 2001, p. 26.

9   Richard Baker, "Lesbians only need apply", *The Age* (Melbourne), September 12, 2003, p. 3.

10   For example, Andrew Milnes, "Queer spaces?", *MCV: Melbourne's Gay and Lesbian Community Voice*, September 19, 2003, pp. 1-4.

11   "Lesfest bans overturned", *MCV*, October 3, 2003, p. 3. See also, Andrew Bolt, "Bully laws that discriminate", *Herald Sun* (Melbourne), October 6, 2003.

12   Adam Carr, "Lesfest cancelled", *B.News*, October 23, 2003, p. 7.

13   Collin Mullane, "Hatching an idea for change", *B.News*, September 11, 2003, p. 4.

14   Kate Jones, "Men stage dance win", *Herald Sun*, December 20, 2003.

15   Shannon McRae, "Keep out if you're straight", *Herald Sun*, January 19, 2006.

16   Matt Doran, "Gay pub can out straight patrons", *Herald Sun*, May 28, 2007.

17   "Going straight", *MCV*, January 9, 2004, p. 3.

18   Kelvin Healey, "No blokes allowed", *Herald Sun*, July 23, 2009, p. 5.

19   Padraic Murphy, "Gay club bans women", *Herald Sun*, September 16, 2010.

20   Padraic Murphy, "No women allowed", *Herald Sun*, June 10, 2011, p. 5.

21   Brent Bozell, "Playing hardball on softball", *TownHall.com*, 17 June 17, 2011. URL: http://townhall.com/columnists/brentbozell/2011/06/17/playing_hardball_on_softball

22   As but one example, see this introductory piece I have written on such adverse effects: "Coming soon to you: The state PC church", *CultureWatch*, June 19, 2009. URL: www.billmuehlenberg.com/2009/06/19/1635/

23   Barbara Bradley Hagerty, "When gay rights and religious liberties clash", *Public Radio NPR*, June 13, 2008. URL: www.npr.org/templates/story/story.php?storyId=91486340

24   Charles Colson, "Gay marriage v. religious freedom", *Breakpoint*, March 8, 2010. URL: www.breakpoint.org/commentaries/14688-gay-marriage-v-religious-freedom

25   Matt Akersten, "Ten dumps TV Bible-basher", *Same Same*, October 5, 2010. URL: www.samesame.com.au/news/local/5950/Ten-dumps-TV-Bible-basher.htm

26   Mark Russell, "Church camp found guilty of discrimination", *Sunday Age* (Melbourne), October 10, 2010.

27   Roger Severino, "Or for poorer? How same-sex marriage threatens religious liberty", in Lynn Wardle, ed., *What's the Harm?* (Lanham, Maryland: University Press of America, 2008), pp. 325-354.

28   Ibid., p. 326.

29   David Orgon Coolidge, "The question of marriage", in Christopher Wolfe, ed., *Homosexuality and American Public Life* (Dallas: Spence Publishing, 1999), pp. 200-238, p. 225.

30   Ibid.

Chapter 7.   Judicial Activism and Homosexuality

1   Phillip Coorey, "Gay marriage victory", *Herald Sun* (Melbourne), November 20, 2003, p. 34.

2   Darrin Farrant, "Joy, anger in IVF victory", *The Age* (Melbourne), July 29, 2000, p. 1.

3   Michelle Pountney, "Baby battle", *Herald Sun*, April 19, 2002, p. 1.

4   Cindy Wockner, "Transsexual marriage is valid", *Daily Telegraph* (Sydney), October 15, 2001.

5   Ian Munro, "Family court ruling tests the meaning of marriage", *The Age*, February 22, 2003, p. 3.

6   Fergus Shiel, "Gay couple 'parents', court finds", *The Age*, December 13, 2003, p. 3.

7   Misha Schubert, "Gays win rights as refugees", *The Australian*, December 10, 2003, p. 1.

8   Deborah Gough, "Court allows girl's bid to become boy", *The Age*, April 14, 2004, p. 1.

9   "Boy gets three parents", *Herald Sun*, April 19, 2004, p. 14.

10   "Find out your rights," *MCV: Melbourne's Gay and Lesbian Community Voice*, January 9, 2004, p. 4.

Chapter 8.   The Homosexual Agenda

1   "Platform of the 1993 March on Washington for Lesbian, Gay, and Bi Equal Rights and Liberation" as cited in Burtoft, *The Social Significance of Homosexuality* (1994), *op. cit.*, pp. 57-68.

2   National Coalition of Gay Organizations, 1972 Gay Rights Platform, as cited in Enrique Rueda, *The Homosexual Network* (Greenwich, Connecticut: Devin-Adair Publishers, 1982), pp. 202, 203.

3   Senate: Hansard (Canberra), Legal and Constitutional Committee; Reference: *Human Rights (Sexual Conduct) Bill*, November 30 – December 1, 1994, p. 349.

4   Ibid.

5   Ibid., p. 396.

6   Ibid., p. 389.

7   Ibid., p. 341.

8   Ibid., p. 365.

9   Ibid.

10   Ibid.

11   Sid Spindler, *Prohibiting Discrimination on the Grounds of Sexuality: Issues Paper No. 1* (1994), p. 1.

12   Ibid., p. 4.

13   Ibid., p. 5.

14   Ibid.

15   Graham Willett, *Living Out Loud: A History of Gay and Lesbian Activism in Australia* (Sydney: Allen & Unwin, 2000).

16   Ibid., p. x.

17   Ibid., pp. 238-239.

18   Ibid., p. 240.

19   In a vote on July 17, 2003, the Uniting Church of Australia did decide to go down the path of gay ordination.

20   Lance Spurr, "Who wants to get married?", *B.News*, July 3, 2003, p. 8.

21   Ibid.

22   Lance Spurr, "The rise of same-sex marriage", *Melbourne Star*, February 5, 2004, p. 5.

23   Dennis Altman, "Responsible gay citizenship", *Sydney Star Observer*, August 26, 2004.

24   Dennis Altman, "Same-sex marriage just a sop to convention", *The Australian Literary Review*, February 2, 2011, pp. 4-5.

25   Miranda Stewart, "It's a queer thing", *The Alternative Law Journal*, vol. 29, no. 2, April 2004, pp. 75-80, p. 75.

26   Helen Razer, "Homosexuality is a bore now so many gays are wedded to a rickety institution", *Sydney Morning Herald*, March 3, 2011.

Chapter 9.   Homosexual Marriage

1   "NSW gives new meaning to the concept of family", *The Age* (Melbourne), April 18, 1995, p. 7.

2   Miranda Stewart, "It's a queer thing", *The Alternative Law Journal*, vol. 29, no. 2, April 2004, *op. cit.*, p. 78.

3   Maggie Gallagher, *The Abolition of Marriage* (Washington DC: Regnery Publishing, 1996), p. 131.

4   Victorian Gay and Lesbian Rights Lobby (VGLRL) spokesperson David McCarthy, cited in Andrew Milnes, "Always a bridesmaid", *MCV: Melbourne's Gay and Lesbian Community Voice*, November 7, 2003, p. 1.

5   "Marriage splits NSW lobby", *MCV*, June 11, 2004, p. 3.

6   Amy Lowell, "Do lesbians need marriage?", *MCV*, June 4, 2004, p. 6.

7   Amy Lowell, "Do open relationships work?", *MCV*, August 27, 2004, p. 6.

8   Cited in James Norman, "The gay conservative and other queer couplings", *The Age*, March 11, 2006, A2 section, p. 20.

9   Ron Thiele, "Gay marriage? Just say no", *B.News*, March 6, 2008, p. 8.

10   Dennis Altman, "Misconstrued comment", *B.News*, December 13, 2007, p. 8.

11   Rev. T. Turner, "Is gay marriage selfish?", *B.News*, December 13, 2007, p. 8.

12   Dennis Altman, "Same-sex marriage just a sop to convention", *op. cit.*

13   Ibid.

14   Lance Spurr, "Who wants to get married?", *B.News*, July 3, 2003, p. 8., *op. cit.*

15   Ibid.

16   Brian Noll, "Get off the marriage band wagon", *B.News*, May 8, 2008, p. 8.

17   Ibid.

18   Zoe Beaumont, "The sanctimony of marriage", *B.News*, August 21, 2008, p. 10.

19   Ibid.

20   Kristen Walker, "The same-sex marriage debate in Australia", *International Journal of Human Rights*, vol. 11, no.1, 2007, pp.109-130, p. 123.

21   Helen Razer, "Homosexuality is a bore now so many gays are wedded to a rickety institution", *Sydney Morning Herald*, March 3, 2011.

22   See their website: http://againstequality.org

23 Clifford Krauss, "Free to marry, Canada's gays say, 'Do I'?", *New York Times*, August 31, 2003, sec. 1, p. 1.

24 Ibid.

25 Ibid.

26 Jim Rinnert, "The trouble with gay marriage", *In These Times*, December 30, 2003.

27 Richard Waghorne, "Gay marriage", *Irish Daily Mail*, April 5, 2011.
URL: http://richardtwaghorne.wordpress.com/2011/04/05/gay-marriage/

28 Ibid.

29 Sotirios Sarantakos, "Same-sex marriage: Which way to go?", *Alternative Law Journal*, vol. 24, no. 2, April 1999, pp. 79-84, p. 82.

30 Cath Pope, "Marriage, right?", *MCV*, May 27, 2005, p. 1.

31 Maggie Gallagher and Joshua K. Baker, "Demand for same-sex marriage: Evidence from the United States, Canada, and Europe", *Institute for Marriage and Public Policy*, vol. 3, no. 1, April 26, 2006, p. 2.

32 William Duncan, "The tenth anniversary of Dutch same-sex marriage: How is marriage doing in the Netherlands?", *iMAPP Research Brief*, vol. 4, no. 3, May 2011, p. 3.

33 Gallagher and Baker, *op. cit.*, p. 6.

34 Samantha Maiden, "Kirby in support of gay marriage", *The Australian*, October 24, 2006.

35 This title comes from the Canadian homosexual paper, *Xtra*.

36 Andrew Sullivan, *Virtually Normal: An Argument About Homosexuality* (London: Picador, 1996), p. 202.

37 Ibid., p. 203.

38 Ibid., pp. 203-204.

39 Elizabeth Kristol, "The marrying kind", *First Things*, January 1996, pp. 45-47, p. 46.

40 Peter Tatchell, "Beyond equality", *New Humanist*, vol. 116, issue 1, Spring 2001.

41 Peter Tatchell, "Ban on same-sex marriage must be lifted", *The Independent* (UK), June 15, 2010.

42 Ibid.

43 Kristen Walker, *op. cit.*, p. 124.

44 Altman, "Same-sex marriage just a sop to convention", *op. cit.*

45 Dennis Altman, "Marriage right vs rite", *Compass*, ABC TV, July 10, 2011.
URL: www.abc.net.au/compass/s3251965.htm

46 Richard Mohr, *A More Perfect Union* (Boston: Beacon Press, 1994), p. 50.

47 Paula Ettelbrick, "Since when is marriage a path to liberation?", *Out/Look*, Fall 1989, p. 8.

48 Kirk and Madsen, *After the Ball* (New York: Plume, 1990), *op. cit.*, p. 330.

49 Ibid.

50 William Aaron, *Straight* (New York: Bantam Books, 1972), p. 208.

51 Michelangelo Signorile, "Bridal wave", *OUT*, December-January 1994, p. 161.

52 Michelangelo Signorile, "I do, I do, I do, I do, I do", *OUT*, May 1996, p. 30.

53 Evan Wolfson, "All together now", in Lynn Wardle, et al. eds., *Marriage and Same-Sex Unions:*

A Debate (Westport, Connecticut: Praeger, 2003), pp. 3-9, p. 3.

54   Adam Carr, "Test gay marriage says lobby", *B.News*, July 3, 2003, p. 3.

55   Farah Farouque, "Gay 'husbands' to test their marriage in court", *The Age*, February 4, 2004, p. 3.

56   Gerard McManus and Simon Kearney, "Same-sex laws probe", *Herald Sun* (Melbourne), June 30, 2002, p. 8.

57   Richard Egan, "Family court redefines man", *Family Update* (Australian Family Association), vol. 17, no. 6, November-December 2001, p. 1.

58   Ian Munro, "Family court ruling tests the meaning of marriage", *The Age*, February 22, 2003, p. 3.

59   Commonwealth Government, *Marriage Act 1961*, sect. 46 (1).

60   The case for this is argued in my research paper, *The Historicity and Universality of the Natural Family*.

61   Richard Posner, *Sex and Reason* (Cambridge, Massachusetts: Harvard University Press, 1992), p. 312.

62   Thaddeus Baklinski, "Canadian court: Marriage officials must marry homosexuals", *LifeSiteNews*, January 10, 2011.

63   Peter Wood, "Sex and consequences", *The American Conservative*, July 28, 2003, pp. 8-12, p. 10.
URL: www.amconmag.com/article/2003/jul/28/00008/

64   Douglas Farrow, "Culture wars are killing marriage", *National Post* (Canada), May 7, 2003.

65   Ibid.

66   William Bennett, "Gay marriage: Not a very good idea", *Washington Times*, May 21, 1996.

67   Cited in Matthew Cullinan Hoffman, "Attorney for man accused of incest asks: if homosexual sex is legal, why not this?", *LifeSiteNews*, December 17, 2010.
URL: www.lifesitenews.com/news/attorney-for-man-accused-of-incest-asks-if-homosexual-sex-is-legal-why-not

68   Sam Schulman, "Gay marriage – and marriage", *Commentary* (New York), November 2003.

69   National Coalition of Gay Organizations, "The 1972 Gay Rights Platform", Chicago, 1972.
URL: www.article8.org/docs/general/platform.htm

70   Judith Levine, *Harmful to Minors: The Perils of Protecting Children from Sex* (University of Minnesota Press, 2002 / New York: De Capo Press, 2003).

71   Judith Levine, "Stop the wedding! Why gay marriage isn't radical enough", *The Village Voice*, July 23-29, 2003.

72   Allan Hall, "Switzerland considers repealing incest laws", *The Telegraph* (UK), December 15, 2010.
URL: www.telegraph.co.uk/news/worldnews/europe/switzerland/8198917/Switzerland-considers-repealing-incest-laws.html

73   "Marriage for petrosexuals", *B.News*, October 23, 2003, p. 4.

74   Stephen Bertman, "The transformation of marriage", *The Futurist*, March-April 2004, pp. 44-47, at p. 47.

75   Ibid., p. 44.

76   Ibid., p. 46.

77   Ibid., p. 47.

78   Ibid., p. 47.

79   Bennett, *Broken Hearth, op. cit.*, p. 115.

80   David Frum, "Modern marriage, modern trouble", in Katherine Anderson, Don Browning and Brian Boyer, eds., *Marriage: Just a Piece of Paper?* (Grand Rapids: Eerdmans, 2002), p. 364.

81   Thomas Stoddard, "Why gay people should seek the right to marry", in William Rubenstein, ed., *Lesbians, Gay Men and the Law* (New York: The New Press, 1993), p. 400.

82   As just one example, see Elizabeth F. Emens, "Monogamy's law: Compulsory monogamy and polyamorous existence", *New York University Review of Law & Social Change*, vol. 29, no. 2, 2004, pp. 283-286.

83   URL: www.pro-polygamy.com (Accessed February 21, 2011.)

84   Dale O'Leary, *One Man, One Woman* (Manchester, New Hampshire: Sophia Institute Press, 2007), p. 247.

85   Cited in Don Lattin, "Committed to marriage for the masses: Polyamorists say they relate honestly to multiple partners", *San Francisco Chronicle*, April 20, 2004. URL: http://articles.sfgate.com/2004-04-20/bay-area/17423451_1_same-sex-marriage-universalists-gay-rights-movement

86   Jessica Bennett, "Polyamory: the next sexual revolution", *Newsweek*, July 29, 2009.

87   Linda Kirkman, "Poly is the new gay", *La Trobe Opinions* (La Trobe University, Melbourne), November 29, 2010. URL: www.latrobe.edu.au/news/articles/2010/opinion/poly-is-the-new-gay

88   Katrina Fox, "Marriage needs redefining", *The Drum Opinion* (Australian Broadcasting Corporation), March 2, 2011. URL: www.abc.net.au/unleashed/44576.html

89   Julie McCrossin, "Always a bridesmaid, never a bride: Recognising same-sex relationships", *The Sydney Papers*, Winter 1999, pp. 145-151, p. 145.

90   Rodney Croome, "Fundamental flaws and dangers in moves against same-sex marriage", *Canberra Times*, August 16, 2004, p. 13.

91   Richard Waghorne, *op. cit.*

92   Ibid.

93   Emma-Kate Symons, "Block on gay marriage is just like apartheid", *The Australian*, April 27, 2004, p. 1.

94   See, for example, Keith Boykin, "Whose dream? Why the black church opposes black marriage", *The Village Voice* (New York), May 18, 2004. URL: www.villagevoice.com/2004-05-18/news/whose-dream/1/

95   Cheryl Wetzstein, "Blacks angered by gays' metaphors", *Washington Times*, March 2, 2004, p. A3.

96   Greg Koukl, "Same-sex marriage – challenges and responses", *Stand to Reason* (Signal Hill, California), May 2004. URL: www.str.org/site/News2?page=NewsArticle&id=6553

97   Sherif Girgis, Robert George and Ryan Anderson, "What is marriage?", *Harvard Journal of*

Law & Public Policy, vol. 34, no. 1, Winter 2010, pp. 245-287, p. 249.

98   Francis J. Beckworth, "Interracial marriage and same-sex marriage", *Public Discourse* (The Witherspoon Institute, Princeton, New Jersey), May 21, 2010.
URL: www.thepublicdiscourse.com/2010/05/1324

99   Altman, "Same-sex marriage just a sop to convention", *op. cit.*

100   Glenn Stanton and Bill Maier, *Marriage on Trial* (Downers Grove, Illinois: InterVarsity Press, 2004), p. 37.

101   Stanley N. Kurtz, "What is wrong with gay marriage?", *Commentary* (New York), September 2000, pp. 35-41, p. 37.

102   Hadley Arkes, "Homosexuality and the law", in Christopher Wolfe, ed., *Homosexuality and American Public Life* (Dallas: Spence Publishing, 1999), pp. 157-178, p. 157.

103   Peter Sprigg, "Questions and answers: What's wrong with letting same-sex couples legally 'marry'?", *Family Research Council*, issue no. 256, October 17, 2003.

104   David Blankenhorn, *The Future of Marriage* (New York: Encounter Books, 2007), p. 153.

105   Lynn Wardle, "Image, analysis, and the nature of relationships", in Lynn Wardle, et al., eds., *Marriage and Same Sex Unions: A Debate* (Westport, Connecticut: Praeger, 2003), pp. 115-118, p. 117.

106   Girgis, George and Anderson, *op. cit.*, pp. 256-257.

107   Richard Waghorne, *op. cit.*

108   John Cloud, "Will gay marriage be legal?", *Time* magazine, February 21, 2000.
URL: www.time.com/time/magazine/article/0,9171,996172,00.html#ixzz0hMcRgILK

109   Jonathan Rauch, *Gay Marriage: Why it is Good for Gays, Good for Straights, and Good for America* (New York: Times Books, 2004), p. 71.

110   Rodney Croome, "Let no wedge tear gay unions asunder", *The Australian*, April 29, 2004, p. 11.

111   Altman, "Same-sex marriage just a sop to convention", *op. cit.*

112   Kirk and Madsen, *op. cit.*, p. 165.

113   Arthur Leonard, "On legal recognition for same-sex partners", in Lynn Wardle et al. eds., *Marriage and Same Sex Unions: A Debate* (Westport, Connecticut: Praeger, 2003), pp. 65-77, p. 70.

114   Shelby Steele, "Selma to San Francisco?", *Wall Street Journal*, March 20, 2004.

115   Kurtz, *op. cit*, pp. 40-41.

116   Peter Sprigg, *Outrage* (Washington: Regnery, 2004), p. 86.

117   David Orgon Coolidge, "The question of marriage", in Christopher Wolfe, ed., *Homosexuality and American Public Life* (Dallas: Spence Publishing, 1999), p. 238.

Chapter 10.   Homosexual Adoption Rights

1   Catherine Naylor, "ACT same-sex couples can now adopt", *Canberra Times*, February 11, 2004, p. 2.

2   Michael Ebert, "Joseph Nicolosi, PhD, is the fugitive", *Focus on the Family Citizen*, June 20, 1994, pp. 10-12.

3   Cited in Don Feder, "Dangers of gay parenting are underrated", *Boston Globe*, September 27, 1993.

4   Glenn Stanton and Bill Maier, *Marriage on Trial* (Downers Grove, Illinois: InterVarsity Press, 2004), p. 71.

5   Ibid.

6   Cited in Feder, *op. cit.*

7   Testimony of Suzanne Cook before the Oregon State Senate, April 3, 1997.

8   Kylie Smith, "I prefer suicide to lesbian mum", *Herald Sun* (Melbourne), November 24, 2002, p. 6.

9   Pattrick Smellie, "Mum no more", *The Australian*, January 24, 1995.

10   Sotirios Sarantakos , "Children in three contexts", *Children Australia*, vol. 21, no. 3, 1996, pp. 23-31.

11   Paul Cameron, "Homosexual parents testing 'common sense' – A literature review emphasizing the Golombok and Tasker longitudinal study of lesbians' children", *Psychological Reports*, 85, 1999, p. 282.

12   Robert Lerner and Althea Nagai, *Out of Nothing Comes Nothing: Homosexual and Heterosexual Marriage Not Shown to be Equivalent for Raising Children* (Washington DC: Ethics and Public Policy Center, 2000).

13   David Demo and Martha Cox, "Families with young children: A review of research in the 1990s", *Journal of Marriage and the Family,* 62, November 2000, pp. 876-895, at p. 889.

14   Steven Nock, Affidavit to the Ontario Supreme Court of Justice regarding Hedy Halpren et al., 2001.

15   S. Golombok, et al., "Children in lesbian and single-parent households: Psychosexual and psychiatric appraisal", *Journal of Child Psychology and Psychiatry,* vol. 24, no. 4, October 1983, pp. 551-572, p. 569.

16   Lynn Wardle, "The potential impact of homosexual parenting on children", *University of Illinois Law Review*, 1997, No. 3, pp. 833-920, p. 835.

17   Judith Stacey and Timothy Biblarz, "(How) does the sexual orientation of parents matter?", *American Sociological Review*, 66, 2001, pp. 159-183.

18   P.A. Belcastro, et al., "A review of data-based studies addressing the affects of homosexual parenting on children's sexual and social functioning", *Journal of Divorce and Remarriage*, 20, 1993, pp. 105-106.

19   Mary Beth Style, "Homosexuality and adoption", in Christopher Wolfe, ed., *Same-Sex Matters* (Dallas: Spence Publishing, 2000), pp. 107-127, p. 116.

20   See, for example, my two research papers, "The Benefits of Marriage" (Melbourne, 2004), and "The Case for the Two-Parent Family" (Melbourne 2004).

21   Wendy Manning and Kathleen Lamb, "Adolescent well-being in cohabiting, married, and single-parent families", *Journal of Marriage and Family*, vol. 65, no. 4, November 2003, pp. 876-893, at p. 890.

22   Yongmin Sun, "The well-being of adolescents in households with no biological parents", *Journal of Marriage and Family*, vol. 65, no. 4, November 2003, pp. 894-909, at p. 894.

23   Ibid., p. 905.

24   Stanton and Maier, *op. cit.*, pp. 70-71.

25   Mary Beth Style, *op. cit.*, p. 114.

26   Tammy Bruce, *The Death of Right and Wrong* (Roseville, California: Prima Publishing, 2003), p. 88.

27   Dawn Stefanowicz, *Out From Under: The Impact of Homosexual Parenting* (Enumclaw, Washington: Annotation Press, 2007).

28   Tony Wood and Lee Matthews, "Men making babies", *Melbourne Star*, April 14, 2005, p. 4.

29   Cath Pope, "Marriage, right?", *MCV: Melbourne's Gay and Lesbian Community Voice*, May 27, 2005, p. 1.

30   Bill Maier, "Same-sex marriage", in Joe Dallas and Nancy Heche, eds., *The Complete Christian Guide to Understanding Homosexuality* (Eugene, Oregon: Harvest House, 2010), pp. 363-376, p. 373.

31   Patricia Morgan, *Children as Trophies? Examining the Evidence on Same-Sex Parenting* (Newcastle upon Tyne, UK: The Christian Institute, 2002). URL: www.christian.org.uk/pdfpublications/childrenastrophies.pdf

32   Ibid., p. 34.

33   Ibid., p. 35.

34   Ibid., p. 45.

35   Ibid., p. 48.

36   Ibid., p. 49.

37   Ibid., p. 57.

38   Ibid., p. 67.

39   Ibid., p. 89.

40   Ibid., p. 80.

41   Ibid., pp. 81-82.

42   Ibid., p. 83.

43   Ibid., p. 87.

44   Ibid., pp. 111-112.

45   Ibid., p. 130.

46   Ibid., p. 132.

47   Melissa Jenkins, "Love lost after twins", *Herald Sun* (Melbourne), September 20, 2007, p. 9.

Chapter 11.   Homosexuality and Children

1   Although the new reproductive technologies are beginning to make this possible.

2   Pat Califia and Daniel Tsang, eds., *The Age Taboo* (Boston: Alyson Publications and Gay Men's Press, 1981), p. 144.

3   As cited in Thomas Schmidt, *Straight & Narrow: Compassion & Clarity in the Homosexuality Debate* (Downers Grove, Illinois: InterVarsity Press, 1995), p. 148.

4   Patricia Neil Warren, "Future shock", *The Advocate*, October 3, 1995, p. 80.

5   Cal Thomas, "Good and bad get ugly", *World* magazine, August 21, 1999, p. 19.

6   As reported in Kathryn Jean Lopez, "The cookie crumbles: The Girl Scouts go PC", *National Review*, October 23, 2000.

7   Bruce Loudon, "Scout's gay move anger", *Herald Sun* (Melbourne), March 24, 1997, p. 23.

8   Scott Emerson, "Sexually explicit gay cards banned", *The Australian*, March 9, 1995, p. 3.

9   Zoe Velonis, "Comics come out", *Brother/Sister*, April 29, 2000, pp. 12-13.

10   Stephen McGinty, "Camped crusaders up, up and a-gay", *The Australian*, February 28, 2000, p. 11.

11   Troy Gurr, "Super Queer!", *MCV: Melbourne's Gay and Lesbian Community Voice*, April 15, 2005, p. 8.

12   For example, *MCV*, March 5, 2004, p. 24.

13   Nikki Voss and Catherine Lambert, "Gay dolls are outed", *Herald Sun*, November 2, 2003, p. 13.

14   Leslea Newman, *Heather Has Two Mommies* (Los Angeles: Alyson Publications, 1989).

15   Michael Willhoite, *Daddy's Roommate* (Los Angeles: Alyson Publications, 1990).

16   Alexandra Carlton, "Her own write", *Who*, March 24, 2003, p. 36.

17   Liam Houlihan, "'Gay school' for tots row", *Herald Sun*, June 3, 2004, p. 2.

18   Kelly Burke, "See Jed's dads rile the minister", *Sydney Morning Herald*, February 12, 2005.

19   Larissa Dubecki, "Schools unable to stop photos on gay website", *The Age* (Melbourne), February 22, 2002, p. 3.

20   Chris Tinkler, "Gay photos storm", *Herald Sun*, August 1, 2004, p. 5.

21   "Back to school", *DNA* magazine, July 2004, pp. 40-51.

22   John from Footscray, "High school hijinx?", *MCV*, August 6, 2004, p. 5.

23   Kenton Penley Miller and Mahamati, *Not Round Here: Affirming Diversity, Challenging Homophobia*: Rural Service Providers Training Manual (Sydney: Outlink/Australian Human Rights and Equal Opportunity Commission, 2000). URL: www.humanrights.gov.au/pdf/human_rights/Not_round_here.pdf

24   "Lesbian, gay, bisexual, trans and intersex equality", Australian Human Rights Commission (AHRC) [formerly Australian Human Rights and Equal Opportunity Commission (HREOC)]. URL: www.hreoc.gov.au/human_rights/gay_lesbian/ (Accessed December 2, 2003).

25   Greg Callaghan, "Worst days of their lives", *The Australian*, April 10, 2000, p. 11.

26   Malcolm Brown, "It's OK to be gay, said the judge to the schoolboys", *The Age*, February 25, 2000, p. 3.

27   Jasper Copping, "'Gay lessons' in maths, geography and science", *The Telegraph* (UK), January 22, 2011. URL: www.telegraph.co.uk/education/educationnews/8275937/Gay-lessons-in-maths-geography-and-science.html

28   Ibid.

29   Daniel Villarreal, "Can we please just start admitting that we *do* actually want to indoctrinate kids?", *Queerty*, May 12, 2011. URL: www.queerty.com/can-we-please-just-start-admitting-that-we-do-actually-want-to-

indoctrinate-kids-20110512

30   Ibid.

31   "Gay-friendly centre angers parents", *Daily Telegraph* (Sydney), May 29, 2006.

32   Darren Devlyn, "Gay neighbour moving in", *Herald Sun*, August 20, 2004, p. 3.

33   "TV reduces homophobia", *MCV*, April 22, 2005, p. 5.

34   David Hirst, "Teachers urged to educate students on homosexuality", *The Australian*, January 9, 1987.

35   "New program to tackle homophobia in schools", ABC Radio 1233 Newcastle (Australian Broadcasting Corporation), January 21, 2011. URL: www.abc.net.au/news/stories/2011/01/21/3118010.htm?site=newcastle

36   Jamie Walker, "Under-10s 'should be taught about sex'", *The Australian*, March 13, 1992.

37   Joanne Painter, "Teachers consider classes on sex and gays", *The Age*, January 19, 1995.

38   Carolyn Jones and Justine Ferrari, "Teachers propose mandatory HIV classes", *The Australian*, January 18, 1995.

39   Cheryl Critchley, "Call to give lessons on gays", *Herald Sun*, October 2, 1995.

40   Kevin Donnelly, "Teacher unions make classrooms the new battleground", *News Weekly* (National Civic Council, Melbourne), April 22, 1995, p. 7.

41   Ibid.

42   Daryl Higgins, ed., *Alsorts: A Sexuality Awareness Guide* (Melbourne: The ALSO Foundation/ Deakin University, 2002).

43   Julie Lewis, "Books may counter anti-gay attitudes", *Sydney Morning Herald*, March 7, 1995.

44   Jeremy Calvert, "Sex survey shocks", *Herald Sun*, October 28, 2003, p. 7.

45   Jeremy Calvert, "Sex survey probe", *Herald Sun*, October 29, 2003, p. 15.

46   Daniel Hoare, "Gay sex questions 'in the curriculum'", *The Australian*, October 29, 2003, p. 3.

47   "School's out for award winners", *MCV*, December 12, 2003, p. 3.

48   Kelvin Healey, "Gay school guide", *Herald Sun*, June 4, 2006, p. 9.

49   Vicki Harding, ed., *Learn to Include: Teacher's Manuel* (Dulwich Hill, New South Wales: Learn to Include Education Series, 2005), p. 31.

50   Ibid., p. 8.

51   "Gay-friendly centre angers parents", *Daily Telegraph* (Sydney), May 29, 2006, *op. cit.*

52   Justine Ferrari, "Author defends gay childcare books", *The Australian*, May 30, 2006, p. 9.

53   "Taking aim at bullying", *MCV*, January 16, 2004, p. 4.

Introduction to Part Two

1   Joe Dallas, *Desires in Conflict: Answering the Struggle for Sexual Identity* (Eugene, Oregon: Harvest House, 1991), p. 268.

2   These include: D.S. Bailey, *Homosexuality and the Western Christian Tradition* (New York: Longmans, Green, and Co., 1955); John Boswell, *Christianity, Social Tolerance, and*

Homosexuality (Chicago: University of Chicago Press, 1980); Pim Pronk, *Against Nature? Types of Moral Arguments Regarding Homosexuality* (Grand Rapids: Eerdmans, 1993); and Robin Scroggs, *The New Testament and Homosexuality* (Philadelphia: Fortress Press, 1983). See my critique of Boswell at: www.billmuehlenberg.com/2007/07/19/pushing-agendas-through-advocacy-scholarship/

3   For example, Letha Scanzoni and Virginia Mollenkott, *Is the Homosexual My Neighbor?* (San Francisco: Harper and Row, 1978).

Chapter 1.   Ten Ploys of the Revisionists

1   Muriel Porter, *Sex, Marriage, and the Church* (Melbourne: Dove, 1996), p. 130.

2   G.K. Chesterton, *Orthodoxy* (London: Dodd, Mead, 1908), pp. 74, 75.

3   Bruce Waltke, *An Old Testament Theology* (Grand Rapids: Zondervan, 2007), p. 468.

4   John Goldingay, *Old Testament Theology*, Vol. 3: "Israel's Life" (Downers Grove, Illinois: IVP, 2009), p. 617.

5   Allen Ross, *Holiness to the Lord* (Grand Rapids, Michigan: Baker Books, 2002), pp. 246-247.

6   Goldingay, *op. cit.*, p. 380.

7   Ross, *op. cit.*, p. 247, n. 8.

8   Muriel Porter, "Why Anglican schism would hurt those who force it", *The Age* (Melbourne), October 18, 2003, Insight, p. 11.

9   Although Jesus does refer to the Sodom episode in Luke 17:32.

10   Manfred Brauch, *Abusing Scripture* (Downers Grove, Illinois: InterVarsity Press, 2009), p. 233.

11   James De Young, *Homosexuality: Contemporary Claims Examined in Light of the Bible and Other Ancient Literature and Law* (Grand Rapids: Kregel, 2000), p. 32.

12   John Stott, *Issues Facing Christians Today* (London: Marshall Pickering, 1990), pp. 344-345.

13   Ibid., p. 346.

14   Kenneth Mathews, *Genesis 1-11:26* (Nashville: Broadman and Holman, 1996).

15   John Jefferson Davis, *Evangelical Ethics: Issues Facing the Church Today* (Phillipsburg, NJ: Presbyterian and Reformed, 1985), p. 114.

16   Greg Bahnsen, *Homosexuality: A Biblical View* (Grand Rapids: Zondervan, 1978), p. 28.

17   Ibid., p. 29.

18   Bob Davies, "A Biblical response to the pro-gay movement," Exodus International paper, p. 1.

19   Stanley Grenz, *Sexual Ethics* (Louisville: Westminster John Knox Press, 1990, 1997), p. 58.

20   Robert Gagnon, *The Bible and Homosexual Practice: Texts and Hermeneutics* (Nashville: Abingdon Press, 2001), pp. 193-194.

21   Thomas Schmidt, *Straight and Narrow?: Compassion and Clarity in the Homosexuality Debate* (Downers Grove, Illinois: InterVarsity Press, 1995), p. 53.

22   See, for example, Tom Horner, *Jonathan Loved David: Homosexuality in Biblical Times* (Philadelphia: Westminster Press, 1978).

23   Gagnon, *op. cit.*, pp. 151-152.

24   Stanley Grenz, *Welcoming But Not Affirming: An Evangelical Response to Homosexuality*

(Louisville: Westminster John Knox Press, 1988), p. 60.

25   Norman Geisler, *Christian Ethics*, 2nd ed. (Grand Rapids: Baker Books, 1989, 2010), p. 287.

26   Paul Knobel, letter to the editor, *The Australian*, June 27, 2003, p. 10.

27   See especially 1 Cor 7:7, 17 where Paul speaks about this gift of singleness.

28   D.A. Carson, "Matthew", in Frank Gaebelein, ed., *The Expositors' Bible Commentary*, vol. 8 (Grand Rapids: Zondervan, 1984), pp. 1-599, p. 419.

29   R.T. France, *The Gospel of Matthew* (Grand Rapids: Eerdmans, 2007), pp. 724-725.

30   Ibid., p. 725.

31   For a lengthy discussion of the occurrence, identity and significance of the thorn, see John Wilkinson *The Bible and Healing* (Grand Rapids: Eerdmans, 1998), pp. 195-235.

32   Gordon Fee, *God's Empowering Presence: The Holy Spirit in the Letters of Paul* (Peabody, Mass: Hendrickson Publishers, 1994), p. 352.

33   Ralph Martin, *2 Corinthians*, World Biblical Commentary (WBC), vol. 40 (Waco, Texas: Word Books, 1986), p. 416.

34   This line of revisionistic thinking may have first appeared in L. William Countryman, *Dirt, Greed and Sex: Sexual Ethics in the New Testament and Their Implications for Today* (Philadelphia: Fortress Press, 1988).

35   Grenz, *Welcoming But Not Affirming, op. cit.*, p. 155.

36   Digby Hannah, et. al., letter to the editor, *The Victorian Baptist Witness*, April 2003, p. 10.

37   Stanton Jones and Mark Yarhouse, *Homosexuality: The Use of Scientific Research in the Church's Moral Debate* (Downers Grove, Illinois: InterVarsity Press, 2000), p. 18.

38   See Part One Chapter 5: "Once Homosexual, Always Homosexual?"

39   Neil Whitehead argues that genetic influence could be as low as 10 per cent, with the balance coming from the environment. See his *My Genes Made Me Do It!* (Lafayette, Louisiania: Huntington House, 1999).

40   Jones and Yarhouse, *op. cit.*, p. 181.

41   Alan Chambers, *God's Grace and the Homosexual Next Door* (Eugene, Oregon: Harvest House Pub., 2006), p. 36.

42   Frank Turek, *Correct, Not Politically Correct* (CrossExamined, 2008), pp. 71-72.

43   Ibid., pp. 76-77.

44   Linda Belleville, *Sex, Lies, and the Truth* (Eugene, Oregon: Wipf & Stock, 2010), p. 103.

45   John Stott, *Issues Facing Christians Today* (London: Marshall Pickering, 1984, 1990), p. 351.

46   See Part One: Chapter 2, "Homosexual Practices", and Chapter 9, "Homosexual Marriage".

47   John Walton, *Genesis*, The New International Version Application Commentary (Grand Rapids: Zondervan, 2001), p. 490.

48   Senator John Woodley, "Human Rights Sexual Conduct Bill 1994, Second Reading", *Senate: Hansard* (Canberra), December 9, 1994, p. 4285.

49   Schmidt, *op. cit.*, p. 84.

50   Andreas Kostenberger, "Marriage and family in the New Testament", in Ken Campbell, ed., *Marriage and Family in the Biblical World* (Downers Grove, Illinois: InterVarsity Press, 2003), pp. 240-284, at p. 243.

51   James White and Jeffrey Niell, *The Same Sex Controversy* (Minneapolis: Bethany House, 2002), p. 37.

52   Bahnsen, *op. cit.*, p. 82.

53   Woodley, *op. cit.*, p. 4285.

54   Timothy Dailey, *Dark Obsession* (Nashville: Broadman and Holman, 2003), p. 127.

55   Dennis, Altman, *AIDS and the New Puritanism* (New York: Pluto Press, 1986), pp. 98, 188.

56   Ibid.

57   Woodley, *op. cit.*, p. 4286.

58   Cited in F. LaGard Smith, *Sodom's Second Coming* (Eugene, Oregon: Harvest House Pub., 1993), p. 82.

59   Roger Magnuson, *Informed Answers to Gay Rights Questions* (Sisters, Oregon: Multnomah, 1994), pp. 122, 123.

60   Chambers, *op. cit.*, p. 166.

61   Joe Dallas, "Rebutting pro-gay theology", in Joe Dallas and Nancy Heche, eds., *The Complete Christian Guide to Understanding Homosexuality* (Eugene, Oregon: Harvest House, 2010), pp. 143-159, p. 148.

62   Michael Saia, *Counseling the Homosexual* (Minneapolis: Bethany House, 1988), p. 61.

63   Grenz, *Welcoming But Not Affirming, op. cit.*, p. 93.

64   Joe Dallas, *A Strong Delusion* (Eugene, Oregon: Harvest House Pub., 1996), p. 174.

65   James Bone, "I've been called by God, says gay cannon", *The Australian*, October 21, 2003, p. 8.

66   Gordon D. Fee, *Galatians* (Blandford Forum, Dorset, UK: Deo Publishing, 2007), pp. 142-143.

67   Ben Witherington, *Grace in Galatia: A Commentary on St Paul's Letter to the Galatians* (Edinburgh: T&T Clark, 1998), pp. 280-281.

68   Paul Copan, *When God Goes To Starbucks* (Grand Rapids: Baker Books, 2008), p. 82.

69   William Webb, *Slaves, Women and Homosexuals: Exploring the Hermeneutics of Cultural Analysis* (Downers Grove, Illinois: InterVarsity Press, 2001), pp. 87-88.

70   Ibid., pp. 88-89.

71   Ibid., p. 90.

72   Ibid.

Chapter 2.   Challenging the Biblical Texts

1   Cited in Catherine Watson, "Love God, and love your neighbour", *MCV: Melbourne's Gay and Lesbian Community Voice*, April 12, 2002, p. 7.

2   D.S. Bailey, *Homosexuality and the Western Christian Tradition* (New York: Longmans, Green, and Co., 1955).

3   John Feinberg and Paul Feinberg, *Ethics for a Brave New World*, 2nd ed. (Wheaton, Illinois: Crossway Books, 1993, 2010), p. 321.

4   The numbers vary. Hamilton says there are 948 instances of the verb, with 15 referring

to sexual knowledge. Victor Hamilton, *The Book of Genesis: Chapters 18 to 50*, The New International Commentary on the Old Testament (Grand Rapids: Eerdmans, 1995), p. 33.

5   Hamilton, *ibid.*, p. 34.

6   Ibid., p. 35.

7   Ibid., p. 34.

8   Robert Gagnon, *The Bible and Homosexual Practice: Texts and Hermeneutics* (Nashville: Abingdon Press, 2001), p. 91.

9   Gordon Wenham, *The Book of Leviticus*, The New International Commentary on the Old Testament (Grand Rapids: Eerdmans, 1979), p. 250.

10   James De Young, *Homosexuality: Contemporary Claims Examined in Light of the Bible and Other Ancient Literature and Law* (Grand Rapids: Kregel, 2000), p. 283.

11   Stanley Grenz, *Welcoming But Not Affirming: An Evangelical Response to Homosexuality* (Louisville: Westminster John Knox Press, 1988), p. 47.

12   William Webb, *Slaves, Women and Homosexuals: Exploring the Hermeneutics of Cultural Analysis* (Downers Grove, Illinois: InterVarsity Press, 2001), p. 178.

13   Norman Geisler, *Christian Ethics*, 2nd ed. (Grand Rapids: Baker Books, 1989, 2010), p. 284.

14   Walter Kaiser, *Toward Old Testament Ethics* (Grand Rapids: Academie Books, 1983), p. 118.

15   Webb, *op. cit.*, pp. 169-170.

16   Donald Wold, *Out of Order: Homosexuality in the Bible and the Ancient Near East* (Grand Rapids: Baker Books, 1998), p. 119.

17   Nobuyoshi Kiuchi, *Leviticus*, Apollos Old Testament Commentary (Downers Grove, Illinois: InterVarsity Press, 2007), p. 342.

18   Ephraim Radner, *Leviticus*, Brazos Theological Commentary on the Bible (Grand Rapids: Brazos Press, 2008), p. 221.

19   John Goldingay, *Old Testament Theology*, Vol. 3: "Israel's Life" (Downers Grove, Illinois: IVP, 2009), p. 381.

20   Kenneth Mathews, *Leviticus* (Wheaton, Illinois: Crossway Books, 2009), p. 159.

21   Arthur Cundall and Leon Morris, *Judges & Ruth*, Tyndale Old Testament Commentaries (Downers Grove, Illinois: InterVarsity Press, 1968), p. 197.

22   K. Lawson Younger, *Judges, Ruth*, The New International Version Application Commentary (Grand Rapids: Zondervan, 2002), p. 360.

23   Daniel Block, *Judges, Ruth*, New American Commentary (Nashville: Broadman and Holman, 1999), p. 543.

24   Ibid., p. 544.

25   Herbert Wolf, *Judges*, in Frank Gaebelein, ed., *The Expositor's Bible Commentary* (Grand Rapids: Zondervan, 1992), pp. 373-506, p. 493.

26   Ibid., p. 489.

27   Geisler, *op. cit.*, pp. 264-265.

28   Wold, *op. cit.*, p. 162.

29   James Dunn, *Romans 1-8*, Word Biblical Commentary (Dallas: Word Books, 1988), pp. 65-66.

30   Webb, *op. cit.*, p. 82.

31   Joseph Fitzmyer, *Romans*, The Anchor Bible (New York: Doubleday, 1992), pp. 275-276.

32   Douglas Moo, *Romans*, The New International Commentary on the New Testament (Grand Rapids: Eerdmans, 1996), p. 116.

33   Leon Morris, *The Epistle to the Romans*, Pillar New Testament Commentary (Grand Rapids: Eerdmans, 1998), p. 92.

34   Thomas Schreiner, *Romans*, Baker Exegetical Commentary on the New Testament (Grand Rapids: Baker Books, 1998), p. 96.

35   John Stott, *The Message of Romans*, The Bible Speaks Today (Leicester, UK: Inter-Varsity Press, 1994), p. 78.

36   Ben Witherington, *Paul's Letter to the Romans: A Socio-Rhetorical Commentary* (Grand Rapids: Eerdmans, 2004), p. 69.

37   C.K. Barrett, *The Epistle to the Romans*, Black's New Testament Commentaries (London: A&C Black, 1957, 1971), p. 39.

38   R.C. Sproul, *Romans* (Wheaton, Illinois: Crossway Books, 2009), p. 51.

39   Dunn, *op. cit.*, p. 65.

40   Morris, *op. cit.*, pp. 92-93.

41   Greg Bahnsen, *Homosexuality: A Biblical View* (Grand Rapids: Baker, 1978, 1994), p. 50.

42   Richard B. Hays, *The Moral Vision of the New Testament* (San Francisco: Harper Collins, 1996), p. 384.

43   Linda Belleville, *Sex, Lies, and the Truth* (Eugene, Oregon: Wipf & Stock, 2010), p. 104.

44   Fitzmyer, *op. cit.*, p. 276.

45   Sproul, *op. cit.*, pp.50-51.

46   John Jefferson Davis, *Evangelical Ethics: Issues Facing the Church Today* (Phillipsburg, New Jersey: Presbyterian and Reformed, 1985), p. 120.

47   Ibid., p. 121.

48   C.K. Barrett, *A Commentary on the First Epistle to the Corinthians*, Black's New Testament Commentaries (London: A&C Black, 1968), p. 140.

49   Andreas Kostenberger, "Marriage and family in the New Testament", in Ken Campbell, ed., *Marriage and Family in the Biblical World* (Downers Grove, Illinois: InterVarsity Press, 2003), p. 243.

50   David Garland, *1 Corinthians*, Baker Exegetical Commentary on the New Testament (Grand Rapids: Baker, 2003), p. 212.

51   Anthony Thiselton, *The First Epistle to the Corinthians*, The New International Greek Testament Commentary (Grand Rapids: Eerdmans, 2000), p. 452.

52   Roy E. Ciampa and Brian S. Rosner, *The First Letter to the Corinthians*, The Pillar New Testament Commentary (Grand Rapids: Eerdmans, 2010), p. 242.

53   William Mounce, *Pastoral Epistles*, Word Biblical Commentary (Nashville: Thomas Nelson, 2000), p. 39.

54   Ben Witherington, *A Socio-Rhetorical Commentary on Titus, 1-2 Timothy and 1-3 John* (Downers Grove, Illinois: InterVarsity Press, 2006), p. 198.

55   See for example, Marion Soards, *1 Corinthians*, New International Biblical Commentary (Peabody, Mass.: Hendrickson Publishers, 1999), p. 126.

56   Cited in Brian Rosner, *Paul, Scripture, and Ethics* (Grand Rapids: Baker, 1999), p. 120.

57   George Knight, *The Pastoral Epistles*, The New International Greek Testament Commentary (Grand Rapids: Eerdmans, 1992), p. 86.

58   Jerome Quinn and William Wacker, *The First and Second Letters to Timothy*, Eerdmans Critical Commentary (Grand Rapids: Eerdmans, 2000), p. 101.

59   Philip Towner, *The Letters to Timothy and Titus*, The New International Commentary on the New Testament (Grand Rapids: Eerdmans, 2006), pp. 127-128.

60   Ibid., p. 128.

61   Thomas Schreiner, *1,2 Peter, Jude*, New American Commentary (Nashville: Broadman and Holman, 2003), p. 339.

62   Douglas Moo, *2 Peter, Jude*, The NIV Application Commentary (Grand Rapids: Zondervan, 1996), p. 107.

63   Ben Witherington, *A Socio-Rhetorical Commentary on 1-2 Peter* (Downers Grove, Illinois: InterVarsity Press, 2007), p. 355.

64   Schreiner, *1,2 Peter, Jude, op. cit.*, pp. 451-452.

65   Jerome Neyrey, *2 Peter, Jude*, The Anchor Bible (New York: Doubleday, 1993), pp. 10-11, 61.

66   Gene Green, *Jude & 2 Peter*, Baker Exegetical Commentary on the New Testament (Grand Rapids: Baker, 2008), p. 72.

67   Hays, *op. cit.*, p. 394.

68   See for example the discussion by Duane Christensen, *Deuteronomy 21:10-34:12*, Word Biblical Commentary (Nashville: Thomas Nelson, 2002), pp. 549-551.

69   Daniel Heimbach, *True Sexual Morality* (Wheaton, Illinois: Crossway Books, 2004), p. 187.

70   Pim Pronk, *Against Nature? Types of Moral Arguments Regarding Homosexuality* (Grand Rapids: Eerdmans, 1993), p. 279.

Made in the USA
Charleston, SC
09 April 2014